Alice & Bob Learn
Application Security

Alice & Bob Learn Application Security

Tanya Janca

WILEY

I dedicate this book to my tireless cheering squad: Lexy, Matteus, Ash, and Vane. Your constant support, encouragement, and celebration of each milestone kept me going. Also, thank you for not judging me for how much ice cream I ate during my editing.

About the Author

Tanya Janca, also known as SheHacksPurple, is the founder of We Hack Purple, an online learning academy, community, and podcast that revolves around teaching everyone to create secure software. She is also the co-founder of WoSEC: Women of Security, is a project leader for OWASP DevSlop, and is a chapter leader for OWASP Victoria. Tanya has been coding and working in IT for over twenty years, has won numerous awards, and has been everywhere from startups to public service to tech giants (Microsoft, Adobe, and Nokia). She has worn many hats: startup founder, pentester, CISO, AppSec Engineer, and software developer. She is an award-winning public speaker, active blogger and streamer, and has delivered hundreds of talks and trainings on six continents. She values diversity, inclusion, and kindness, which shines through in her countless initiatives.

About the Technical Editors

Dominique Righetto started his career in software development before moving, eight years later, to the security side while continuing to live on the border between the two worlds. Dominique is strongly interested in the offensive and defensive aspects of application security. When he moved into the field of security, his objective was (and always has been) to help development teams integrate security into their projects, using a pragmatic point of view. Dominique has been an active member of the OWASP foundation since 2011, where he contributes to different projects, mainly those concerning the web and mobile domain (his domains specialization). Adept at the open source philosophy, he contributes to various open source projects in his spare time. His homepage is `righettod.eu`.

Elie Saad is an experienced information security officer working in the banking industry. He leads and contributes to various standardization initiatives at OWASP and regularly publishes articles on the subject. His main drive is to provide guidance for software developers to own and champion security. He has presented several local talks to bring security closer to newcomers and has been a podcast guest on *Security Journey*, raising the awareness of various AppSec projects. He is an advocate for breaking down the fragmented culture in the AppSec world. In addition, Elie enjoys taking time to appreciate the simpler things in life, a nice breather in the mountains, and a tasteful glass of whiskey (single malt, of course). You can find him on Twitter (`@7hunderSon`) and on GitHub (thunderson). You can also reach him via email at `eliesaad7@gmail.com`.

Acknowledgments

I would like to thank Jim Minatel, my publisher, for helping me decide that I was ready to write a book, and what type of book to write. Thank you, Adaobi Obi Tulton, my editor, for your endless patience, guidance, and very-helpful-check-ins that kept me on track for the largest project of my professional life. Thank you to Dominique Righetto and Elie Saad, my technical editors. I could never afford to pay you for how hard you both worked to ensure I did not make any grave technical errors. I do not have words to convey my appreciation for your time, expertise, and support. Thank you all for coming on this journey with me.

Contents at a Glance

Contents

Introduction

Why application security? Why should you read this book? Why is security important? Why is it so *hard*?

If you have picked up this book, you likely already know the answer to this question. You have seen the headlines of companies that have been "hacked," data breached, identities stolen, businesses and lives ruined. However, you may not be aware that the number-one reason for data breaches is insecure software, causing between 26% and 40% of leaked and stolen records (Verizon Breach Report, 2019).[1] Yet when we look at the budgets of most companies, the amount allocated toward ensuring their software is secure is usually much, much lower than that.

Most organizations at this point are highly skilled at protecting their network perimeter (with firewalls), enterprise security (blocking malware and not allowing admin rights for most users), and physical security (badging in and out of secure areas). That said, reliably creating secure software is still an elusive goal for most organizations today. Why?

Right now, universities and colleges are teaching students how to code, but not teaching them how to ensure the code they write is secure, nor are they teaching them even the basics of information security. Most post-secondary programs that do cover security just barely touch upon application security, concentrating instead on identity, network security, and infrastructure.

Imagine if someone went to school to become an electrician but they never learned about safety. Houses would catch fire from time to time because the electricians wouldn't know how to ensure the work that they did was safe. Allowing engineering and computer science students to graduate with inadequate security training is equally dangerous, as they create banking software, software that runs pacemakers, software that safeguards government secrets, and so much more that our society depends on.

This is one part of the problem.

Another part of the problem is that (English-language) training is generally extremely expensive, making it unobtainable for many. There is also no clear career path or training program that a person can take to become a secure coder, security architect, incident responder, or application security engineer. Most people end up with on-the-job training, which means that each of us has a completely different idea of how to do things, with varying results.

Adding to this problem is how profitable it is to commit crimes on the internet, and with attribution (figuring out who did the crime) being so difficult, there are many, many threats facing any application hosted on the internet. The more valuable the system or the data within it, the more threats it will face.

The last part of this equation is that application security is quite difficult. Unlike infrastructure security, where each version of Microsoft Windows Server 2008 R2 PS2 is exactly the same, each piece of custom software is a snowflake; unique by design. When you build a deck out of wood in your backyard and you go to the hardware store to buy a 2x4 that is 8 feet long, it will be the same in every store you go to, meaning you can make safe assumptions and calculations. With software this is almost never the case; you must never make any assumptions and you must verify every fact. This means brute-force memorization, automated tools, and other one-size-fits-all solutions rarely work. And that makes application security, as a field, very challenging.

Pushing Left

If you look at the System Development Life Cycle (SDLC) in Figure I-1, you see the various phases moving toward the right of the page. Requirements come before Design, which comes before Coding. Whether you are doing Agile, Waterfall, DevOps, or any other software development methodology, you always need to know what you are building (requirements), make a plan (design), build it (coding), verifying it does all that it should do, and nothing more (testing), then release and maintain it (deployment).

Requirements   Design   Code   Testing   Release

Figure I-1: System Development Life Cycle (SDLC)

Often security activities start in the release or testing phases, far to the right, and quite late in the project. The problem with this is that the later in the process that you fix a flaw (design problem) or a bug (implementation problem), the more it costs and the harder it is to do.

Let me explain this a different way. Imagine Alice and Bob are building a house. They have saved for this project for years, and the contractors are putting the finishing touches on it by putting up wallpaper and adding handles on the cupboards. Alice turns to Bob and says, "Honey, we have 2 children but only one bathroom! How is this going to work?" If they tell the contractors to stop working, the house won't be finished on time. If they ask them to add a second bathroom, where will it go? How much will it cost? Finding out this late in their project would be disastrous. However, if they had figured this out in the requirements phase or during the design phase it would have been easy to add more bathrooms, for very little cost. The same is true for solving security problems.

This is where "shifting left" comes into play: the earlier you can start doing security activities during a software development project, the better the results will be. The arrows in Figure I-2 show a progression of starting security earlier and earlier in your projects. We will discuss later on what these activities are.

Figure I-2: Shifting/Pushing Left

About This Book

This book will teach you the foundations of application security (AppSec for short); that is, how to create secure software. This book is for software developers, information security professionals wanting to know more about the security of software, and anyone who wants to work in the field of application security (which includes penetration testing, aka "ethical hacking").

If you are a software developer, it is your job to make the most secure software that you know how to make. Your responsibility here cannot be understated; there are hundreds of programmers for every AppSec engineer in the field, and we cannot do it without you. Reading this book is the first step on the right path. After you've read it, you should know enough to make secure software and know where to find answers if you are stuck.

Notes on format: There will be examples of how security issues can potentially affect real users, with the characters Alice and Bob making several appearances throughout the book. You may recall the characters of Alice and Bob from other security examples; they have been being used to simplify complex topics in our industry since the advent of cryptography and encryption.

Out-of-Scope Topics

Brief note on topics that are out of scope for this book: incident response (IR), network monitoring and alerting, cloud security, infrastructure security, network security, security operations, identity and access management (IAM), enterprise security, support, anti-phishing, reverse engineering, code obfuscation, and other advanced defense techniques, as well as every other type of security not listed here. Some of these topics will be touched upon but are in no way covered exhaustively in this book. Please consume additional resources to learn more about these important topics.

The Answer Key

At the end of each chapter are exercises to help you learn and to test your knowledge. There is an answer key at the end of the book; however, it will be incomplete. Many of questions could be an essay, research paper, or online discussion in themselves, while others are personal in nature (only you can answer what roadblocks you may be facing in your workplace). With this in mind, the answer key is made up of answers (when possible), examples (when appropriate), and some skipped questions, left for online discussion.

In the months following the publication of this book, you will be able to stream recorded discussions answering *all* of the exercise questions online at youtube.com/shehackspurple under the playlist "Alice and Bob Learn Application Security." You can subscribe to learn about new videos, watch the previous videos, and explore other free content.

You can participate *live* in the discussions by subscribing to the SheHacksPurple newsletter to receive invitations to the streams (plus a lot of other free content) at newsletter.shehackspurple.ca.

It doesn't cost anything to attend the discussions or watch them afterward, and you can learn a *lot* by hearing other's opinions, ideas, successes, and failures. Please join us.

What You Must Know to Write Code Safe Enough to Put on the Internet

In This Part

Security Fundamentals

Before learning how to create secure software, you need to understand several key security concepts. There is no point in memorizing how to implement a concept if you don't understand when or why you need it. Learning these principles will ensure you make secure project decisions and are able to argue for better security when you face opposition. Also, knowing the reason behind security rules makes them a lot easier to live with.

The Security Mandate: CIA

The mandate and purpose of every IT security team is to protect the *confidentiality*, *integrity*, and *availability* of the systems and data of the company, government, or organization that they work for. That is why the security team hassles you about having unnecessary administrator rights on your work machine, won't let you plug unknown devices into the network, and wants you to do all the other things that feel inconvenient; they want to protect these three things. We call it the "CIA Triad" for short (Figure 1-1).

Let's examine this with our friends Alice and Bob. Alice has type 1 diabetes and uses a tiny device implanted in her arm to check her insulin several times a day, while Bob has a "smart" pacemaker that regulates his heart, which he accesses via a mobile app on this phone. Both of these devices are referred to as IoT medical device implants in our industry.

Figure 1-1: The CIA Triad is the reason IT Security teams exist.

NOTE   IoT stands for Internet of Things, physical products that are internet connected. A smart toaster or a fridge that talks to the internet are IoT devices.

Confidentiality

Alice is the CEO of a large Fortune 500 company, and although she is not ashamed that she is a type 1 diabetic, she does not want this information to become public. She is often interviewed by the media and does public speaking, serving as a role model for many other women in her industry. Alice works hard to keep her personal life *private*, and this includes her health condition. She believes that some people within her organization are after her job and would do anything to try to portray her as "weak" in an effort to undermine her authority. If her device were to accidentally leak her information, showing itself on public networks, or if her account information became part of a breach, this would be highly embarrassing for her and potentially damaging to her career. Keeping her personal life private is important to Alice.

Bob, on the other hand, is open about his heart condition and happy to tell anyone that he has a pacemaker. He has a great insurance plan with the federal government and is grateful that when he retires he can continue with his plan, despite his pre-existing condition. Confidentiality is not a priority for Bob in this respect (Figure 1-2).

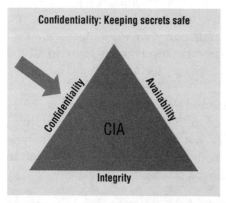

Figure 1-2: Confidentiality: keeping things safe

NOTE   Confidentiality is often undervalued in our personal lives. Many people tell me they "have nothing to hide." Then I ask, "Do you have curtains on your windows at home? Why? I thought that you had nothing to hide?" I'm a blast at parties.

Integrity

Integrity in data (Figure 1-3) means that the data is current, correct, and accurate. Integrity also means that your data has not been altered during transmission; the correct value must be maintained during transit. Integrity in a computer system means that the results it gives are precise and factual. For Bob and Alice, this may be the most crucial of the CIA factors: if either of their systems gives them incorrect treatment, it could result in death. For a human being (as opposed to a company or nation-state), there does not exist a more serious repercussion than end of life. The integrity of their health systems is crucial to ensuring they both remain in good health.

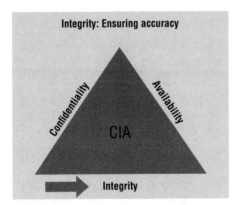

Figure 1-3: Integrity means accuracy.

CIA is the very core of our entire industry. Without understanding this from the beginning, and how it affects your teammates, your software, and most significantly, your users, you cannot build secure software.

Availability

If Alice's insulin measuring device was unavailable due to malfunction, tampering, or dead batteries, her device would not be "available." Since Alice usually checks her insulin levels several times a day, but she is able to do manual testing of her insulin (by pricking her finger and using a medical kit designed for this purpose) if she needs to, it is somewhat important to her that this service is available. A lack of availability of this system would be quite inconvenient for her, but not life-threatening.

Bob, on the other hand, has irregular heartbeats from time to time and never knows when his arrhythmia will strike. If Bob's pacemaker was not available when his heart was behaving erratically, this could be a life-or-death situation if enough time elapsed. It is vital that his pacemaker is available and that it reacts in real time (immediately) when an emergency happens.

Bob works for the federal government as a clerk managing secret and top-secret documents, and has for many years. He is a proud grandfather and has been trying hard to live a healthy life since his pacemaker was installed.

> **NOTE**   Medical devices are generally "real-time" software systems. Real-time means the system must respond to changes in the fastest amount of time possible, generally in milliseconds. It cannot have delays—the responses must be as close as possible to instantaneous or immediate. When Bob's arrhythmia starts, his pacemaker must act immediately; there cannot be a delay. Most applications are not real-time. If there is a 10-millisecond delay in the purchase of new running shoes, or in predicting traffic changes, it is not *truly* critical.

Figure 1-4: Resilience *improves* availability.

> **NOTE**   Many customers move to "the cloud" for the sole reason that it is extremely reliable (almost always available) when compared to more traditional in-house data center service levels. As you can see in Figure 1-4, resilience improves availability, making public cloud an attractive option from a security perspective.

The following are security concepts that are well known within the information security industry. It is essential to have a good grasp of these foundational ideas in order to understand how the rest of the topics in this book apply to them. If you are already a security practitioner, you may not need to read this chapter.

Assume Breach

"There are two types of companies: those that have been breached and those that don't know they've been breached yet."[2] It's such a famous saying in the information security industry that we don't even know who to attribute it to anymore. It may sound pessimistic, but for those of us who work in incident response, forensics, or other areas of investigation, we know this is all too true.

The concept of *assume breach* means preparation and design considerations to ensure that if someone were to gain unapproved access to your network, application, data, or other systems, it would prove difficult, time-consuming, expensive, and risky, and you would be able to detect and respond to the situation quickly. It also means monitoring and logging your systems to ensure that if you don't notice until after a breach occurs, at least you can find out what did happen. Many systems also monitor for behavioral changes or anomalies to detect potential breaches. It means preparing for the worst, in advance, to minimize damage, time to detect, and remediation efforts.

Let's look at two examples of how we can apply this principle: a consumer example and a professional example.

As a consumer, Alice opens an online document-sharing account. If she were to "assume breach," she wouldn't upload anything sensitive or valuable there (for instance, unregistered intellectual property, photos of a personal nature that could damage her professional or personal life, business secrets, government secrets, etc.). She would also set up monitoring of the account as well as have a plan if the documents were stolen, changed, removed, shared publicly, or otherwise accessed in an unapproved manner. Lastly, she would monitor the entire internet in case they were leaked somewhere. This would be an unrealistic amount of responsibility to expect from a regular consumer; this book does not advise average consumers to "assume breach" in their lives, although doing occasional online searches on yourself is a good idea and not uploading sensitive documents online is definitely advisable.

As a professional, Bob manages secret and top-secret documents. The department Bob works at would never consider the idea of using an online file-sharing service to share their documents; they control every aspect of this valuable information. When they were creating the network and the software systems that manage these documents, they designed them, and their processes, *assuming breach*. They hunt for threats on their network, designed their network using zero trust, monitor the internet for signs of data leakage, authenticate to APIs before connecting, verify data from the database and from internal APIs, perform red team exercises (security testing in production), and monitor their network and applications closely for anomalies or other signs of breach. They've written automated responses to common attack patterns, have processes in place and ready for uncommon attacks, and they analyze behavioral patterns for signs of breach. They operate on the idea that data may have been breached already or could be at any time.

Another example of this would be initiating your incident response process when a serious bug has been disclosed via your responsible disclosure or bug bounty program, assuming that someone else has potentially already found and exploited this bug in your systems.

According to Wikipedia, *coordinated disclosure* is a vulnerability disclosure model in which a vulnerability or an issue is disclosed only after a period of time that allows for the vulnerability or issue to be patched or mended.

Bug bounty programs are run by many organizations. They provide recognition and compensation for security researchers who report bugs, especially those pertaining to vulnerabilities.

Insider Threats

An insider threat means that someone who has approved access to your systems, network, and data (usually an employee or consultant) negatively affects one or more of the CIA aspects of your systems, data, and/or network. This can be malicious (on purpose) or accidental.

Here are some examples of malicious threats and the parts of the CIA Triad they affect:

- An employee downloading intellectual property onto a portable drive, leaving the building, and then selling the information to your competitors (confidentiality)

- An employee deleting a database and its backup on their last day of work because they are angry that they were dismissed (availability)

- An employee programming a back door into a system so they can steal from your company (integrity and confidentiality)

- An employee downloading sensitive files from another employee's computer and using them for blackmail (confidentiality)

- An employee accidentally deleting files, then changing the logs to cover their mistake (integrity and availability)

- An employee not reporting a vulnerability to management in order to avoid the work of fixing it (potentially all three, depending upon the type of vulnerability)

Here are some examples of accidental threats and the parts of the CIA Triad they affect:

- Employees using software improperly, causing it to fall into an unknown state (potentially all three)

- An employee accidentally deleting valuable data, files, or even entire systems (availability)

- An employee accidentally misconfiguring software, the network, or other software in a way that introduces security vulnerabilities (potentially all three)

- An inexperienced employee pointing a web proxy/dynamic application security testing (DAST) tool at one of your internal applications, crashing the application (availability) or polluting your database (integrity)
  We will cover how to avoid this in later chapters to ensure all of your security testing is performed safely.

WARNING   Web proxy software and/or DAST tools are generally forbidden on professional work networks. Also known as "web app scanners," web proxies are hacker tools and can cause great damage. Never point a web app scanner at a website or application and perform active scanning or other interactive testing without permission. It must be *written* permission, from someone with the authority to give the permission. Using a DAST tool to interact with a site on the internet (without permission) is a criminal act in many countries. Be careful, and when in doubt, always ask before you start.

Defense in Depth

Defense in depth is the idea of having multiple layers of security in case one is not enough (Figure 1-5). Although this may seem obvious when explained so simply, deciding how many layers and which layers to have can be difficult (especially if your security budget is limited).

"Layers" of security can be processes (checking someone's ID before giving them their mail, having to pass security testing before software can be released), physical, software, or hardware systems (a lock on a door, a network firewall, hardware encryption), built-in design choices (writing separate functions for code that handles more sensitive tasks in an application, ensuring everyone in a building must enter through one door), and so on.

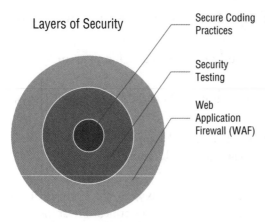

Layers of Security

Secure Coding
Practices

Security
Testing

Web
Application
Firewall (WAF)

Figure 1-5: Three layers of security for an application; an example of defense in depth

Here are some examples of using multiple layers:

- **When creating software**: Having security requirements, performing threat modeling, ensuring you use secure design concepts, ensuring you use secure coding tactics, security testing, testing in multiple ways with multiple tools, etc. Each one presents another form of defense, making your application more secure.

- **Network security**: Turning on monitoring, having a SIEM (Security information and event management, a dashboard for viewing potential security events, in real time), having IPS/IDS (Intrusion prevention/detection system, tools to find and stop intruders on your network), firewalls, and so much more. Each new item adds to your defenses.

- **Physical security**: Locks, barbed wire, fences, gates, video cameras, security guards, guard dogs, motion sensors, alarms, etc.

Quite often the most difficult thing when advocating for security is convincing someone that one defense is not enough. Use the value of what you are protecting (reputation, monetary value, national security, etc.) when making these decisions. While it makes little business sense to spend one million dollars protecting something with a value of one thousand dollars, the examples our industry sees the most often are usually reversed.

NOTE   Threat modeling: Identifying threats to your applications and creating plans for mitigation. More on this in Chapter 3.

SIEM system: Monitoring for your network and applications, a dashboard of potential problems.

Intrusion prevention/detection system (IPS/IDS): Software installed on a network with the intention of detecting and/or preventing network attacks.

Least Privilege

Giving users exactly how much access and control they need to do their jobs, but nothing more, is the concept of *least privilege*. The reasoning behind least privilege is that if someone were able to take over your account(s), they wouldn't get very far. If you are a software developer with access to your code and read/write access to the single database that you are working on, that means if someone were able to take over your account they would only be able to access that one database, your code, your email, and whatever else you have access to. However, if you were the database *owner* on all of the databases, the intruder could potentially wipe out everything. Although it may be unpleasant to give up your superpowers on your desktop, network, or other systems, you are reducing the risk to those systems significantly by doing so.

Examples of least privilege:

- Needing extra security approvals to have access to a lab or area of your building with a higher level of security.
- Not having administrator privileges on your desktop at work.
- Having read-only access to all of your team's code and write access to your projects, but not having access to other teams' code repositories.
- Creating a service account for your application to access its database and only giving it read/write access, not database owner (DBO). If the application only requires read access, only give it what it requires to function properly. A service account with only read access to a database cannot be used to alter or delete any of the data, even if it could be used to steal a copy of the data. This reduces the risk greatly.

NOTE   Software developers and system administrators are attractive targets for most malicious actors, as they have the most privileges. By giving up some of your privileges you will be protecting your organization more than you may realize, and you will earn the respect of the security team at the same time.

Supply Chain Security

Every item you use to create a product is considered to be part of your "supply chain," with the chain including the entity (supplier) of each item (manufacturer, store, farm, a person, etc.). It's called a "chain" because each part of it depends on the previous part in order to create the final product. It can include people, companies, natural or manufactured resources, information, licenses, or anything else required to make your end product (which does not need to be physical in nature).

Let's explain this a bit more clearly with an example. If Bob was building a dollhouse for his grandchildren, he might buy a kit that was made in a factory. That factory would require wood, paper, ink to create color, glue, machines for cutting, workers to run and maintain the machines, and energy to power the machines. To get the wood, the factory would order it from a lumber company, which would cut it down from a forest that it owns or has licensed access to. The paper, ink, and glue are likely all made in different factories. The workers could work directly for the factory or they could be casual contractors. The energy would most likely come from an energy company but could potentially come from solar or wind power, or a generator in case of emergency. Figure 1-6 shows the (hypothetical) supply chain for the kit that Bob has purchased in order to build a doll house for his children for Christmas this year.

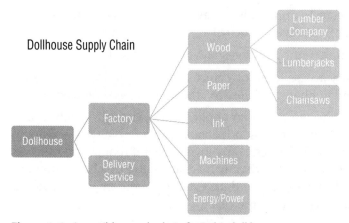

Figure 1-6: A possible supply chain for Bob's doll house

What are the potential security (safety) issues with this situation? The glue provided in this kit could be poisonous, or the ink used to decorate the pieces could be toxic. The dollhouse could be manufactured in a facility that also processes nuts, which could cross-contaminate the boxes, which could cause allergic reactions in some children. Incorrect parts could be included, such as a sharp component, which would not be appropriate for a young child. All of these situations are likely to be unintentional on the part of the factory.

When creating software, we also use a supply chain: the frameworks we use to write our code, the libraries we call in order to write to the screen, do advanced math calculations, or draw a button, the application programming interfaces (APIs) we call to perform actions on behalf of our applications, etc. Worse still, each one of these pieces usually depends on other pieces of software, and all of them are potentially maintained by different groups, companies, and/or people.

Modern applications are typically made up of 20–40 percent original code[3] (what you and your teammates wrote), with the rest being made up of these third-party components, often referred to as "dependencies." When you plug dependencies into your applications, you are accepting the risks of the code they contain that your application uses. For instance, if you add something to process images into your application rather than writing your own, but it has a serious security flaw in it, your application now has a serious security flaw in it, too.

This is not to suggest that you could write every single line of code yourself; that would not only be extremely inefficient, but you may still make errors that result in security problems. One way to reduce the risk, though, is to use fewer dependencies and to vet carefully the ones that you do decide to include in your software. Many tools on the market (some are even free) can verify if there are any known security issues with your dependencies. These tools should be used not only every time you push new code to production, but your code repository should also be scanned regularly as well.

SUPPLY CHAIN ATTACK EXAMPLE

The open source Node.js module called event-stream was passed on to a new maintainer in 2018 who added malicious code into it, waited until millions of people had downloaded it via NPM (the package manager for Node.JS), and then used this vulnerability to steal bitcoins from Copay wallets, which used the event-stream library in their wallet software.[4]

Another defense tactic against using an insecure software supply chain is using frameworks and other third-party components made by known companies or recognized and well-respected open source groups, just as a chef would only use the finest ingredients in the food they make. You can (and should) take care when choosing which components make it into the final cut of your products.

There have been a handful of publicly exposed supply chain attacks in recent years, where malicious actors injected vulnerabilities into software libraries, firmware (low-level software that is a part of hardware), and even into hardware itself. This threat is real and taking precautions against it will serve any developer well.

Security by Obscurity

The concept of *security by obscurity* means that if something is hidden it will be "more secure," as potential attackers will not notice it. The most common implementation of this is software companies that hide their source code, rather than putting it open on the internet (this is used as a means to protect their intellectual property *and* as a security measure). Some go as far as obfuscating their code, changing it such that it is much more difficult or impossible to understand if someone is attempting to reverse engineer your product.

> **NOTE**   *Obfuscation* is making something hard to understand or read. A common tactic is encoding all of the source code in ASCII, Base64, or Hex, but that's quite easy to see for professional reverse engineers. Some companies will double or triple encode their code. Another tactic is to XOR the code (an assembler command) or create their own encoding schema and add it programmatically. There are also products on the market that can perform more advanced obfuscation.

Another example of "security by obscurity" is having a wireless router suppress the SSID/Wi-Fi name (meaning if you want to connect you need to know the name) or deploying a web server without a domain name hoping no one will find it. There are tools to get around this, but it reduces your risk of people attacking your wireless router or web server.

The other side of this is "security by being open," the argument that if you write open source software there will be more eyes on it and therefore those eyes will find security vulnerabilities and report them. In practice this is rarely true; security researchers rarely review open source code and report bugs for free. When security flaws are reported to open source projects they don't necessarily fix them, and if vulnerabilities are found, the finder may decide to sell them on the black market (to criminals, to their own government, to foreign governments, etc.) instead of reporting them to the owner of the code repository in a secure manner.

Although security by obscurity is hardly an excellent defense when used on its own, it is certainly helpful as one layer of a "defense in depth" security strategy.

Attack Surface Reduction

Every part of your software can be attacked; each feature, input, page, or button. The smaller your application, the smaller the attack surface. If you have four pages with 10 functions versus 20 pages and 100 functions, that's a much smaller attack surface. Every part of your app that could be potentially exposed to an attacker is considered attack surface.

Attack surface reduction means removing anything from your application that is unrequired. For instance, a feature that is not fully implemented but you have the button grayed out, would be an ideal place to start for a malicious actor because it's not fully tested or hardened yet. Instead, you should remove this code before publishing it to production and wait until it's finished to publish it. Even if it's hidden, that's not enough; reduce your attack surface by removing that part of your code.

TIP Legacy software often has very large amounts of functionality that is not used. Removing features that are not in use is an excellent way to reduce your attack surface.

If you recall from earlier in the chapter, Alice and Bob both have medical implants, a device to measure insulin for Alice and a pacemaker for Bob. Both of their devices are "smart," meaning they can connect to them via their smart phones. Alice's device works over Bluetooth and Bob's works over Wi-Fi. One way for them to reduce the attack surface of their medical devices would have been to not have gotten smart devices in the first place. However, it's too late for that in this example. Instead, Alice could disable her insulin measuring device's Bluetooth "discoverable" setting, and Bob could hide the SSID of his pacemaker, rather than broadcasting it.

Hard Coding

Hard coding means programming values into the code, rather than getting the values organically (from the user, database, an API, etc.). For example, if you have created a calculator application and the user enters 4 + 4, presses Enter, and then the screen shows 8, you will likely assume the calculator works. However, if you enter 5 + 5 and press Enter but the screen still shows 8, you may have a situation of hard coding.

Why is hard coding a potential security issue? The reason is twofold: you cannot trust the output of the application, and the values that have been hard coded are often of a sensitive nature (passwords, API keys, hashes, etc.) and anyone with access to the source code would therefore have access to those hard-coded values. We always want to keep our secrets safe, and hard coding them into our source code is far from safe.

Hard coding is generally considered a symptom of poor software development (there are some exceptions to this). If you encounter it, you should search the entire application for hard coding, as it is unlikely the one instance you have found is unique.

Never Trust, Always Verify

If you take away only one lesson from this book, it should be this: never trust anything outside of your own application. If your application talks to an API, verify it is the correct API, and that it has authority to do whatever it's trying to do. If your application accepts data, from *any source*, perform validation on the data (ensure it is what you are expecting and that it is appropriate; if it is not, reject it). Even data from your own database could have malicious input or other contamination. If a user is attempting to access an area of your application that requires special permissions, reverify they have the permission to every single page or feature they use. If a user has authenticated to your application (proven they are who they say they are), ensure you continue to validate it's the same user that you are dealing with as they move from page to page (this is called *session management*). Never assume because you checked one time that everything is fine from then on; you must *always* verify and reverify.

> **NOTE**   We verify data from our own database because it may contain *stored cross-site scripting* (XSS), or other values that may damage our program. Stored XSS happens when a program does not perform proper input validation and saves an XSS attack into its database by accident. When users perform an action in your application that calls that data, when it is returned to the user it launches the attack against the user in their browser. It is an attack that a user is unable to protect themselves against, and it is generally considered a critical risk if found during security testing.

Quite often developers forget this lesson and assume trust due to context. For instance, you have a public-facing internet application, and you have extremely tight security on that web app. That web app calls an API (#1) within your network (behind the firewall) all the time, which then calls another API (#2) that changes data in a related database. Often developers don't bother authenticating (proving identity) to the first API or have the API (#1) verify the app has authorization to call whatever part of the API it's calling. If they do, however, in this situation, they often perform security measures only on API #1 and then skip doing it on API #2. This results in anyone inside your network being able to call API #2, including malicious actors who shouldn't be there, insider threats, or even accidental users (Figure 1-7).

Application calling APIs; when to authenticate

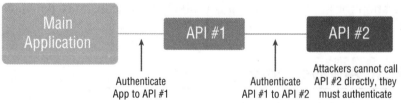

Figure 1-7: Example of an application calling APIs and when to authenticate

Here are some examples:

- A website is vulnerable to stored cross-site scripting, and an attacker uses this to store an attack in the database. If the web application validates the data from the database, the stored attack would be unsuccessful when triggered.

- A website charges for access to certain data, which it gets from an API. If a user knows the API is exposed to the internet, and the API does not validate that who is calling it is allowed to use it (authentication and authorization), the user can call the API directly and get the data without paying (which would be malicious use of the website), it's theft.

- A regular user of your application is frustrated and pounds on the keyboard repeatedly, accidentally entering much more data than they should have into your application. If your application is validating the input properly, it would reject it if there is too much. However, if the application does not validate the data, perhaps it would overload your variables or be submitted to your database and cause it to crash. When we don't verify that the data we are getting is what we are expecting (a number in a number field, a date in a date field, an appropriate amount of text, etc.), our application can fall into an unknown state, which is where we find many security bugs. We never want an application to fall into an unknown state.

Usable Security

If security features make your application difficult to use, users will find a way around it or go to your competitor. There are countless examples online of users creatively circumventing inconvenient security features; humans are very good at solving problems, and we don't want security to be the problem.

The answer to this is creating *usable* security features. While it is obvious that if we just turned the internet off, all our applications would be safer, that is obviously an unproductive solution to protecting anyone from threats on the internet. We need to be creative ourselves and find a way to make the easiest way to do something also be the most secure way to do something.

Examples of usable security include:

- Allowing a fingerprint, facial recognition, or pattern to unlock your personal device instead of a long and complicated password.

- Teaching users to create passphrases (a sentence or phrase that is easy to remember and type) rather than having complexity rules (ensuing a special character, number, lower- and uppercase letters are used, etc.). This would increase entropy, making it more difficult for malicious actors to break the password, but would also make it easier to use for users.

■ Teaching users to use password managers, rather than expecting them to create and remember 100+ unique passwords for all of their accounts.

Examples of users getting around security measures include:

■ Users tailgating at secure building entrances (following closely while someone enters a building so that they do not need to swipe to get in).

■ Users turning off their phones, entering through a scanner meant to detect transmitting devices, then turning it back on once in the secure area where cell phones are banned.

■ Using a proxy service to visit websites that are blocked by your workplace network.

■ Taking a photo of your screen to bring a copyright image or sensitive data home.

■ Using the same password over and over but incrementing the last number of it for easy memory. If your company forces users to reset their password every 90 days, there's a good chance there are quite a few passwords in your org that follow the format currentSeason_currentYear.

Factors of Authentication

Authentication is proving that you are indeed the real, *authentic*, you, to a computer. A "factor" of authentication is a method of proving who you are to a computer. Currently there are only three different factors: something you *have*, something you *are*, and something you *know*:

■ *Something you have* could be a phone, computer, token, or your badge for work. Something that should only ever be in *your* possession.

■ *Something you are* could be your fingerprint, an iris scan, your gait (the way you walk), or your DNA. Something that is physically unique to *you*.

■ *Something you know* could be a password, a passphrase, a pattern, or a combination of several pieces of information (often referred to as security questions) such as your mother's maiden name, your date of birth, and your social insurance number. The idea is that it is something that only *you* would know.

When we log in to accounts online with only a username and password, we are only using one "factor" of authentication, and it is significantly less secure than using two or more factors. When accounts are broken into or data is stolen, it is often due to someone using only one factor of authentication to protect the account. Using more than one factor of authentication is usually referred to as multi-factor authentication (MFA) or two-factor authentication (2FA), or two-step login. We will refer to this as MFA from now on in this book.

TIP Security questions are passé. It is simple to look up the answers to most security questions on the internet by performing Open Source Intelligence Gathering (OSINT). Do not use security questions as a factor of authentication in your software; they are too easily circumvented by attackers.

When credentials (usernames with corresponding passwords) are stolen and used maliciously to break into accounts, users that have a second factor of authentication are protected; the attacker will not have the second factor of authentication and therefore will be unable to get in. When someone tries to brute force (using a script to automatically try every possible option, very quickly) a system or account that has MFA enabled, even if they eventually get the password, they won't have the second factor in order to get in. Using a second factor makes your online accounts significantly more difficult to break into.

Examples of MFA include:

- **Multi-factor**: Entering your username and password, then having to use a second device or physical token to receive a code to authenticate. The username and password are one factor (something you know) and using a second device is the second factor (something you have).

- **Not multi-factor**: A username *and* a password. This is two examples of the *same* factor; they are both something that you know. Multi-factor authentication means that you have more than one of the different types of factors of authentication, not one or more of the same factor.

- **Not multi-factor**: Using a username and password, and then answering security questions. These are two of the *same* fact, something you know.

- **Multi-factor**: Username and password, then using your thumb print.

NOTE Many in the information security industry are in disagreement as to whether or not using your phone to receive an SMS (text message) with a pin code is a "good" implementation of MFA, as there are known security flaws within the SMS protocol and some implementations of it. It is my opinion that having a "pretty-darn-good second factor," rather than having only one factor, is better. Whenever possible, however, ask users to use an authentication application instead of SMS text messages as the second factor.

Exercises

These exercises are meant to help you understand the concepts in this chapter. Write out the answers and see which ones you get stuck on. If you have trouble answering some of the questions, you may want to reread the chapter. Every chapter will have exercises like these at the end. If there is a term you are unfamiliar with, look it up in the glossary at the end of the book; that may help with your understanding.

If you have a colleague or professional mentor who you can discuss the answers with, that would be the best way to find out if you are right or wrong, and why. Some of the answers are not Boolean (true/false) and are just to make you contemplate the problem.

1. Bob sets the Wi-Fi setting on his pacemaker to not broadcast the name of his Wi-Fi. What is this defensive strategy called?

2. Name an example of a value that could be hard coded and why. (What would be the motivation for the programmer to do that?)

3. Is a captcha *usable* security? Why or why not?

4. Give one example of a good implementation of usable security.

5. When using information from the URL parameters do you need to validate that data? Why or why not?

6. If an employee learns a trade secret at work and then sells it to a competitor, this breaks which part(s) of CIA?

7. If you buy a "smart" refrigerator and connect it to your home network, then have a malicious actor connect to it and change the settings so that it's slightly warmer and your milk goes bad, which part(s) of CIA did they break?

8. If someone hacks your smart thermostat and turns off your heat, which part(s) of CIA did they break?

9. If a programmer adds an Easter egg (extra code that does undocumented functionality, as a "surprise" for users, which is unknown to management and the security team), does this qualify as an insider threat? If so, why? If not, why not?

10. When connecting to a public Wi-Fi, what are some of the precautions that you could take to ensure you are doing "defense in depth"?

11. If you live in an apartment with several roommates and you all have a key to the door, is one of the keys considered to be a "factor of authentication"?

CHAPTER 2

Security Requirements

When you create any application or embark on any project, you must have requirements for what you are going to build. This is true no matter what development methodology you use (Waterfall, Agile, DevOps), language or framework you write it in, or type of audience you serve; without a plan you cannot build something of substance.

If you have studied computer science or computer engineering, the image shown in Figure 2-1 is likely burned into your brain. It is commonly known as the System Development Life Cycle (SDLC), and it consists of five phases: Requirements, Design, Code, Testing, and Release. As this book progresses, we will refer back to this image in order to explain when each activity we talk about can and/or should occur. This chapter will revolve around the Requirements phase.

Figure 2-1: The System Development Life Cycle (SDLC)

> **TIP** SDLC is sometimes defined as the *software* development life cycle, focusing on software rather than system. The two definitions are used interchangeably.

When you have your very first project meeting (often called a "project kickoff meeting"), there should be a person from the security team present, to take part in the project from its very inception. Even though this person will not be working full time on the project, they should be part of the team and make themselves available regularly to ensure that all security questions and concerns are addressed in a timely manner. Assigning a security person to a project team is sometimes called the *partnership model* or the person is referring to as being "matrixed into the team." No matter what you call it, this person is there to ensure that security's interests (CIA) are represented throughout the entire project.

> **NOTE**   The exact origin of the Partnership model is unknown. I first learned of it from the Netflix AppSec Team. The expression of being "matrixed into a project" was first introduced to me at the Treasury Board Secretariat of Canada and is, again, of unknown origin.

This chapter will assume that you have a basic understanding of how IT projects and software development processes work.

> **TIP**   Create a Support Level Agreement (SLA) between the security team and the other teams in order to define what a reasonable amount of time is to wait for a response to requests to the security team. Often security teams become the bottle-neck of projects, and when an SLA is in place, this is less likely to happen. For best results, set conservative goals at first, and aim to improve over time.

Requirements

Software project requirements should always include security questions. Following are the types of questions that security professionals should be asking when assisting with requirements gathering and analysis:

- Does the system contain, or come in contact with, confidential, sensitive, or Personally Identifiable Information (PII) data?
- Where and how is the data being stored? Will this application be available to the public (internet) or internally only (intranet)?
- Does this application perform sensitive or essential tasks (such as transferring money, unlocking doors, or delivering medicine)?
- Does this application perform any risky software activities (such as allowing users to upload files)?
- What level of availability do you need?
- Does it require 99.999% up time? (Note: almost no systems actually require that level of up time.)

Ideally, when creating a list of requirements, the security representative should ask questions and then add the appropriate security requirements to the list of requirements for the project. For instance; "Will your application allow users to upload files? Yes? Okay then, let's add the following security requirements to that project requirements document to ensure they design it securely from the start."

As someone creating software, it is part of your responsibility to protect the security, safety, and privacy of your users. These requirements will help ensure that you do.

The following sections detail security requirement definitions and explanations. At the end of this chapter you'll find a checklist of requirements that could be added to any web application project requirements document.

Encryption

Cryptography is a type of math that can be applied to information in order to make its value no longer understandable; it is used to hide secrets and ensure privacy of communications. *Encryption* is two-way, in that you can jumble up the information into an unreadable mess, and then "decrypt" it back into its original form. *Hashing* is one-way; the original value can never be recovered.

Encryption is used quite often to protect secrets or to transmit data, because the system needs that data back later. The value is in the data. Hashing is most often used to prove identity, to authenticate to a system, to verify the integrity of your data, or some sort of challenge or verification; for example, no one cares what your password actually is, they just want to know if they should let you into the system or not. The data is not the value; proving your identity is (you know the original value, the password, which proves your identity). Hashing a value also means that if the value is ever leaked, it is unusable; leaked passwords (that are in an altered and hashed format) don't do the thief any good, as you would enter them into the system and they would not be recognized as your password.

> **NOTE** Although there are currently concerns about quantum computing making our current forms of cryptography and encryption obsolete, this book will presume that has not happened yet. There is no known date as to when this will occur, and no one, including me, currently has a working quantum-resistant encryption algorithm or strategy that is proven as of this writing. As such, this topic is out of scope for this book.

In order to ensure the confidentiality of your data, it should be encrypted in transit (on its way to and from the user, the database, an API, etc.) and at rest (while in the database). It should be noted that this ensures no one will learn your secrets; if someone were to gain unauthorized access to your data or intercept your traffic with a sniffing tool, they would not be able to understand what they have found. This does not, however, protect the availability of your data, or its integrity. Someone could still delete or change the data in your database (it would be obvious it was changed or removed, but also quite inconvenient if your backups and rollbacks are not perfectly seamless). A malicious actor could intercept your traffic and change or block your messages, which again would cause problems. That said, protecting your secrets (the "C" in CIA) is vital, and thus no matter what system you are creating, you will want to ensure the data is encrypted (not hashed) in transit and at rest.

Some may argue that data should even be encrypted while in use (in memory), but unless you are dealing with extremely sensitive data, this is generally not expected as a project requirement. To protect highly sensitive data, it is recommended that you flush the memory when your program exits, logs out, or is otherwise ended.

Never Trust System Input

Any input to your system could potentially be tampered with or otherwise cause your application to malfunction or fail. Whether this input is intentionally malicious or not, if it causes your application to go into an unknown state (a state you have not planned for or programmed to handle), this is a very dangerous place to be. When your application falls into an unknown state, this is where malicious actors are able to force your application to do things you never dreamed of, including breaking one or more of the CIA factors. Your program must be able to handle every type of input *gracefully*, even bad input.

Input to your application means literally anything and everything that is not a part of your application or that could have been manipulated outside of your application.

> **NOTE**   One of the main risks to computer software is when data (values in variables, from an API or from a database) is executed as though it were part of the code of your application. Having code run that is not supposed to be a part of your application is generally characterized as an "injection" vulnerability and has been widely recognized by security professionals as the #1 threat to secure software[5] since the start of our industry. This risk is the motivation for many of the project requirements included in this chapter, but most especially this one.

Following are examples of input to your application:

■ User input on the screen (for instance, entering search phrases into a field)

■ Information from a database (even the database you designed for your app)

- Information from an API (even one you wrote)
- Information from another application that your application integrates with or otherwise accepts input from (this includes serverless apps and scripts)
- Values in the URL parameters, cookie values, configuration files
- Data or commands from cloud workflows
- Images that you've included from other sites (with or without permission)
- Values used from online storage

This is not an exhaustive list. Please be aware that *anything* from outside your program could potentially be damaging.

NOTE   *Cloud workflows* are triggers that are usually used to call serverless apps, but may be used to trigger an action within your application.

Serverless applications are applications or scripts that run in the cloud, without the need of a server running all the time. This means they are not using infrastructure resources unless they are running. When a serverless application is called, it launches a container, the app or script runs to completion on that container, and then it self-destructs, releasing the infrastructure resources.

Examples of parts of your application that could be manipulated outside of your program include:

- URL parameters (a user could change them)
- Information in a cookie that does not have the "secure" and "HTTPS only" flags set
- Hidden fields (they are not safe from attackers)
- HTTPS request headers
- Values entered on the screen that can be manipulated after they have passed your JavaScript validation if using a web proxy (more on this later in the chapter)
- Front-end frameworks that are not included as part of your project but instead hosted elsewhere on the internet and called from your application in real time
- Third-party code that you include in your application when it is compiled (libraries, includes, frameworks, etc.)
- Images that you include in your application that are hosted elsewhere on the internet

- Configuration files that are not managed by you

- APIs or any other service that your application calls

- Scripts that you do not control

Sometimes developers forget that even frameworks and online services that are well trusted, respected, and supported are still possible attack vectors.

In order to effectively apply the concept "never trust system input" you must always validate all input (every single time) before you use the input. Input is considered untrustworthy until after validation. By "validate" I mean you perform tests to ensure the input is appropriate and what you are expecting, and if it's not, reject it. There are special cases where you should sanitize input (remove anything that is potentially bad), and that will be discussed later. For this section we are discussing validating input to your application.

Input validation examples include:

- You are expecting a date of birth, so you verify that the value you receive is indeed in date format and/or convert it into date format, and that it is within the previous 100 years (for example, `age > current year - 100 && age < current year`). If it is not in proper date format ("aaaaaaaa" for example), you reject it. If it states the person is 5,000 years old, you reject it. If the person's age is such that they have not been born yet, reject it. Issue a proper error message stating the format is incorrect, and what the format should be. Or, if it is not within your age range of 100 years, issue an error message stating that the age is not correct.

- The field is a person's first name, and you have dedicated 80 characters for this field. Verify that the input you receive is 80 characters or less, and that the characters are appropriate for a name. For instance, if it contains %, [, {, <, or |, it is unlikely to be a real name, and you should reject this input with an appropriate error message. However, with many anglophone names such as O'Connor containing apostrophes ('), you will need to ensure you accept this input but handle it carefully (encode the value; more on that soon). For non-anglophone names you will need to accept accents (é, å, etc.), letters from alphabets other than the Greek one used for English, hyphens, etc.

- The field is an email address; there are regular expressions available online for validating email addresses, and validators in your framework. I suggest that you use the tried, tested, and true validation functions in your framework, which are quite complex but work perfectly.

- Your program does a search in the database and displays a string from the record it found to the screen. Validate that this input is what you are expecting, just as you would if it came from a user. Ensure that it is not stored cross-site scripting (XSS), or something else potentially malicious. Always output encode[6] it before displaying to the screen.

NOTE   XSS is JavaScript injected into your application by a malicious actor that is executed in the browser, on the device the user is using to view your web app. If we output encode all of our output before putting it on the screen, XSS attacks are rendered as text and not executed, producing something similar to "<script>. . . ." on the screen. It's ugly, but it is also harmless.

■ You call an API; you send a postal code, and it returns the rest of the address. Verify that the address is in the correct format and is what you are expecting. If it's thousands of characters, that's likely incorrect; 500 should be enough to call any API. If it's all numbers, that's likely incorrect. If it contains characters that are commonly found in code ([, {, <, /, etc.), that's likely incorrect. Only accept the input into your program if it passes your validation. Lastly, the data as it flows between the application and the API should be encrypted to protect the privacy of your user. Encryption can be forced within the application itself, by using a service mesh, or by any other reliable mechanism.

■ An application calls your application and passes a URL in the parameters. This is a dangerous action from a security perspective and is generally referred to as an *open redirect*. Whenever possible, your application should only accept information from other applications over secure channels (TLS), and you should also validate the data they send you. Preferably you should find a different way to pass a value like this, as a malicious actor could change the URL and potentially send your users to a dangerous site. However, if this is the only option available, you should flip ahead to Chapter 4, "Secure Code," which explains how to handle this.

■ If you are writing an application in a language that is not memory-safe (for example, C/C++), you will need to do something called *bounds checking*[7] to ensure the input does not overflow your variable types. In C/C++ it is possible to input more than the maximum amount for an integer and cause it to "rollover"[8] into the negatives, which would obviously be problematic. It is also possible to overflow strings, which results in the well-known vulnerability called *buffer overflow*,[9] wherein an attacker can overwrite parts of memory. In a best-case buffer-overflow scenario your application crashes, the crash triggers an alert, and your incident response team stops the attacker from getting any further. In the worst case the attacker uses the crash information to refine and improve their attack until they are able to take over your web server and infiltrate your network. The risks cannot be understated when discussing overflow vulnerabilities; take this vulnerability category seriously.

It is essential that your application validates the input first, then uses it. There is no purpose in performing validation of the data *after* you have used it. It must be the very first thing you do after receiving input into your application.

NOTE   When issuing an error message to the screen to reject user input, if you decide to show the user's input, be aware that it may be malicious and therefore potentially cause your program to malfunction. *Always* encode the output using HTML encoding (which is a function available in all modern programming frameworks), assuming you are in an HTML context.

TIP   The type of output encoding will depend on the context of the data that you are reflecting to the screen. For instance, if you are using text within JavaScript strings, you need to Unicode-escape them; however, if you are embedding user input within an event handler there would be two levels of output encoding (the JavaScript and then the HTML). If possible, avoid these types of situations. If that is not possible, consult the OWASP XXS Prevention Cheat Sheet.[10]

NOTE   If you are writing or rewriting a low-level application from scratch, always choose Rust over C or C++. Rust is a new-ish programming language that can perform low-level tasks well like C and C++, but unlike C/C++, *Rust is memory-safe*. This means that bounds checking is no longer required, and it is impossible to overflow variables to create potential security vulnerabilities. Memory safety is no joke; browser maker Mozilla (Firefox) estimates that 73% of the vulnerabilities in their style component alone would never have happened if it had been written in Rust as opposed to C/C++.[11] This one design decision alone could reduce your attack surface so dramatically that there is no acceptable business reasoning that could excuse writing new applications in C when Rust is available. "But we all already know how to program in C" is not an acceptable reason not to learn and use the Rust programming language.

Encoding and Escaping

The most commonly known security vulnerability in web applications is *cross-site scripting* (XSS); it's estimated to be present in over two-thirds[12] of web applications on the internet as of this writing. There are multiple mitigations for this risk: the Content Security Policy Header (CSP), input validation, and output encoding (*this* requirement). The output encoding requirement only exists in order to prevent XSS, and as this risk is so prevalent and this mistake is so easy to make, it is most definitely worth the effort to add *all three* of these defenses to *all* of your applications.

TIP   Adding all three defenses for XSS to your application is a great example of applying the "defense in depth" principle to your application.

Escaping a character or value means removing the special powers that it would have if it were executed as code, instead of being treated as data (as it should be). It is usually done by adding a backslash (\) character before the special character in question.

Encoding is changing a value from whatever format it is in into whatever format you are encoding for (URL encoding, base64 encoding, HTML encoding). Encoding can easily be reversed and is not to be mistaken for or used instead of encryption. The purpose of encoding is not to protect the value you are encoding, but to change it into the format that you want to use it as. For instance, if you are going to output something to the screen, you must *output encode* it using the feature for this in your framework (all modern frameworks have this feature). The output encoding will ensure that if the value that you are outputting to the screen contains code (such as a cross-site scripting attack), it will only output the text value, not interpret (execute) the code in the browser as JavaScript. Output encoding renders XSS attack code powerless.

The commandment here is likely obvious; encode (and escape if need be) all output.

NOTE XSS is a special type of injection vulnerability, in that when an attack is successful, the code (JavaScript) is executed on the client side (in the browser), whereas most other types of injection vulnerabilities are executed on the server side (at the interpreter level, operating system level, etc.). The defense for XSS is a combination of input validation and output encoding/escaping, whereas all other injection vulnerabilities depend mainly on input validation and configuration settings on the server side. It is also more common than every other serious type of vulnerability on the web. Thus, despite the fact that XSS is a type of injection vulnerability, it is always segregated as its own class of vulnerability.

Third-Party Components

As stated previously, every line of code you include from a library, framework, plugin, or other third-party component is risk that you accept into your application; if it is insecure your application is now also insecure if it accesses/ uses/calls that part of the component. Even if the insecure line of code in the component is not used by your application, it can sometimes still make your application vulnerable, depending on the situation. Verifying that all third-party components are not known to be vulnerable is a quick-and-easy win in regard to understanding how secure your application is. Fixing the issues found may not be quick or easy, but it goes a long way to ensuring your application is secure, and thus is always recommended as a project and maintenance requirement.

KNOWN VULNERABLE

What does "known vulnerable" mean? When creating custom software, it is, by definition, unique. Each piece of custom software is a snowflake, and thus, every new vulnerability a person would find in it is unknown to the public. Software that is not custom is often just called "software," such as an operating system or COTS. (COTS stands for Commercial/Customizable/Configurable Off The Shelf. It's software that anyone can purchase that is installed but also highly configurable. Examples include SharePoint, WordPress, Microsoft Office, and Adobe Illustrator.) When a penetration tester, security researcher, or other "hacker" finds a vulnerability in any software (custom or not), ideally they would report it to whoever made the software (this is called "coordinated disclosure"), or if there is a bug bounty program, they could submit it as part of the program and potentially be paid. If it is not custom software, once the bug is reported and a patch is issued (usually a software update from the user/s perspective), the bug is published in several places online (such as Mitre's CVE database[13]) for all to see, and thus it is considered to be a "known" vulnerability. The version of the software with the vulnerability is then considered to be "known to be vulnerable" and would usually be picked up by automated tools that scan for this.

After a bug is found in software, an operating system, or a COTS product, but before a patch is issued, this bug is called a "zero day" or "0 day," to make it clear there is no known fix for the problem. Often security teams will refer to patches in terms of days since they've been issued, for instance "this vulnerability is 90+ days old and we still haven't patched!", hence why "zero" was chosen.

NOTE   If you listen to a podcast or read a news article stating someone "dropped oh day," they mean that the person publicly released details about a security vulnerability for which there is no known fix. This is usually done to create social pressure to force the company to issue a fix, or to show off their skills as a security researcher. It is my opinion and advice that anyone with information on a security vulnerability should always report it to the maker of the software before publishing it publicly. Not to protect the company that makes the software, but to protect the users of the software; they are not at fault and endangering them is in opposition of the purpose and mandate of the Information Security industry. </rant>

There are many, many tools on the market that can verify if your third-party components are known to be vulnerable. This book is not going to recommend specific tools or vendors, but instead it will offer strategic uses of such tools. The first strategy is that if you can afford it, use two tools, not one. They all check different databases and in different ways, and therefore may not catch the same things. The second strategy is that you should regularly scan your code repository (daily, or at least weekly), as well as scan every time you release code to production. You should scan your repository because some of your applications will be published rarely, but new vulnerabilities are still being found all the time. The older the components are that you are including in your code, the more time there has been for security researchers and malicious actors to review them, and potentially find vulnerabilities in them. You should scan every time you release your code because you (or your teammates) may have added a new component or upgraded a component to a version that is known to be vulnerable but not realized it. Building this into your CI/CD pipeline (or whatever other process you use to publish your code) would protect you from unintentionally including harmful third-party code.

Note that this step is the scan for *known* vulnerabilities in third-party code. There are likely to be more vulnerabilities that remain unknown. Checking for known vulnerabilities is the bare minimum in regard to creating secure software. If you are building software that requires a very high level of assurance, you should test and review every single line of code that your application depends on. A best practice when it comes to third-party components is to only include the ones that you need, as opposed to including every cool new thing you see on the internet. Although this will be a tough sell with developers (let's face it, new tech is exciting and fun), if you can explain the risks involved and propose an alternative or solution, rather than just saying no, you are more likely to have positive results.

PRIVACY WARNING

Alice wanted to attach her online encrypted personal calendar to her desktop calendar software, so she could see her work calendar and personal calendar in the same place. She read the help page for the desktop calendar software and it said to set her calendar Share settings to "Public." Alice was shocked! She has an encrypted calendar because she wants to keep her information *private*. She filed a complaint for the help page, explaining that it should warn the users about the potential privacy issues that could happen if they set it that way. Alice got new desktop calendar software.

Security Headers: Seatbelts for Web Apps

Security headers are settings that tell the browser and server how to handle various things for your web application; they only apply to web assets that use a browser (web apps and Software as a Service, or SaaS, products that are accessed via a browser). They do not apply to software that you install on your computer, operating systems, or embedded systems like firmware. Security headers are a lot like seatbelts; they aren't sexy or exciting, they aren't difficult to use or time consuming, and if you create a habit of using them, they can save you in an emergency (such as a car accident or an attack against your web application, respectively). Security headers can usually be applied on either the web server or your code. To apply them you generally will add one line of code or check a box to configure your web server; it's not a difficult task. You can do it; I believe in you.

Now let's talk about what each header is for, why you do or do not need to use each one, and what settings you should choose. Feel free to copy and paste these settings directly into your applications if you feel they would be helpful; but always test before pushing to prod.

> **TIP**   Visit `OWASP.org` or `SecurityHeaders.com` to learn even more about security headers!

Security Headers in Action

For the OWASP DevSlop Project, my friend Franziska Bühler and I made several videos and blog posts about adding security headers to our website. Here is an example of potential code you could use for ASP.Net:

```
<! - Start ASP.Net Security Headers ->
<httpProtocol>
<customHeaders>
<add name="X-XSS-Protection" value="1; mode=block"/>
<add name="Content-Security-Policy" value="default-src 'self'"/>
<add name="X-frame-options" value="SAMEORIGIN"/>
<add name="X-Content-Type-Options" value="nosniff"/>
<add name="Referrer-Policy" value="strict-origin-when-cross-origin"/>
<remove name="X-Powered-By"/>
</customHeaders>
</httpProtocol>
<! - End Security Headers ->
```

X-XSS-Protection

This header has been deprecated. Not only is it no longer supported by modern browsers, but it is recommended by several industry experts that it should no longer be used at all, due to the vulnerabilities it can create. Although it can help in *some* cases with *some* very old browsers, it causes more harm than good, and therefore should no longer be used as of this writing.

Content-Security-Policy (CSP)

The first thing a malicious actor does when they realize a website is vulnerable to XSS is call out to their own script, located somewhere else on the internet, which is usually significantly longer than the vulnerable app would allow or would be otherwise detected and blocked. Most applications only allow 20–100 characters for most fields, meaning an attacker wouldn't be able to install a complete piece of malware or do as much damage as they would like to, so they call out to somewhere else on the internet where their harmful code is ready and waiting.

Content Security Policy makes you list all of the sources for content (scripts, images, frames, fonts, etc.) that your site will use that are outside of your domain, which would stop a vulnerable web application from calling out and running the secondary part of the attack. It reduces the risk and potential damage of this type of attack drastically. That said, developers tend to find it time consuming to keep track of their sources and so this is not a popular security header among developers. It is my viewpoint that it would be used much more often if developers understood the risks and the protection it offers from these risks. If you are having trouble convincing a developer to apply this header, consider lending them this book; hopefully they'll thank you later.

> **NOTE** *Never* turn CSP on without the developer's consent and assistance. You shouldn't enable security features without coordinating with affected teams in general, but especially for this security header. It would almost certainly break the website's look and feel and some of its features, but more importantly, it will break trust with the developer team. Don't rush into this one; test it thoroughly before you deploy for the first time.

The absolute easiest setting is to just block everything, which is a good choice if your site is static and/or boring (doesn't call any content from anywhere). The settings for this would be as follows:

```
Content-Security-Policy: default-src 'self'; block-all-mixed-content;
```

But let's be honest; few modern websites are so simple. That's okay, we got this.

This is a list, courtesy of OWASP (the Open Web Application Security Project), of the various sources you can define in your policy:

- **default-src**: As you would expect, this is the default setting. It's sort of a "catch all." If anything is trying to load and it's not clearly defined in the rest of the policy, this will apply. It is often set to "self," to say that if we don't explicitly allow it somewhere else in the policy the answer is "don't load it." Always set this to "self" if you are unsure.

> **NOTE** Frame Ancestors and Form Action are exceptions to this rule; they do not fallback to default-src.

- **script-src**: A list of domains (where scripts are located) or the exact URL of the script that are allowed to run as part of your site. Every other script from any other place on the internet, except those in your domain and what you list here, will not run. This protects against XSS attacks.

> **WARNING**   The "unsafe-inline" keyword can be used as part of your configuration in order to undo all of the locking down we just did in our Content Security Policy; it allows any script from anywhere to run. The use of unsafe-inline in your applications should not be final; it should be temporary, for testing. Use unsafe-inline as you work your way up to a mature and complete CSP implementation, but it should never be final or used as a permanent solution. Also, make sure to audit for this setting in production during security assessments.

Each of the following items follows this pattern: if you list it, then that type of resource can be used or loaded as part of your web application, plus those from within your own domain. Every other type of resource not listed here, when using the CSP header, will be blocked.

- object-src = plugins (valid sources for <object>, <embed>, and <applet> elements)
- style-src = styles (Cascading Style Sheets, or CSS)
- img-src = images
- media-src = video and audio
- frame-src = frames
- font-src = fonts
- `plugin-types = limits types of plugins that can be run`
- **script-nonce**: This is a complicated one, but noteworthy. A nonce is string of characters created to be used one single time in order to prove that a specific script is the one you mean to call. This is an extra-added level of security within the CSP security header. Using this setting means you require the nonce in order to run the script.

> **TIP**   Nonces are a complex topic, and the implementation of the nonce feature within CSP has changed over time. With this in mind I direct you to the OWASP Cheat Sheet on this topic for updates and a significantly longer explanation: `cheatsheetseries.owasp.org/cheatsheets/Content_Security_Policy_Cheat_Sheet.html`.

- **report-uri**: CSP will make a report for you about what it has blocked and other helpful information. This URI is to tell it where to send the report. As of this writing there are only four security headers that provide a reporting feature, and quite frankly, it's really cool. Having metrics and information about the types of attacks your site is receiving is a gift.

WARNING   The URL of the reports are public, meaning an attacker could potentially view your reports and also perform a denial-of-service attack (DOS or DDOS) in order to hide their misdeeds.

This is by far the most complex of all the security headers. For more information on this topic visit `csp-evaluator.withgoogle.com` (from Google) and `scotthelme.co.uk`.

For example:

```
Content-Security-Policy: default-src 'self'; img-src
https://*.wehackpurple.com; media-src https://*.wehackpurple.com;
```

allows the browser to load images, videos, and audio from *.wehackpurple.com.

```
Content-Security-Policy: default-src 'self'; style-src
https://*.jquery.com; script-src https://*.google.com;
```

allows the browser to load styles from `jquery.com` and scripts from `google.com`.

TIP   Security headers that provide reports: CSP, Expect-CT, Public-Key-Pins, and XSS-Protection. Very handy!

NOTE   DOS or DDOS stands for denial of service, with the extra "D" meaning "distributed." The purpose of a DOS attack is to overload the resources of the victim such that no one can use them. This could cause a website to crash, online stores to lose sales, and other forms of blocking access to online resources. When DOS attacks first started, they often came from one only source, meaning that IP address could be blocked and the attack would be subverted. Over time attackers learned that having many (hundreds or even thousands) of different IPs launching an attack was significantly more damaging and difficult to defend against. Most DOS attacks as of this writing are distributed (DDOS), often using compromised IoT devices as part of the attack.

X-Frame-Options

This header helps to protect against clickjacking attacks,[15] which means a malicious website framing your legitimate website, and being able to steal information or "clicks." Although you may have a specific situation where you want your site to be framed by one or more specific sites, allowing any site to frame yours is likely a bad idea as this can lead to situations where a user thinks they are on your site, when in fact they are clicking on an invisible site that is most likely malicious in nature (which is called "clickjacking"). This can lead to keylogging and stealing user's credentials. In order for this type of vulnerability to be exploited the user has to participate by clicking a phishing link or a link on a malicious site, meaning it doesn't happen in the wild as often as some other attacks, but the potential damage is high when it does.

> **WARNING**   X-Frame-Options is deprecated and Content-Security-Policy (CSP) is used in its place for modern browsers. X-Frame-Options is used for backward compatibility of older browsers and will hopefully be phased out slowly from active use.

To allow the site to use frames from within your own domain, set X-Frame-Options to "sameorigin":

```
X-Frame-Options: SAMEORIGIN
```

To allow no frames, from anywhere, set to X-Frame-Options to "deny":

```
X-Frame-Options: DENY
```

X-Content-Type-Options

Part of the beauty of writing software is being creative and taking poetic license in the way you use a programming language; finding new and imaginative ways to use your language and framework. However, sometimes this leads to ambiguity, which can lead to security vulnerabilities if an application is unsure of its next instruction. This is called "falling into an unknown state," and we *never* want our applications to fall into an unknown state. Unless you are a penetration tester or security researcher that is; in that case it is your favorite place in the world as you will most certainly find software vulnerabilities there.

This security header instructs a browser not to "sniff" (infer/guess) the content type of media used in a web app, and instead to rely solely on the type specified by the application. Browsers like to think that they can anticipate the type of the content that they are serving in attempts to be helpful, but unfortunately this has turned into a known vulnerability that can be exploited, to the detriment of your website. This security header only has one possible setting:

```
X-Content-Type-Options: nosniff
```

Referrer-Policy

When you surf from site to site on the internet, each site sends the next site a value called the "referrer," which means a link to the page you came from. This is incredibly helpful for people analyzing their traffic, so they know where people are coming from. However, if you are visiting a site of a sensitive nature (a mortgage application, or a site detailing a specific medical condition, for example), you may not want the specifics sent to the next page you visit. In order to protect your user's privacy, as the website creator you can set the referrer value to only pass the domain and not which page the user was on (`wehackpurple.com` versus `wehackpurple.com/embarrassing-blog-post-title`), or to not pass any value at all. You can also change the value of the referrer based on whether you are "downgrading" from HTTPS to HTTP.

In order to only pass on the protocol and domain information, set the referrer to "origin." No other context can change this setting.

```
Referrer-Policy: origin
```

For example, a document at `https://wehackpurple.com/page.html` will send the referrer `https://wehackpurple.com/`.

This setting will send only the protocol and domain if the user is leaving your domain. Within your domain it passes the entire path. This will serve most situations for non-sensitive websites:

```
Referrer-Policy: strict-origin-when-cross-origin
```

No value in the referrer field, context does not matter:

```
Referrer-Policy: no-referrer
```

This setting can get quite complex if you need it to, but generally only sending the origin domain when leaving your domain will fit most business situations and protect your user's privacy adequately. If in doubt, you can always send nothing to ensure your user's privacy is respected.

For more information, Mozilla is a leader in this area and always offers stellar advice and technical guidance:

```
developer.mozilla.org/en-US/docs/Web/HTTP/Headers/Referrer-Policy
```

Bonus Resource: Scott Helme, a security researcher who shares a lot of information and tools on security headers, is a great resource to learn more about this topic: `scotthelme.co.uk`

Strict-Transport-Security (HSTS)

This security header forces the connection to be HTTPS (encrypted), even if the user attempted to connect to the website via HTTP. This means the data going and back and forth will be encrypted by force. Users, including attackers, cannot downgrade to HTTP (unencrypted); the browser will force it to switch to HTTPS before loading any data.

DEFINITIONS

Platform as a Service (PaaS): A cloud computing service that hosts software in the cloud (usually web applications), which is maintained by the cloud provider. There is no need to patch or upgrade a PaaS; your cloud provider performs these tasks for you.

Certificate Authority (often known as a CA): A trusted company or organization that verifies the identity of whoever is purchasing a certificate.

Electronic Frontier Foundation (EFF): An international non-profit organization that works to protect the privacy and other rights on the internet.

"Let's Encrypt": Run by the Electronic Frontier Foundation (EFF), this offers encryption certificates for free. As of this writing Let's Encrypt is the only consumer Certificate Authority that offers certificates to the public for free.

Wild Card Certificate: A "wild card" certificate covers all of your subdomains, not only your main domain. You will want to get one of these if you have subdomains. Subdomains are everything where the '*' is in this formula: `*.yourdomain.whatever`.

For example, *.wehackpurple.com would include newsletter.wehackpurple.com, store.wehackpurple.com, and www.wehackpurple.com.

In order for this security header to work correctly you need to have a certificate that is issued by a certificate authority (CA), installed on your web server, PaaS, container, or wherever else you are hosting your app. This certificate will be used as part of the encryption process, and you cannot turn on HSTS without one. You will want to get one called a "wildcard" certificate if you have subdomains. You will also want a certificate that lasts as long as possible (one year as opposed to 3 months), so that you don't have to waste time "rotating your certs" very often.

Then you will need to figure out how long your certificate lasts, in seconds. No, I'm not kidding, they decided to time it in *seconds*. Hint: one year is 31,536,000 seconds:

```
Strict-Transport-Security: max-age=31536000; includeSubDomains
```

TIP   You can submit your domain to `hstspreload.org` and add the suffix "preload" to your declaration. Google will preload your site to ensure that no one is ever able to connect to your site unencrypted. Although major browsers have announced their intentions to adopt this functionality, it is not part of the official HSTS specification.[16]

The adjusted syntax of the preceding example would become Strict-Transport-Security: max-age=31536000; includeSubDomains; preload.

Feature-Policy

As of this writing, this is the newest security header supported by modern browsers. With the advent of HTML 5 and many cool new features in more modern browsers, this security header allows or disallows these new types of features for your web application.

The setting choices are:

- **none**: Not allowed at all
- **self**: Allowed but only your own domain can use/call this feature
- **src** (iframes only): The document loaded into the iframe must come from the same origin as the URL in the iframe's src attribute[16]
- *****: Any domain can use/call this feature
- **<origin(s)>**: This feature is allowed for specific URLs[17]

Here is an example that allows only your own speaker and full screen to run on your site:

```
Feature-Policy: camera 'none'; microphone 'none'; speaker 'self';
vibrate 'none'; geolocation 'none'; accelerometer 'none';
ambient-light-sensor 'none'; autoplay 'none'; encrypted-media 'none';
gyroscope 'none'; magnetometer 'none'; midi 'none'; payment 'none';
picture-in-picture 'none'; usb 'none'; vr 'none'; fullscreen *
```

These settings were used for the OWASP DevSlop Project website. We forbid almost all features; we only allowed the use of the speaker when called from our own site. We also allowed any domain to set the browser to full screen. When in doubt, be more restrictive, not less. Your users will thank you.

X-Permitted-Cross-Domain-Policies

This security header specifically applies only to Adobe products (Reader and Flash) being a part of your application. Adobe Flash is incredibly insecure and is no longer supported by Adobe, and thus should not be used in modern websites or applications.

The purpose of this header is to ensure that files from your domain are allowed (or not) to be accessed by the Adobe products from other sites. If you intend to allow Adobe Reader hosted in places other than your domain to access the documents on your site, you would want to name the domains here. Otherwise, set it to "none" to ensure that no other domains are allowed to use Adobe products to access your documents/resources:

```
X-Permitted-Cross-Domain-Policies: none
```

Expect-CT

"CT" refers to Certification Transparency, an open framework that provides oversite for Certificate Authorities (CAs). From time to time CAs accidentally issue certificates to less-than-ideal sites, and sometimes even outright malicious sites. The entire Certificate Authority system was designed in order to create trust and verify that whoever was the holder of a certificate would be a site that could be trusted by browsers and users. If CAs are providing certificates to malicious sites, whether it be through error, negligence, or by being complicit, it is not acceptable. The Certificate Transparency Framework logs details about various transactions to track when CAs have issued certificates inappropriately.

If a CA has made several "bad calls" when issuing certificates, a browser or organization may choose to no longer "trust" the certificates that they issue.

You may wonder what this has to do with you as a software developer, application support professional, or security professional. In order to help maintain the integrity of the entire Certificate Authority system, we must log our certificates into the online CT registry. If a site's certificate is not in the registry, modern web browsers will issue warnings to users that your website is untrustworthy. No one in your business wants browsers telling users their website is unsafe.

When you turn on this security header:

1. Your user's browser will check the CT logs to see if your certificate is there, for better or worse.

2. If set to "enforce," your user's browser will enforce certificate transparency, which means if your certificate is not in the registry or is otherwise "CT unqualified," it will terminate the connection between your site and the user. If not in enforce mode, a report is sent to the report URL.

It is advised at first you deploy in "reporting only" mode, then once you are certain your certificates are acceptable and correctly registered, you upgrade to "enforce" mode.

The "max-age" field (measured in seconds) is the length of time for the browser to apply this setting (it is cached in the browser for this length of time).

WARNING   Just like the CSP Reports, the Expect-CT Report URLs are not private. Any information in them could be accessed by anyone, including those with less-than-honest intentions.

Below are two examples of implementation of the Expect-CT header:

Reporting only:

```
Expect-CT: max-age=86400, report-uri="https://wehackpurple.com/report"
```

Reporting and Blocking:

```
Expect-CT: max-age=86400, enforce, report-uri="https://wehackpurple.com/
report"
```

The following is another example from the OWASP DevSlop project, this time for .Net CORE applications. This example requires that you add an additional Nuget package ("Nwebsec.AspNetCore.Middleware")[18] to your project, as per the first line in the example:

```
<PackageReference Include="Nwebsec.AspNetCore.Middleware"
Version="2.0.0"/>

//Security headers .Net CORE, not the same as ASP.net
app.UseHsts(hsts => hsts.MaxAge(365).IncludeSubdomains());
app.UseXContentTypeOptions();
app.UseReferrerPolicy(opts => opts.NoReferrer());
app.UseXXssProtection(options => options.EnabledWithBlockMode());
app.UseXfo(options => options.Deny());
app.UseCsp(opts => opts
.BlockAllMixedContent()
.StyleSources(s => s.Self())
.StyleSources(s => s.UnsafeInline())
.FontSources(s => s.Self())
.FormActions(s => s.Self())
.FrameAncestors(s => s.Self())
.ImageSources(s => s.Self())
.ScriptSources(s => s.Self())
);
//End Security Headers
```

Public Key Pinning Extension for HTTP (HPKP)

Public Key Pinning is a system that was created to protect against fraudulent certificates. The idea of this system was that only one or two Certificate Authorities would be trusted for a particular URL/site. At first it was implemented using static pins (built into the browser directly and manually, specifically in Chrome and Firefox), but eventually other website owners wanted to "pin" certificates as well, and this was done dynamically by website owners. The certificate would be pinned for a period of time (usually a year) and to a specific cryptographic identity (keys). However, if you lose your keys, it means you've lost control of your website for up to a year, as it won't work without them. In the meantime, you have essentially "bricked" your website URL (made it unusable), and thus your security feature has caused catastrophic business damage. This situation is called "HPKP Suicide."

Although the potential benefits of this security header are great, the risks make it unadvisable to use this security feature unless you require an extremely high level of assurance and have a team that is extremely knowledgeable on this topic and ready to accept this business risk.

WARNING   This security header is considered deprecated/no longer supported.

Securing Your Cookies

The HTTP protocol was never designed to handle user sessions (keeping track of someone being logged in, or having items in a shopping cart; keeping track of anything as a user moves from page to page within your site is referred to as "state"). Cookies are used to pass information about a user session back and forth from the browser to your web server and can be saved for future use to give the user a more personalized experience (for instance, it can remember their language preference). Although many websites use cookies to store information for marketing and tracking purposes, and even selling the information to other companies, the ethical aspects in regard to privacy of the data kept within cookies is not a topic we will delve into here.

When you are setting cookies in your application, there are settings that you will need to use in order to ensure the data within your cookie remains safe, and they are discussed in the following sections.

Please note: Sometimes developers decide to use local storage instead of cookies. There is an entirely different set of precautions to take in order to protect local storage, and that will not be covered in this section. Also, your session should *always* be passed in a session cookie (not a persistent cookie, and never saved into local storage). *Always use a session cookie for your session.*

Also, just in case you forgot, always validate the input that you put into your cookies. If the data you are getting doesn't make sense, reject it and try again. Your cookie data is very valuable, and you must take care to always protect your session (more on that in the following chapters).

The Secure Flag

The secure flag ensures that your cookie will only be sent over encrypted (HTTPS) channels. If an attacker attempts to downgrade your session to HTTP, your web application will refuse to send the cookie. You should always turn this setting on:

```
Set-Cookie: Secure; (plus all of your other settings)
```

The HttpOnly Flag

The naming of this flag is not intuitive, as it has nothing to do with forcing the connection to be unencrypted (HTTP), and thus makes it confusing for programmers. When this flag is set on a cookie it means that the cookie cannot be accessed via JavaScript; it can only be changed on the server side. The reason for using this setting on your cookie is to protect against XSS attacks attempting to access the values in your cookie. You always want to set this value, in all cookies, as another layer of defense against XSS attacks against the confidentiality of the data in your cookie:

```
Set-Cookie: HttpOnly; (plus all of your other settings)
```

Persistence

If you are collecting sensitive user data or managing your session, your cookie should not be persistent; it should self-destruct at the end of the session to protect that data. A cookie that self-destructs at the end of your session is a called a "session cookie." If the cookie does not self-destruct at the end of the session, it is called a "persistent cookie" or a "tracking cookie." Talk with the privacy team and business analysts to determine whether you want the cookie to be persistent or not.

For persistent cookies, you can set the expiry via the "expires" attribute setting, and/or set a specific maximum age that the cookie can reach via "max-age" setting.

Expires: Jan 1, 2021

```
Set-Cookie: Expires=Mon, 1st Jan 2021 00:00:00 GMT; (plus all of your
other settings)
```

Max-age of 1 hour

```
Set-Cookie: Max-Age=3600; (plus all of your other settings)
```

Domain

If you want your cookie to be able to be accessed by domains outside of your own, you must explicitly list them as trusted domains using the "domain" attribute. Otherwise browsers will assume your cookies are "host-only," meaning only your domain can access them and it will block all other access. This type of built-in protection is considered "secure by default"; if only all software settings worked this way!

```
Set-Cookie: Domain=app.NOTwehackpurple.com; (plus all of your other
settings)
```

WARNING   If you do not set the subdomain (`NOTwehackpurple.com` instead of `app.NOTwehackpurple.com`), every application and page hosted within that domain will be able to access your cookie. You probably don't want that.

Path

Many URLs on the web are actually many separate applications all listed under different paths and subdomains. To the user they appear as one giant web page, but in reality, they could be thousands of different applications. If you are working in such a situation, it is likely that you should limit access to your cookie to only your specific area of the location where your application resides—its "path." You set the path attribute to limit your cookie's scope:

```
Set-Cookie: path=/YourApplicationsPath; (plus all of your other
settings)
```

Same-Site

The same-site attribute was created by Google to combat the cross-site request forgery (CSRF) vulnerability. CSRF, affectionately known as "sea surf," is an attack against users who are logged in to a legitimate site, where an attacker attempts to take actions on the user's behalf without their consent or knowledge. It's usually done via a phishing email.

Imagine Alice is going to be on a TV show to talk about the company she works for. Alice wants to look great on the show, and she has decided to buy a brand new outfit online. Alice logs in to her favorite clothing site and is looking through all the new items they have when she notices she has received an email. The email is a phishing email, with a link to the site that she is currently logged in to, and the link includes code instructions for the site to purchase a product and send it to the attacker, not Alice. If Alice clicks this link, and the site does not have proper defenses, the entire attack could happen without her even realizing it. The attack only works if Alice is currently logged in to the site in the phishing email.

You might think this sounds far fetched, but think back to logging in to any of the websites that you usually use. Do you always press the Log Out button? Do you sometimes leave a site open for a few days? No one is perfect, and it is our job is to protect the users of our sites, even if they make a mistake such as clicking a phishing link.

With this in mind, this cookie attribute enforces the rule that cookies can only come from within the same site. Cookies cannot come from cross-site (not your site) origins. The options are "None" (cookies can be sent from anywhere), "Strict" (only from your domain), and "Lax" (if you want cookies to be sent when coming from a link or another page, only send non-sensitive information in these cookies). If you don't set this value in your cookies, the default on modern browsers is "lax:/" and on older browsers it's "none."[19]

Lax means users can remain logged in and surf to other sites and then return and your cookies will still work. Lax is usually used for navigation and other features your application does *before* a user logs in. It will block obvious CSRF attacks (POST requests). It's not foolproof, but it's a good compromise if you can't talk them into using "strict."

```
Set-Cookie: same-site=Strict; (plus all of your other settings)

Set-Cookie: same-site=Lax; //only blocks POST requests, allows links
```

Cookie Prefixes

Prefixes for cookies are new and not accepted by all browsers; however, they are a defense-in-depth measure (additional layer) for cases where cookies are accidentally mishandled in your application. For instance, if a subdomain has been compromised, and your cookie is set to your entire domain in the "Path" setting, the compromised domain could attempt access to your cookie. Prefixes are within the name of the cookie, and therefore the server will see it, encrypted or not. Prefixes can be used to ensure your cookie is only accessed within a specific subdomain using the "host" prefix. More information on this topic is available on the Mozilla and Chrome websites.

Data Privacy

Most websites now have a privacy policy stating that websites must state which data they are collecting and how they are using it. If your workplace has such a policy, ensure you follow it. If your workplace doesn't, perhaps you need one. Food for thought.

Data Classification

All data collected, used, or created by your application must be classified and labeled to ensure that anyone doing work on your project knows how to handle the data. Depending upon which country you live in and where you work (private company or governmental agency), the classification system you use may be different. Ask your privacy or security team if you need guidance.

Let's look at some examples of why we need to classify data and how.

Bob works for the federal government, and they have their own data classification system (Figure 2-2). In his current role he deals with data that is Classified, Secret, and Top Secret, and there is a strict system to identify these files and data types, which Bob always follows. Classified, Secret, and Top Secret, in Bob's country of Canada, means that if exposed the data would cause harm to Canada as a nation, as opposed to a specific person. In his previous role Bob dealt with data that was much less sensitive, and those data classifications were public (anyone can see them), Protected A (could cause harm or embarrassment to an individual), Protected B (will cause harm to a person or persons), and Protected C (could result in death or otherwise irreparable damage to one or more persons).

Data Classifications Used at Bob's Job

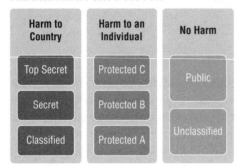

Figure 2-2: Data classifications Bob uses at work

By always classifying (deciding its level of sensitivity) and labeling the data that he collects, Bob ensures that everyone on the team knows how to handle the data correctly. If it's unlabeled, people could make a mistake, and unknowingly leak or leave unprotected very valuable and/or sensitive data. Many database systems allow you to add classification levels to data fields or tables (such as Microsoft SQL Server). If the one you are using doesn't provide this functionality natively, you can add an extra field to your table to label it yourself (or one for each field, if the sensitivity level varies). Even if data is "unclassified" or "public," it should be labeled.

Always follow the rules and regulations according to your data's classification. If you don't know what the rules or regulations are, ask. If there are no rules where you work, you can either adopt and follow the standard put forth by your country's government or NIST's "Guide for Mapping Types of Information and Information Systems to Security Categories."

NOTE   Although not appropriate as a project requirement, there should exist technical documentation explaining how to handle all the levels of sensitive data, coupled with ready-to-use code or libraries to handle the data. Ideally this code or library would centralize the management and processing of the data for uniform results.

Passwords, Storage, and Other Important Decisions

Alice has several different accounts for work, home, and as part of her hobbies. Bob is in the same situation—he has literally hundreds of passwords that he is supposed to remember between his job and personal life. In order to remember them all, Alice uses a password manager, while Bob just uses the same couple of passwords over and over again (which is called "password reuse" by security professionals).

TIP   This section contains requirements that may not be appropriate for a project, and instead be more appropriate as a standard for your IT shop as a whole, such as using a password manager. Do what makes sense for your organization.

A *password manager* is software that securely stores users' passwords and helps them create unique, long, and complex passwords. People use password managers so they don't need to remember several passwords; they just need the single password that they use to get into the manager (plus the passwords that cannot be stored in there, such as your phone or computer's password). Having a password manager create passwords for you ensures that they will be random (not predicable from a computer or human standpoint) and unique (that you won't reuse passwords like Bob).

Most password managers have plugins for your browsers so that once you sign into the password manager you just press a button to log in to any site you are visiting. It copies the username and password into the browser for you, meaning no typing errors. Really good password managers will also inform you if you are using the same password in multiple places, if your username and password have been part of a data breach, if you have chosen a poor password (you can still make up your own passwords when using a manager), and if a site that you have an account on offers MFA (multi-factor authentication) so that you can enable the MFA feature.

Password managers also usually have an area to take secure notes (you can save your SIN number, credit card info, etc., there). It is my advice that all avid computer users make use of password managers, not only for the added security it provides over your life, but to save your time in regard to resetting and forgetting passwords. Password managers are for end users; they are not to be used by computers.

One of the great things about using a password manager and using unique passwords everywhere is that if one of the websites you use has a data breach and their users' usernames and passwords (known as "credentials") are leaked onto the internet or fall into the hands of malicious actors, it will only affect one single account, not all of your accounts. Quite often when credentials are stolen as part of a data breach they are used as part of a *credential stuffing attack*, which means an attacker takes the stolen credentials and uses them as part of an automated attack against one or more other sites to see which have been reused, allowing the attacker to access accounts on other sites. Some attackers go so far as to script "adjustments" on the passwords, such as changing "Password1" to

"Password2," Password3," and so on, to try variations of the passwords. Using variations of the stolen passwords is called a *rainbow credential stuffing attack*.

If Alice and Bob both used the same site that had a data breach, since Alice uses unique passwords everywhere, she would just need to reset that one password and worry about that one account. Bob, on the other hand, would have a lot of work and worrying to do! Another way that Alice and Bob could protect themselves against this type of attack is to turn on MFA for every account that is valuable or potentially damaging to them (banking, work, email, accounts with credit cards attached, very personal accounts, health accounts, etc.)

Password manager + unique passwords everywhere + MFA = personal defense in depth

Software developers and tech workers are expected to remember an impossible number of passwords as part of their jobs, and they should always have access to a workplace-provided password manager.

Secret stores are similar to password managers, except they are built for computer systems to use, not people. A secret store is a software vault that encrypts your secrets, and then allows your application to access them programmatically (via the code in your app or CI/CD pipeline build process). You can store certificates, credentials (username and password), connection strings, hashes, and anything else that you consider a "secret" that your application will use.

Service accounts are accounts used by computers, not people. It is the identity of a computer system on your network, as opposed to a person. When you create an application and it needs to access a database, you should create a service account for your application to connect to the database, rather than using your own account. There are many reasons for this, with the most obvious being that if you quit and work somewhere else, they still need all the software to work after you're gone. Other reasons include monitoring (if each app has its own account then your monitoring team can see what the apps are doing, versus what *you* are doing), incident investigation (we want to see who did what and it could potentially look as though you had acted inappropriately if your username is everywhere), least privilege (your account likely has lots of permissions all over the place, and if someone got into your account they could take over all of the apps too), etc. You should always ensure you practice least privilege when creating and enabling service accounts.

> **TIP** Service account passwords should never expire unless there is a (suspected) breach. They should also be extremely complex and as long as possible. Service accounts should never be allowed (have privileges) to log in to workstations or access any other resource than what they were originally created for.

What about the passwords of the users of your application? Where should those be stored? They should be stored in the database (or other centralized place of management such as an identity provider), in a *salted* and *hashed* format. If you recall from earlier, hashing means a one-way cryptographic process, it cannot be undone. The process of salting is adding a unique, long value to a value before you hash it, in order to increase entropy and to make it even more difficult for a potential attacker to crack or guess a password. This means that when your application has a user login, it will run the hashing and salting functions against the value the user entered, then compare the result to what is stored in the database. If the usernames and passwords were ever stolen, they would be useless to an attacker, because if they entered the hashed and salted value into the application it would perform the functions against it, changing the value, and then it would no longer match the value in the database.

NOTE   *Cracking* refers to using an automated tool to guess a password, with the help of a word list, over and over again until it figures out the password. This process is also called *brute forcing*—guessing over and over at something until you gain access, using automation.

Your salt should be at least 28 characters (but preferably much longer), be generated by a secure random number generator, and it should be unique for each user of your application. Store the salt value in the database along with the hashed value of the salt + password, for each user. The salt is not a secret, unlike a pepper (explained in a moment), which is a secret.

Newer techniques for ensuring that passwords are extremely difficult to crack include "work factor" and "peppering."

A *work factor* means that you repeat the hashing algorithm X amount of times, with X being the work factor.[20] Your work factor should be at least 2, but can be incremented if need be (based on changes to hardware improvements in our industry, level of sensitivity of your data and/or accounts, or anything else in your application's changing threat landscape).

Peppering, or a cryptographic "pepper,"[20] is similar to a salt in that it is added to a password before the password is hashed and it should be generated by a secure random number generator. However, a pepper is a secret and should not be stored in the database like a salt (it should be stored in a secret store, as it is a secret), it should be quite long (minimum 32 characters but preferably 128), and the pepper is unique for each application, but the same for all users of that application.

It is possible to both salt and pepper your passwords; however, generally only a salt is required for most systems. Decide this with your security team.

TIP   Ideally your system's users can be managed as part of an identity management solution, meaning you can offload this difficult security work to a system made for this purpose.

WARNING   If a pepper needs to be rotated, it is possible it will invalidate all of the passwords for all of the users of your application. You must be careful when rotating your pepper. This risk is a big deal and will make your users and clients upset if a reset occurs, so design with pepper rotation in mind if you decide to use peppering.

Ensure passwords for your application's users are long, but not necessarily complex; having an uppercase letter, a lowercase letter, a number, and a special character is good, but demanding how many they have of each is frustrating for users. Only ask for one of each category for "complexity" requirements. Allow users to enter passwords of up to 64 characters. The longer the better; encourage use of passphrases. Do not force users to change their passwords after a certain amount of time, unless a breach is suspected. Verify that new users' passwords have not previously been in a breach by comparing sha1 hashes in a range, using a service such as HaveIBeenPwned.

WARNING   When verifying if a user's password has already been in a breach, ensure you protect the anonymity of your users. There are several models for this such as K-anonymity; read more at `haveibeenpwned.com/API/v3#SearchingPwnedP asswordsByRange`.

Never verify if it was the username or password that was incorrect when alerting the user that they have failed when logging in. Giving this information away allows potential attackers to harvest usernames (verifying that a user does or does not use your system).

TIP   Security questions are not a modern verification method as most users select questions for which the answer is publicly available (on social media, for instance), and thus security questions should be avoided if possible.

Forgotten password features should verify the user's identity before sending a password reset link via email or SMS, either by using another form of authentication or security questions. If the user fails authentication, never reveal which part failed. Never allow the user to reset the password directly on your system; always send it using an "out of band" form of communication (via an email or SMS link) as a second form of authentication. The reset link should be one-use only, and expire within 1 hour if not used. Always log that the password has been reset (or an attempt, if the user was not successful), and send an email or SMS listed on that account to confirm that the password has been reset. If a user attempts to reset their password 10 times unsuccessfully in 24 hours, lock their account on the IP address that the requests are coming from, log the situation, and trigger an alert. If an IP address is attempting to reset a password for an account that does not exist, treat that IP as though the account does exist in order to prevent attackers from enumerating (gathering) valid usernames. Review Figure 2-3 to see a flowchart of a safe forgotten password progression.

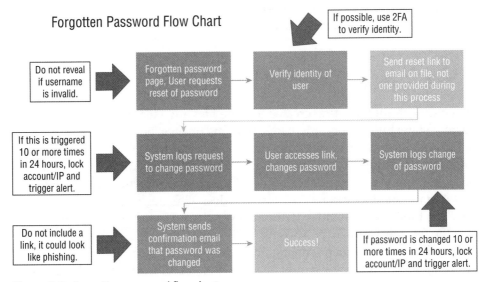

Figure 2-3: Forgotten password flowchart

Rules for Passwords

- Hash and salt all user passwords. Make the salt at least 28 characters.

- All application secrets must be stored in a secret store.

- All accounts used within the application must be service accounts (not a human being's account). They must be unique for each application and should follow the concept of least privilege.

- Have all people on your team use password managers that are managed by your organization and create a policy that they must never reuse passwords, including variations of the same password.

- Turn on MFA for all important accounts, at work and at home. Whenever possible use an authenticator app or device rather than SMS as your second factor of authentication.

- Do not force password changes on a schedule, only after a breach or suspicious activity.

- Always use a *modern* hashing algorithm.

- When in doubt, follow your government's policy on password storage, and if there is none then follow NIST's password policy. It was created by a team of experts and vetted by industry, resulting in the best possible advice.

> **TIP**   You can find modern hashing algorithms and additional advice on password storage at `cheatsheetseries.owasp.org/cheatsheets/ Password_Storage_Cheat_Sheet.html`.

HTTPS Everywhere

When the internet was first created, no one had any idea it would turn into its current state; billions of daily users, trillions of sites, being the main method of communication for most of the world. Thus, it wasn't planned for. Security, privacy, how to transfer funds, etc., was not built into the protocols, and we have been creating workarounds ever since. Originally everything on the internet was unencrypted (clear text), because the designers never dreamed we would have the tools we have today that could watch and read traffic over networks and the internet (known as "sniffing" network traffic), and even interrupt that traffic, change it, and then send it onto its destination, without the receiver ever realizing it. This is why we now need to encrypt all traffic over the internet. However, not everyone is on board with this idea yet, so let's discuss the "why" before the "how."

When a user visits your website over the internet, you have no idea where they are coming from. They could be at a café on an open Wi-Fi, at a conference in a big hotel, at home on a network they share with the apartment next door, or in a very secure military environment. Unfortunately, you need to design your application for the worst-case scenario on that list, not the best one, which means designing your app to ensure you protect users who are using an insecure network.

Situations where someone might be sniffing traffic are where people are on an insecure network, such as at a café, or when neighbors share their Wi-Fi with each other. You have no idea who else is on there, potentially watching people as they visit your website.

There are also many situations where people are 100% for sure watching your traffic, such as when you are staying at a hotel, at work, or connecting to any network where they are doing "deep packet inspection." This is more common than you may realize.

NOTE   *Deep packet inspection* refers to data processing that inspects packets (data) being sent over a network, which results in actions such as blocking, re-routing, and/or logging.[21]

When someone is sniffing networking traffic, they can not only see what a user is seeing (violating their privacy), but they can change the information that is being sent to them. It is currently common practice at big brand hotels to replace all advertisements on unencrypted sites to their own advertisements; this is one potential example of changing the information your users see. Another example would be to inject malware, malicious scripts, or misinformation into the site they are visiting. The possible damage to your users is actually surprisingly high, even though the odds of a serious attack happening against your users is somewhat low (unless you work on a very, very large/popular site). If that wasn't enough of an incentive to use only HTTPS, modern browsers now alert users that the site they are visiting is not secure (either through a graphic or with text in the browser) if the traffic is over HTTP instead of HTTPS. Talk about bad for business!

Now that we are convinced that we always need to use HTTPS, let's define *The Rule*:

Only allow your site to be accessible via HTTPS. Redirect from HTTP to HTTPS. If someone attempts to downgrade a connection, redirect them. This can be done via security headers in your code, or settings on your server. How to do this was covered earlier in this chapter in the "Security Headers: Seatbelts for Web Apps" section.

TLS Settings

Ensure you are using the latest version of TLS for encryption (currently 1.3, but 1.2 is still appropriate as of this writing if your provider isn't able to support 1.3). Because this changes so often, you are encouraged to search online for current best practices.

More best practices in this area are discussed in Chapter 3, "Secure Design."

TLS TIPS

For TLS recommendations see: `bettercrypto.org/#webservers` and `https://ssl-config.mozilla.org`

 For assistance in compatibility Configuration see: `wiki.mozilla.org/Security/Server _ Side _ TLS`

 To test your configuration see: `testssl.sh`

Comments

Developers write comments (commentary throughout their code that is not executed, it's just text) in order to help themselves or future developers understand what's happening in the program. However, sometimes developers put things into comments that they should not, such as database passwords or other secrets, information about the company or users that should not be shared, or other sensitive information. When comments are put in front-end code (JavaScript, HTML, CSS) they are not always removed at packaging time, and a reverse engineer can often find those comments if they are looking. As such, we should never put sensitive information in comments, ever.

> **TIP**   There are many tools available for your CI/CD pipeline or to scan your repository that search for secrets in your code. Use one, always!

Backup and Rollback

All the data that your application uses, creates, or stores must be backed up regularly (as per your organization's data classification policy), with a second, geographically differing location for weekly backups. The system must be capable of data rollback, in the event of malware, security incident, or ransomware. Your backup and restore procedures must be tested and practiced.

Framework Security Features

Programming frameworks are maintained by teams of experts and tested by hundreds or thousands of developers regularly. They also have hackers, both the ethical and unethical variety, testing framework security features. This means that the security features in a framework, compared to the ones you write yourself, have significantly more people, experience, time, and testing behind them, resulting in framework security features being almost guaranteed to be more secure than code you would write yourself to perform a security activity. As such, you should use the security features in your framework rather than writing your own.

Experienced web application penetration testers and application security engineers all have one or more stories of a software developer that decided to "roll their own crypto"; rather than use the cryptography features in their framework a developer decided they would either base64 encode the value (sometimes multiple times), or write their own function to jumble the values. Unfortunately for those developers, the easiest challenges in a Capture the Flag (CTF) contest often involve finding such simple and inadequate attempts at security, meaning such "defenses" are generally easily discovered and circumvented.

Other examples include writing your own output encoding function, trying to manage session yourself manually, saving session data into local storage rather than a secure cookie, etc. If your framework offers a security feature, use it. If it does not, consider adding an additional framework or component to your application that does include features to perform the activity you need, and only write your own if absolutely required.

Technical Debt = Security Debt

Technical debt is a concept in software development that reflects the implied cost of additional rework caused by choosing an easy (limited) solution now, instead of using a better approach that would take longer.

—Wikipedia[22]

Technical debt can include hard coding, not upgrading your servers or frameworks for extended periods of time, not patching, choosing shortcuts in order to "just get things out," etc. Technical debt often causes an organization to be slow in reacting to change, meaning they are unable to respond in a timely manner in time of incident or other threats to security. Both of these situations lead to weakening defenses and the inability for an organization to effectively defend itself.

Bob is quite used to working with large amounts of technical debt from one of the governmental departments he used to work for. They had so many processes and approvals, sometimes he wasn't even sure how to get a change out. They had CAB (Change Approval Board) and TAG (Technical Architecture Group) to pass, but first he had to get his boss's boss's boss's boss to sign off on his change. Having someone four levels above him approve changes just didn't make sense to Bob. How could that person understand if his change would conflict with the other tech they had when the person approving the change is a director general? That person doesn't write code. He was often frustrated and felt as though management just didn't trust him to do his job, making things slower than necessary, with no real added benefit.

When Bob worked at this department, they had a very serious security incident. He overheard the software developers telling the security team they have a 16-month release cycle for new features and if they wanted an emergency release it would take at least 4 months. The security person's face said it all: it was going to be a very bad day for the department. When Bob was offered a job at a new department that had more modern software development practices he jumped at the chance; the crippling technical dept at his previous department had been a real drain on his day-to-day work, and he wanted to work at a place where he felt his management team trusted him to do his job.

When organizations are unable to make changes without long lead times or herculean efforts, this is technical debt preventing them from being productive. When organizations spend most of their time just trying to keep the lights on, constantly fighting fires, this will most certainly result in security problems as well.

File Uploads

If performing a file upload, if at all possible, find a well-respected third-party component designed for this purpose to use for this portion of your application, rather than writing it yourself. This will reduce the risk as it will have already had extensive testing (only choose a third-party component where this is the case). Allowing members of the public (as opposed to authorized users from within your own organization) to upload files is the riskiest software functionality that common applications will ever perform. Usually user input is considered the most dangerous part of an application, but allowing users to upload a file (which could potentially be malicious) takes "dangerous user input" to an entirely new level of potential risk.

Alice remembers accidentally bringing a virus to work; it was so embarrassing. At home she has a Mac, but at work they have Windows. She had brought a USB full of music that she downloaded at home and had been listening to for ages. When she plugged it into her Windows machine at work, the EXE file she hadn't noticed started running and. . . the security team was at her desk in no time.

Alice is an extremely intelligent person, but she's not a security professional, and everyone can make a mistake. Your programs need to account for both malicious actors and people who make an error with what types of files they upload to your application.

When accepting an uploaded file from a user, assume the worst. Verify its type and size, rename the file, do not allow the user to set the path as to where it would be stored, and store it in a safe place away from the rest of your application and web server. Once you have accepted the file, scan it with at least one tool that can verify if the file is questionable. If your business unit will allow it, restrict the files to only specific types that are less dangerous. For instance, accept JPG, TXT, and PNG, but do not accept PDF or EXE file types.

The OWASP Cheat Sheet series, an open source project under the umbrella of the Open Web Application Security Project, has a brilliant and extensive list of precautions to take when allowing file uploads. Familiarize yourself with it if you must write this functionality from scratch: cheatsheetseries.owasp.org/ cheatsheets/Protect_FileUpload_Against_Malicious_File.html.

Malicious file uploads are such a serious and crucial topic that the Canadian government's cyber security arm, the Communications Security Establishment of Canada (CSE), created and open-sourced a free tool to check uploaded files; it is called AssemblyLine (cyber.gc.ca/en/assemblyline). It does not share information back to the Canadian government like many other online tools that are available for no financial cost online.

Errors and Logging

All errors should be caught and handled gracefully; there should never be a stack trace or database error on the screen. Not only so that your application looks professional and users have a pleasant user experience, but so that attackers are not given extra information to use against your application when creating their attacks. When errors happen, an application should never fail into an unknown state. It should always roll back any transaction it was performing, and "close" anything it may have opened (this is called "fail-closed"). Such a situation should also always be logged, so that if an incident were to arise the incident responders would have something to work with when they investigate, and so that auditors can verify that the system is and has been working correctly.

Your security team likely has something called a SIEM, a Security Incident and Event Management system, which ingests all the log files from all of your network tools. It can ingest the logs from your application as well. Talk to the team to learn the format in which they want to receive the logs and ensure that your application's logs are in that format, and then ensure that the SIEM will have access to your logs when your application moves into production.

Never log sensitive information, such as passwords, Social Insurance Numbers, complete credit card numbers (last 4 digits are okay), date of birth plus a person's first and last name, etc. Any combination of information that combined would make personally identifiable information (PII) should not be logged. When in doubt, ask your privacy team and business analyst(s).

If an activity happens within your application that appears to be a security event or incident, your app should not only log the situation, but it should raise an alert. An alert can be an email to the security team, the person on call from the Ops team, or whatever your organization decides is appropriate. Decide this in advance, during the requirements phase. Also, do not have the email go to a person's account; send it to a team or service account, so that if that person quits the alert is not being sent to nowhere. Test this functionality periodically to ensure it still works; alerts that don't trigger, or that aren't received, help no one.

Events that would potentially trigger a security alert include falling into an unknown state, having access denied to a feature or document, a workflow bypass attempt, a user exceeding usage quotas (for instance, attempting to log in 10 times in 1 second, or 100 times in an hour—human beings do not act like this), the application crashing, a user using a certain (large) amount of bandwidth, CPU, or storage, calls to an HTTP verb that you have blocked, etc. You will need to decide what is appropriate for your organization and your application with the business analysts and security team.

TIP   For more potential alerts and logging, visit `cheatsheetseries.owasp`
`.org/cheatsheets/Error_Handling_Cheat_Sheet.html`.

Input Validation and Sanitization

JavaScript is a special type of programming language because it runs in the browser, commonly known as the client side, because the people (clients) who use our web applications have to use a browser to access them, and a browser is on *their* computer, not *our* servers. All other programming languages run on the server side; on your web server, PaaS (Platform as a Service from a cloud provider), or container (more on containers later).

When someone uses a web proxy on a web application, the web proxy places itself *after* your application's JavaScript has run, but *before* the request is sent out over the network to your web server. Someone using a web proxy can easily change the HTTP request before it leaves your computer, thus circumventing any input validation or sanitization you may have written into your JavaScript. As you see in Figure 2-4, it is clear why security validation or sanitization must be done on the server side; it's way too easy to get around security defenses in JavaScript.

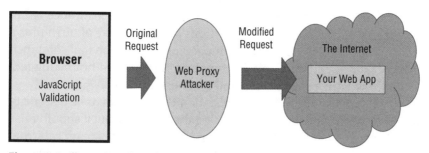

Figure 2-4: Illustration of a web proxy intercepting web traffic

The second thing to ensure when performing validation is that we use something called an "accepted list" or "approved list," rather than a "blocked list." Malicious actors and penetration testers have shown themselves to be capable of getting around blocked lists with relative ease, on a regular basis, with creative uses of the input options that are not blocked. The number of different ways that someone can enter a single quote (the character used most often in SQL Injection attacks) into an input field is actually quite amazing. Rather than attempting to block a long list of different types of attacks, make a list of what *is* allowed and then reject the rest. Your "approved list" should be written with regular expressions (regex), and anything not matching your expression is not allowed. For example, if you wanted to allow only a–z and A–Z for a username, you could use this expression: ^[a-zA-Z]{1,10}$.

WARNING   Regex is occasionally the target of denial-of-service (DOS) attacks, since it is resource-heavy when executed. As such, your application should trigger an alert if this functionality is called repeatedly.

Authorization and Authentication

If your application has different types of access for different types of users, generally referred to as Role-Based Access Control (RBAC), then you must define all of it during the requirements phase. You do not want these changing on you as you are developing the system, it will make your job more difficult than necessary. This is part of authorization (aka AuthZ).

At this point you should also define which authentication (aka AuthN) method/ system and identity method/system should be used: how will your system verify the identity of the users? How will you track their identity? Do you need to track it across several systems or just your website? Deciding all of these systems now is ideal, but during the design phase is also acceptable.

TIP   Implement an automated test suite that verifies that your implementation of AuthZ is actually what you think it is. Being able to automate this testing means you can retest it often to ensure nothing has accidentally been changed.

Parameterized Queries

When an application calls out to a database, the application is instructing the database to perform actions on its behalf. It could be a read, write, update, or delete request, but the point is that your application is speaking *directly* to the database. No person or application should ever be able to speak directly to *your* database except *your* application, *your* software development team, or *your* database administrator. When an attacker performs an SQL or NOSQL attack against an application they are trying to speak directly to the database, attempting to send it commands to perform their wishes rather than the instructions you have programmed for it to follow. This is known as an injection attack and it is the #1 highest risk attack for any web application (as per the OWASP Top Ten, which will be detailed in Chapter 5).

When we use parameterized queries (in SQL they are called stored procedures), we send parameters and the name of the query we want to run to the database, rather than creating a line of code by concatenating user input to create a string and then sending it to the database as a command. The difference is that with parameterized queries if an attacker attempts to add their own code to via user input, the application will send it in one of the parameters, and it will not work.

This is because the parameters are interpreted by the database as data, never as code, which makes injection attacks nearly impossible.

When an application concatenates strings of user input and then sends it to the database directly as a command, this is called "inline SQL," in the SQL language. Writing inline SQL creates a potential SQL Injection vulnerability. Only using parameterized queries instead reliably mitigates this vulnerability. Always used parameterized queries.

URL Parameters

Users have access to the address bar in browsers. So do attackers. Don't put any variables in URL parameters that matter to your application. An ID number can be incremented, and then if your application hasn't been programmed for such a situation, a user may be seeing someone else's account. If a sensitive value is in the URL parameters it will be logged, and that is also a problem. It's very simple for someone to manipulate the values in URL parameters, and the excuse "they weren't supposed to do that" won't fly with your incident response team. Only pass values of zero importance in the URL parameters, such as which language the user wants to view the page in. Never pass anything of importance or anything sensitive in your URL parameters.

Least Privilege

Ensure your application enforces the principle of least privilege, especially in regard to accessing the database or APIs. Your application should also only use a service account to call APIs, parameterized queries, or any other call that requires an account.

Here are some examples how to apply least privilege:

- The service account that calls your database from your application should only have CRUD permissions, never database owner (DBO).

- Ideally one service account will have read-only, for "select" calls, while another will have CRUD access when insert, update, or delete is required. Use the read-only account whenever possible.

- Create a different service account for each API that your application uses, with each one only having the maximum-required permissions (for instance, only "select" or "read" if it is only expected to return data, not modify data).

- Only give your team members access to read/write your projects within your code library, with everyone else only having read access or no access at all if your code is potentially quite sensitive or valuable in nature.

TIP   Using a read-only service account whenever possible, rather than an account with all the CRUD permissions, is an implementation of "least privilege."

Requirements Checklist

Below is a checklist that you can use for all your web application projects. All of these requirements can apply to any web application, and I suggest you include them all as a minimum, plus add your own that fit your unique business needs.

- Encrypt all data at rest (while in the database).
- Encrypt all data in transit (on its way to and from the user, the database, an API, etc.).
- Trust no one: validate (and sanitize if specialize circumstances apply) all data, even from your own database.
- Encode (and escape if need be) all output.
- Scan all libraries and third-party components for known vulnerabilities before use, and regularly after use (new vulnerabilities and versions are released all the time).
- Use all applicable security headers.
- Use appropriate secure cookie settings.
- Classify and label all data that your application will store, collect, or create.
- Hash and salt all user passwords. Make the salt at least 28 characters.
- Store all application secrets in a secret store.
- Ensure all accounts used within the application are service accounts (not a human being's account).
- Have all people on your team use password managers and never reuse passwords.
- Turn on MFA for all important accounts.
- Do not force password changes on a schedule, but only after a breach or suspicious activity.
- Only allow public-facing (internet) sites to be accessible via HTTPS. Redirect from HTTP to HTTPS. Ideally this would be applied to both internal and external applications.
- Ensure you are using the latest version of TLS for encryption (currently 1.3).

- Never hard code anything. *Ever.*

- Never put sensitive information in comments. This includes connection strings and passwords; those belong in a secret store.

- Use the security features within your framework; for instance, cryptography/encryption, session management features, or input sanitization functions. Never write your own if your framework provides them.

- Use only the latest version (or the one before) of your framework and keep it up to date. Technical debt = security debt.

- If performing a file upload, ensure you are following the advice from OWASP for this highly risky activity. This includes scanning all uploaded files with a scanner such as AssemblyLine, available for free from the Communications Security Establishment of Canada (CSE).

- Ensure all errors are logged (but do not log sensitive information), and if any security errors happen, trigger an alert.

- Ensure all input validation (and sanitization) is performed server side, using an approved list or accepted list (not a block list) approach.

- Ensure security testing is performed on your application before being released (more on this in later chapters).

- Perform threat modeling on your application before being released. Learn more in Chapter 3 in the "Threat Modeling" section.

- Perform code review (specifically of security functions) on your application before being released.

- Ensure the application catches all errors and fails safe or fails closed (never fail into an unknown state).

- Ensure all errors provide generic information to the user, never information from a stack trace, query fail, or other technically specific information.

- Define specifics on role-based access in the project requirements.

- Ensure specifics on authentication methods and identity systems are defined in the project requirements.

- Only use parameterized queries, never inline SQL/NOSQL.

- Do not pass variables that are of any importance in the URL parameters.

- Ensure the application enforces the security principle of least privilege, especially in regard to accessing the database and APIs.

- Minimize your attack surface whenever possible.

■ Allow users to cut and paste into the password field, which will allow for use of password managers. Disable password autocomplete features in browsers, to ensure users do not save their passwords into the browser.

■ Disable caching on pages that contain sensitive information. While the Cache HTTP header is not technically a security header, it can be used to enforce this requirement.

■ Ensure passwords for your application's users are long, but not necessarily complex. The longer the better; encourage use of passphrases.

■ Do not force users to change their passwords after a certain amount of time, unless a breach is suspected.

■ Verify that new user's passwords have not previously been in a breach by using a service designed for such a task.

Depending upon what your application does, you may want to add more requirements or remove some. The point of this chapter is to get you thinking about security while you are writing your project requirements. If developers know from the beginning that they need to adhere to these requirements, you are already on your way to creating more secure software.

Exercises

1. List two more potential security requirements for a web application (which are not already listed).

2. List two more potential security requirements for an operating system in a car.

3. List two more potential security requirements for a "smart toaster."

4. List two more potential security requirements for an application that handles credit cards.

5. Which security requirement is the most valuable? Why is it the most valuable one to you and/or your organization?

6. If you had to remove one of the requirements from this chapter from a web app project, which one would it be? Why?

NOTE Reminder: The "answer key" at the back of the book is brief. If you have the opportunity to talk these out with a colleague or friend, you will have a more thorough answer. Join me online to participate live in discussion or view the videos after to discuss these questions at `youtube.com/shehackspurple`.

Secure Design

In the previous chapter we discussed security requirements. When making any product, requirements are a must, and ensuring you have security built into your requirements from the beginning is the first step to ensure your final product will be of high quality. In this chapter we will discuss the next phase of the System Development Life Cycle: Design (Figure 3-1).

Figure 3-1: The System Development Life Cycle (SDLC)

When designing software applications, software architects not only need to worry about business requirements (what the customer has asked for) and functional requirements (user requirements, scheduling, system requirements), but also non-functional requirements that are often taken for granted, such as usability, quality, and the focus of this book: security.

> *Secure by design, in software engineering, means that the software has been designed from the ground up to be secure. Malicious practices are taken for granted and care is taken to minimize impact when a security vulnerability is discovered or on invalid user input.*
>
> —*Wikipedia*[23]

When we talk about designing software, there are several different ways this might be interpreted, so let's define it here.

Software design is planning out how you will build your software, and how it will connect or work with anything else it needs to. This can be a very high-level document that shows how each part fits together; for instance, this front end connects to this database and also calls this API.

Design documents can be extremely formal and detailed, down to writing out which classes will be defined and how, or just a few drawings and data-flow diagrams. The purpose of a design document is to get across to a team how to build the application.

In order to ensure you have enough for the security team, *ask them*. First ensure your development team feels the design document is enough, and after that review it with someone from the security team.

Design Flaw vs. Security Bug

A *design flaw* is an error in the design of the application that allows a user to perform actions they should not be allowed to do (malicious or damaging actions). This is a flaw, a problem with the design. We use secure design concepts, security project requirements, and threat modeling in attempts to avoid or minimize opportunities for design flaws.

A *security bug* is an implementation issue, a problem with the code, that allows a user to use the application in a malicious or otherwise incorrect way. We perform code review, do security testing (many types, during different stages of the project), provide secure coding training, and use secure coding concepts and guidelines in order to protect against security bugs. Review Figure 3-2 to see where flaws and bugs are introduced in the SDLC.

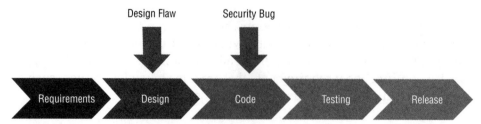

Figure 3-2: Flaws versus bugs

Discovering a Flaw Late

The later you fix a problem in the SDLC, the more it will cost. An article from online magazine Slashdot states that a bug found in the requirements phase of the SDLC may cost $1 to fix, while in design it may cost $10, in coding $100, in testing $1000, and more after release.[24] There are many different estimates of cost all over the internet, but instead of using guesstimates to try to explain the idea, let's consult with Bob. Review Figure 3-3 to see the increasing cost of fixing security issues in each of the phases of the SDLC.

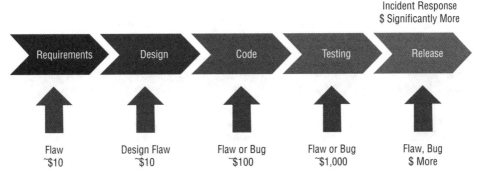

Figure 3-3: Approximate cost to fix security bugs and flaws during the SDLC

Years ago, Bob and his spouse built their dream home; they saved for it for years. When it was almost done, when they were putting on the handles for the cupboards and rolling out the carpets, Bob realized something was wrong. Somehow, throughout all of their planning, they had never thought to ask for more than one bathroom. When they had started saving and planning, they had only one child, but by the time they got to this point they had two and were considering a third. They definitely needed another bathroom.

Bob knew that adding a bathroom this late in the construction would cost quite a bit and make his project late, but he also knew that he could not continue with only one bathroom. When he spoke to the construction company, they explained that they had to reduce the den by half the size in order to add the second bathroom, and it would delay their move by an entire month. It would also add 10 percent to the cost of the project. Bob and his partner begrudgingly gave approval, but Bob learned a very valuable lesson in the process: it's much cheaper, easier, and faster to change the design earlier in the process rather than later.

This is the same situation for software. When you make design changes last minute, they aren't always pretty, they almost always make you miss deadlines, and they are often extremely expensive. Unfortunately, sometimes this last-minute rush introduces new vulnerabilities into your final product.

Pushing Left

The "not enough bathrooms" problem is something that threat modeling would have found, which will be discussed at the end of this chapter. This is also something that secure design concepts might have made visible earlier on in the SDLC. Problems like this are the reason that we need to begin security at the start, not the end, of projects.

If you look at Figure 3-4, it shows the SDLC with arrows pointing to the left of the page. The idea being that the further "left" you start security activities, the earlier you are in the SDLC. Some security practitioners call this "shifting left," others call it "pushing left," but no matter what you call it, it's the most efficient way to ensure that you are creating secure software.

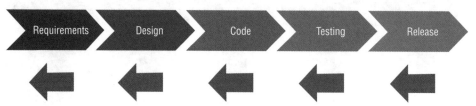

Figure 3-4: Pushing left

Secure Design Concepts

With this in mind, let's talk about several secure design concepts that should be applied (or at least considered) when designing software applications.

Protecting Sensitive Data

In Chapter 2, "Security Requirements," we already determined that we would classify and label all of the data that would be created, gathered, stored, or processed by our application. That's great, now what?

When handling any data, we want to ensure we maintain its CIA. It must be available when we need it (availability), and it must be must accurate (integrity), sensitive or not. If the data is not public/unclassified, then we must also protect it to ensure our secrets *remain* secrets (confidentiality).

> **NOTE**   "Unclassified" means something is not sensitive in nature. Classifying data as "Public" means that it can be released to the public (it has been given a sensitivity level, and the level is that all may see it).

WARNING   If the data in your application contains government secrets, you must follow whatever rules your government has put forth, not this guidance. But for everything else, this advice should be helpful.

For *all* data, we must encrypt it in transit and at rest, use HTTPS only, validate our inputs and encode our outputs, use security headers, avoid putting sensitive information in hidden fields or URL parameters, secure our cookies, ensure users have authorization to view/access data before granting access, and harden our web server and database configurations. Those are the basics; we need to do that for all of our data. But what about our extra-sensitive data?

The first thing that you will need to do is create processes and policies for how to handle sensitive data, if they are not already established at your workplace. If they already exist, you should follow them, and if possible, add some of the items discussed here to further strengthen your policies and procedures.

When data is sensitive, you need to find out how long your application is required to store it and create a plan for disposing of it at end of life. For example, if you must keep data for a time period of 7 years after receiving it, then your system must destroy each record of data automatically after 7 years. Design this into your application; do not assume that users will remember to dispose of the data later (they definitely won't). You must also design a verification that the data has been destroyed successfully and completely. Also, do not forget to plan how the data will be removed from your backup systems, including any duplication of backup systems that may exist.

With many companies moving their data to the public cloud, it is crucial to decide if you will put various types and classifications of information into the cloud or not. Depending upon the country you are in, there may be legal guidance and/or requirements you need to follow. If there is no legal guidance for your situation and you decide to use the public cloud for this purpose, you should use the "bring your own keys" option for your highly sensitive information. This means that you will manage the keys that encrypt and decrypt your data, rather than allowing your service provider to do so on your behalf.

For geographically distributed systems, you will need to decide which areas are allowed to access your data, and where your backups are stored. Again, there may be legal guidance and/or requirements from your government; ensure you are compliant with the laws in your country.

If your data is extremely sensitive, you may choose to use a tokenization system, generally provided by a third party. Tokens replace the data and then are decrypted by the third-party software when the data is used. This would be an additional later of security.

If your system and/or its data is very sensitive, your user's passwords should be hashed, salted, *and* peppered as discussed in Chapter 2. As of this writing, most applications salt and hash passwords, but do not pepper.

Due to encryption standards constantly changing (and improving), specific ciphers, key lengths, and algorithms will not be dictated here. Look up the current standards using your favorite search engine, and make sure you verify the current standards again for new projects (things may have changed).

If possible, set up alerts if any data is leaked online that resembles your data. You do not want to find out this type of information by reading the newspaper; you want to be informed before it gets to that. You can set up alerts like this manually or you can use professional services offered by security vendors. You can also gain value from setting up alerts on various social media, search engine, and data-sharing platforms for keywords (which will result in false positives, so be ready for some "noise"). Some governmental organizations assist in this for businesses in their country; ask your government what types of services or assistance they can offer. In Canada this group is called "Canadian Center for Cyber Security" (cyber.gc.ca[25]), previously known as Canadian Cyber Incident Response Center (CCIRC).

Here are resources from more countries:

- **Luxemburg**: www.circl.lu[26]
- **Japan**: www.jpcert.or.jp/english/at/2020.html[27]
- **United Kingdom (Threat Reports)**: www.ncsc.gov.uk[28]
- **United State of America**: www.us-cert.gov/ncas/alerts[29]
- **New Zealand (Advisories)**: www.cert.govt.nz/it-specialists[30]

If you aren't sure what your government has to offer, look up the CIRT (Cyber Incident Response Team) and ask them.

> **TIP** Even if the data in your application is not sensitive, you must still ensure that it is stored properly, and that your application is secure. The extra precautions in this section are only required if the data or application is highly sensitive, which you will need to determine with your business stakeholders and security team. Please assume the rest of the concepts in the book apply to your data and applications no matter its sensitivity level (unless otherwise stated).

Never Trust, Always Verify/Zero Trust/Assume Breach

We discussed the concepts of zero trust and assume breach in Chapter 1, but how do we apply these concepts when designing our applications? Besides reviewing your design with a security professional and talking it out (which you should definitely do), the following are a few steadfast rules:

- Only use server-side trusted data (data that has been properly validated) to make access control decisions.

- Deny by default—all functions should check to make sure that the user is authorized before proceeding.

- Always fail closed or fail safe, never fail to an open or unknown state. Always roll back if a transaction is not properly completed.

- Verify identity (authenticate), *then* authorize (access control).

- Reverify access on every page and feature of your application, even on reload of a page.

- Verify authentication (AuthN) and authorization (AuthZ) for APIs, both ways (API ⇨ application ⇨ API)

- Block access to any protocol, port, HTTP verb/method and anything else on your server, PaaS, or container that your application does not use.

- One application per server, PaaS, or container, based on your deployment model and budget permitting.

> **NOTE**   Input validation was covered in Chapter 1 as well, and we will touch on it over and over throughout this book. If every software developer mastered the art of input validation, it would eliminate a significant number all types of vulnerabilities in all web applications. It is the most important and valuable lesson in this book. *Never trust, always verify.*

Take the time to review your design with a security professional or another technical person who is not on your team (and therefore unbiased). Look for places in your design where there is implied trust, and then remove the trust and change it to verify. This exercise should take under an hour, can be done on a whiteboard, and recorded with a photo of the whiteboard for later.

Backup and Rollback

A few months ago, Alice's company suffered a ransomware attack. Someone had clicked a link in a phishing email and accidentally infected the entire network. Luckily, Alice always keeps a copy of her essential files on her personal laptop so she can work from home; it's against company policy, but she's been doing it for years. Unfortunately for everyone else at the company, the ransomware software encrypted all of the company's files and no one was able to work; employees were answering emails on their phones for a month, and some of the files were never recovered. Alice never found out the entire cost of what happened, but she was grateful they didn't go out of business, like other companies that she had heard of.

> **NOTE**   Alice saving a copy of her files so that she can work from home is her *circumventing* a security policy that made it difficult for her to perform the duties of her job. The security policy did not create a situation of *usable* security. She needs to work from home to get her job done, so she broke the policy. If the security team provided a *usable but also secure* solution (VPN from home, for instance), she would not break this policy.

Backups aren't valuable unless you can roll back to them efficiently. If it takes one month to roll back, that's a month of work that is lost. It is absolutely essential that your application not only has backups as part of the design, but quick rollback of data and restore of systems:

- Backups must be stored in a geographically differing location than your database and web server.
- Backups must be in a secure location (both physically and digitally) and protected just as you would protect your production database or web server.
- Schedule rollback practice at least once a year. When there are major changes to production systems, ensure a rollback script has been made and tested.
- Your database, your configurations, *and* your application code must be backed up.
- Access to your backups must be monitored, logged, and alerted upon.
- Deletion of backups should be time-delayed in case they are being deleted as part of an attack. Some cloud providers do this by default. Suggested timeline: schedule the delete to occur 14 days *after* the request for deletion of backups of any production databases.
- Practice your rollbacks. Seriously!

> **TIP**   Security incident simulations (also known as security exercises) are a great way to practice in advance of real security incidents. Throwing a ransomware simulation at your team would be an excellent excuse to check if your backups and rollback plans are working according to plan. It is much less expensive, painful, and damaging to practice for an event that never happens, than to be unprepared when it does.

Server-Side Security Validation

When performing web application security testing such as penetration testing, most testers use something called a web proxy or intercept proxy (sometimes combined with a web app scanner, to allow you to do automated testing as well). A web proxy, as the name implies, sits between your browser and your web server, intercepting your traffic. This type of tool is used to communicate with the application directly, sending the requests and responses to and from your web server, after your JavaScript has completed running on the front end (the user's computer/browser). This means that if you write validation code into your JavaScript to make sure that user input is safe for your application, any user with this type of tool could enter valid data into your app, then pause it (intercept the request) after your JavaScript is done validating the data, and change it into malicious data (edit the request, and send it on). If your application validates the data again on the server, this is fine; you might choose to perform very basic data validation in your JavaScript in order to save time. However, if your application does not validate the data on the server, attackers could easily send your application malicious requests using a web proxy. Review Figure 3-5 to see the flow of an HTTP request when using a web proxy.

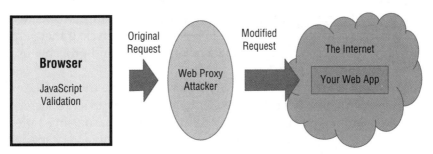

Figure 3-5: Using a web proxy to circumvent JavaScript validation

Unfortunately for web application designers, users of our applications have a lot of power. They can use an insecure or obsolete browser, access our sites from a computer that is infected with malware, change the settings in the browser, edit the parameters in the URL, and even intercept the requests and responses to and from the applications that we create. Users are also able to cloak their location, IP address, type of operating system and browser they are using, and even the web page they came from; the internet was designed to give users a lot of power, for better or worse.

Although it may seem expensive to send every validation back to the server side, it is guaranteed to be less expensive than having an attacker successfully exploit your web application.

Framework Security Features

When Bob was a young man he briefly worked as a programmer, before he decided coding wasn't for him. At first, he thought he could write his own functions, instead of using those provided in his framework. He thought he would do a better job and show his boss how valuable he was as an employee. When he showed his boss, Bob's boss explained that writing his own security features was dangerous. "Several professionals worked on this framework, people who have studied this problem at length and have many years of experience. Bob, do you really think that we have the money to pay you to re-invent the wheel? Do you think we have the time in our project to test to make sure what you wrote works perfectly? Do you really feel, as one person with no special expertise in this area, that you can do a better job than an entire team of experts?" It made Bob feel small, but when he thought about it, he realized his boss was right; he should use the security features in his framework, and never write his own.

This applies to all of us; we should never write our own security features if they exist in our framework. If they do not exist in our frameworks, we should evaluate carefully before we decide to write one ourselves. If there is a commercial, affordable, and trusted option available, we should probably use that before writing our own.

For example, there are many different secret stores available that are free or priced within reach of most organizations. Figuring out how to store secrets, without storing them in your code, is a very complex problem, so using a pre-made solution almost always makes sense. That said, if you have a very special and unique situation, sometimes there is no other choice than to write custom code. Perform an option analysis activity before you make such a decision.

> **TIP**   A secret store is where your application secrets live. It is not like a password manager, which is for human users; a secret store is used by machines. You can and should store your connection strings, credentials, keys, hashes, and other secrets in a secret store.

Security Function Isolation

Whenever possible, isolate security functionality from other functionality in your applications (this applies to hardware design as well). This means if someone breaks the non-security functionality, it won't affect your security functionality (and potentially cause a vulnerability). This is advice is not only part of ITSG-33[31] from the Canadian Government, but also part of NIST's Special Publication 800-53 S-3[32]; these are two very trustworthy sources for security advice.

How do we implement this? For each security control, we separate the code or functionality. We can do this by putting it into a separate object or class, on a different page or dashboard within the application or system, and/or a separate application altogether. We would likely also force the user/app to re-authenticate before allowing it to access the security functionality in order to enforce this requirement. Examples of this include:

- Putting input validation in a separate object or class
- Putting authentication and/or authorization into a separate application
- Identity management performed by your cloud provider or another external system.

The level of separation depends upon the sensitivity of the application you are creating and the power of the security functionality.

The code for the security function could be stored on a separate web server/PaaS/container or file system. There could be a firewall between the two applications or completely separate networks in extreme cases.

Ensure that your identity/authentication system lives in a separate server and follows the hardening guide. Always do this one, no exceptions.

Examples of security functionality that should always be isolated include (security-related) logging and monitoring, intrusion prevention and/or detection, web application firewall (WAF), application control software, file integrity monitoring, alerting, or blocking.

Application Partitioning

Whenever possible, isolate system management (admin) functionality from other functionality in your applications. This means if someone breaks the non-security functionality, it won't affect your system management (access control) functionality. This advice is not only part of ITSG-33[31] from the Canadian Government, but also part of NIST's Special Publication 800-53 S-2.[33]

NOTE The definition from the ITSG-33 standard is: The information system separates user functionality (including user interface services) from information system management functionality.

Similar to the previous entry, this is about separating functionality, except this only applies to administrative capabilities. If there is an administration portion of the application, that functionality is in a separate object/class, on a different page or dashboard, and/or in a separate application. Preferably users would need to log in with a separate set of credentials (with MFA enabled) in order to administer your application.

Secret Management

Before discussing secret management let's define secrets in regard to software. When we are discussing secrets and secret management, we do not mean the secrets that users store inside the software that we build, we mean the secrets that *our software uses* to run properly. If a user has a username and password (credentials) that they use to log in to our application, that is a *user secret*, and that is not what we are discussing in this section. We are discussing the secrets that *computer systems use* to communicate with each other.

When an application logs in to a database, the connection string it used is a secret. When a web server has a certificate and key pair that it uses to enable HTTPS (encryption) for the web app, the private key of the key pair used for that certificate is a secret. Private keys, API keys, hashes, passwords, and anything else that is confidential that is used by the application (not a person or user), is considered a *secret*.

Secret management, when performed manually, is awful. It's time-consuming, complex, and error prone. This is why our industry created secret stores; software that manages this for you that can be accessed programmatically, from your application, your CI/CD pipeline, or from a service account. A human being should never access the secrets in your secret store except when they are first put inside, when they are being updated, or in case of an emergency. Access to a secret store should guarded carefully, monitored, logged, and alerted upon.

A good secret store should provide warnings as to when your certificates will expire and provide details as to when a secret was last rotated. Some have even more features. Take advantage of all the features you can; it's always better than doing it manually.

Re-authentication for Transactions (Avoiding CSRF)

Cross-Site Request Forgery (CSRF)[34] is a vulnerability where an attacker convinces the victim to click a link or to visit a malicious website. The link/site triggers a transaction within an application (let's say the purchase of a fancy new TV, to be shipped to the attacker), and because the user was already logged in to that account (who doesn't leave their browser open for days on end?), the vulnerable web application completes the transaction (purchase) and the user is none the wiser, until the bill arrives. But by then it is too late.

The best way to defend against this is to ask the user for something that only the user could provide, before every important application action (purchase, account deactivation, password change, etc.). This could be asking the user to re-enter their password, complete a captcha, or for a secret token that only the user would have. The most common approach is the secret token (often referred to as an anti-CSRF token). It is so common as of this writing that many modern frameworks (such as .Net, Java, and Ruby on Rails) perform this action on behalf of the programmer, so there is no need to code this functionality yourself. Verify if your framework is already doing it for you, and if not, ensure that you enable it within your framework.

TIP   Users hate captchas. Whenever possible, use an anti-CSRF token instead, which is invisible to the user. Using anti-CSRF tokens instead of making a user enter a captcha or re-enter their password is an example of prioritizing *usable security*.

Segregation of Production Data

Your production data should not be used for testing, development, or any other purpose than what the business intended. This means a masked (anonymized) dataset should be used for all development and testing, and only your "real" data should be in production.

Segregation of production data means fewer systems (and therefore fewer people) will have access to your data. This reduces attack surface, creating less opportunity for potential insider threats.

It also means fewer employees peeking on personal data. Imagine if you have been using a popular messaging platform and you found out that employees were reading your messages, which you thought were private. This would be a violation of your privacy, and most likely also the user agreement. Segregation of production data would eliminate most opportunities for this type of threat, and also mean if something like this did happen, that it would be traceable.

Protection of Source Code

The code that you write for your organization has monetary value, and potentially other types of value (such as competitive advantage, governmental secrets, etc.). It is highly likely that your organization would like to protect the code you write for intellectual property–related reasons; however, some companies publish their code on the internet for all to see (referred to as open source). There are pros and cons for both of these decisions; however, I will argue here that choosing not to share your code online is the more secure option.

Many will be quick to argue that "security through obscurity" is not an effective defense tactic, but I beg to differ. Hiding your code (closed rather than open source) should never be your only defense, but using it as one of many layers of defense is a good idea if the benefits of sharing your code do not outweigh the protection that closed-source offers. Many companies do not put their code in open repositories in order to make it much more difficult for competing companies to try to replicate their products. Yes, a malicious actor can try to reverse engineer popular software, but who has that kind of time?

Many in the open source community argue that if the code is there for all to see that people will notice vulnerabilities quicker and more often in open source projects. However, the numbers tell a different story; studies have shown proprietary (closed source) applications have on average the same number of vulnerabilities as open source projects.[35] The argument seems flawed, as there are few security engineers performing free code reviews on open source projects "just for kicks"; that work is tedious, requires an expert, and is quite time-consuming. With the current shortage of people qualified to perform such work,[36] and this work being very highly paid,[37] there are few who are willing to perform this work for free; certainly not enough to secure all of the open source projects.

On the flip side, if an attacker is targeting you, and if your code is open source, this means that they have all the time in the world to review it for vulnerabilities.

This defense is not bulletproof; it is simply one of many potential layers you can use to protect your applications and intellectual property.

> **NOTE**   Your source code is of great value and should not only have its confidentiality protected, but also its availability and integrity. Ensure that your code repository has backups that follow the same precautions as your application's data backups, ensure your code repository is monitored and logged, and ensure that all changes are tracked according to user, with rollback of code easily accessible if necessary.

Threat Modeling

Unfortunately, when we design software, we tend to focus only on ensuring it does all the things that the client asked for, rather than ensuring that it *only* works that way. This is where threat modeling comes in—the process of identifying potential threats to your business and application and ensure that proper mitigations are in place.

Threat modeling (affectionately known as "evil brainstorming"), in its simplest of forms, is a brainstorming session in search of defining all threats that your business, application, system, or product will likely face. Will people try to intercept your data and sell it to your competitor? Would it have any value if they did? What harm could come if that happened? How can we protect against this? These are some of the types of questions you may find yourself asking during a session. You would then test your app and review its code and design to ensure you have properly avoided these threats, as well as ensure they are covered by your project's security requirements. If your application appears to be vulnerable, you must either change your application to mitigate the threat or accept the risk.

Risk acceptance must be in writing, by people (usually management, C-level executives, and/or project stakeholders) who have the authority to do so. It must also clearly explain the justification for acceptance.

NOTE Threat modeling is a vast topic, and there are several books dedicated to it. These few pages will not do it justice; they are not exhaustive. The purpose of this section is to make you aware that it exists, in hopes that you will perform threat modeling sessions on new applications. No matter how immature your threat modeling process, performing some threat modeling is always better than none.

In order to create a threat model, a representative from each project stakeholder group needs to be present. This means someone from the business, someone representing the customer, a security rep with an offensive mindset, and either the tech architect or someone from the ops team and from the development team. Yes, someone from the tech team needs to be there; they often have the most frightening ideas.

TIP If there is money, someone always wants to steal it. If there is information in your system, there is always someone that wants to see, change, or remove it, who should not. If there are different levels of access within your app, someone will try to escalate (upgrade) their access. Always threat model these scenarios, as a bare minimum.

Next the group discusses what the risks are to the system. "What keeps you up at night?" "If you were going to attack your app, how would you do it?" "What threat actors should we be aware of? Should we prepare for?" etc. You want to look at the system from the viewpoint of an attacker. What could go wrong? How could the system be misused? How can we ensure we protect the user (including from us)? What is the worst-case scenario? This session can be incredibly formal (creating attack trees, for instance), or quite informal (which is how I would suggest you start, if you have never done one before).

A great place to start is take the project user stories and turn them into "abuse stories" or negative use cases. If your application is *supposed* to do X, what would happen if it did Y instead? Starting with this list of stories can give you a lot to work with.

There are several threat modeling methods, but the most popular are attach trees,[38] STRIDE,[39] and PASTA.[40] STRIDE focuses on questions surrounding authentication, authorization, CIA, and repudiation (being able to prove someone did or did not do something). PASTA focuses on business requirements, user stories, data diagrams, and more, making it a bit more labor intensive. Attack trees are illustrated as "trees," with the goal of the attack (for example, steal the money) at the top, with leaves of the tree being possible ways an attacker could achieve the goal (see Figure 3-6 for an example of an attack tree).

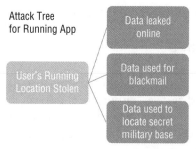

Figure 3-6: Example of very basic attack tree for a run-tracking mobile app

The essential part of all of the methods is that they help you come up with valuable questions and make sure that you have good coverage of all the things that can go wrong. For an informal threat model just think about what is valuable in your application, and how someone might want to steal it (money, data, etc.), manipulate it (to embarrass, to deny access, to show off, etc.), break it, misuse it, etc. Write down all of the questions and answers; this will be your list of concerns. They haven't been validated as risks yet.

> **TIP** You can read about several informal threat models I have performed on my blog (wehackpurple.com) around robots, serverless, lab test data breaches, and more.

Once you have a list of concerns, you will need to evaluate which ones are more (or less) likely and which may require security testing of your app (to see if it is vulnerable or not). You also need to evaluate which ones matter more or less; not all risks are created equal. Eliminate any concerns that seem impossible or would have no damage to your company or application. Sometimes during the brainstorming process people come up with things that just don't apply. That's okay, but those don't make the final list of threats.

Rate all of the remaining items as high, medium, or low in regard to how likely they are to happen, and the level of damage they would cause if they did happen. Now you have a list of threats (the validated list of concerns) and risks (the high/medium/low ratings).

Note: you can also use the Common Vulnerability Enumerator (CVE) rating system, or 1–10. Whatever works best for you and your team, as long as you all use the same system.

> **WARNING** You may be surprised (and frightened) by the justifications for the value of each risk. I once had to deliver the news to a company that the potential damage was "absolutely catastrophic"; if it happened, I was certain they would go out of business. Even though the risk itself was "fairly unlikely," the project team changed their course of action immediately once they understood the potential long-term ramifications.

When you have your list of risks, and how much each one matters (ratings), you need to plan. Will you mitigate (fix/remove) some of the issues? Will you manage some of the risks, by documenting them and keeping an eye on them to see if they get worse? Will you accept some of the risks (documenting that you will do nothing and are okay with that)? Perhaps some are highly unlikely or pose only a tiny threat? Why spend funds on something that is not worrisome? You will likely need to add to your list of security requirements for your project when all the decisions have been made. This is something you will have to discuss with the business and with your risk management team.

> **TIP**   When you talk to non-technical people about the risks, be very careful to ensure that you explain what could happen in terms that they understand. We cannot just say "The sky is falling"; we must be very specific. For example: "If someone was able to control a robot remotely, without authorization, this could cause accidents that could damage the cars we manufacture or cause potential injury or death of an employee." We must always try to "speak their language" when explaining risk.

The entire threat modeling process should be documented, especially the decisions you make at the end, with management sign-off. These decisions must be made with management or someone who has the authority to make large decisions like this. A software developer cannot "accept the risk," nor likely can you as a security engineer; it is probable that you will need a C-level executive to accept risks that are above the level "medium" or "low." Ensure that you get this document signed. It can be used in case there is a security incident in the future, or if you are asking other teams to do work to mitigate the issues and they are pushing back against your requests.

> **AUTHOR STORY**
>
> Once, while in a threat modeling session, I asked two software developers: "If you were going to hack your app, how would you do it?" They looked at each one and then one said sheepishly, "Well...there's that admin module we wrote so that we can administer it from home, maybe that?" The admin module had not been on any design documents and turned out to be a giant security hole. If those programmers had not been at the meeting, we would never have known.

If you are doing an iterative design, you may need to do several shorter threat modeling sessions, for new features or large changes to existing features. If you are doing a large Waterfall-style approach, one thorough session should be enough (assuming no large changes afterward). You will need to decide this for yourself and your organization.

If you are a security engineer, inviting Dev and Ops to threat modeling sessions will improve their awareness of security in the future, and they will have the most wicked of ideas. It will also help you create good relationships with these teams, and make no mistake, you require good relations in order to do your job well.

If you are a software developer, DevOps, or operations person, participating in threat modeling will open your eyes to all the possible threats to your application, and it will be fun. Being creative in this way is surprisingly interesting, and an excellent learning experience. It might also tempt you into joining the security team later on in your career.

Exercises

1. When should data be encrypted? (Select all that apply.)

   a) When an API sends data to another API

   b) On a virtual machine that is powered off

   c) When stored in a database

   d) When sent from the server to the browser

2. What are some possible ways that we can ensure the third-party components we use are secure? How can we minimize risk in this area?

3. Where should you store your application's secrets? How should your application access your secrets?

4. Name three types of "secrets."

5. What are some of the potential threats that a mobile banking application would face? Name three threats and rate how likely they are and how damaging they are based on a scale of low, medium, and high.

6. Name three threats that could apply to a "smart" car. Rate the threats (low, medium, or high) in terms of likelihood and potential damage.

7. Name five different types of security functionality that would potentially be offered in a modern framework.

Secure Code

"Keeping security in mind" when coding is not enough to ensure that secure code is produced; it must be an organizational priority, an official part of your SDLC, and developers must be supported with the appropriate training, time, and resources. This chapter will provide more secure coding guidance, which can be adopted as a standard or guideline for your organization, if you do not already have one.

If you decide to adopt information from this and previous chapters for your organization, it is critical that you "socialize" the information. Hold consultations, have lunch and learns, create posters, design infographics, put it in your intranet web page or wiki, email it to people, and most importantly, answer any and every question anyone has about the information. If you want people to adopt more secure practices, you need to ensure that you support them in every way possible.

Selecting Your Framework and Programming Language

Quite often we work in an environment where our programming language and/or framework is already chosen for us. We work in a "Dot Net Shop" or a "Java Shop," and it is unlikely anyone will be making any big changes in the near future. That said, you may have more flexibility and influence than you realize. Let's see what Alice and Bob have to say about this.

Alice isn't a techie, but she *is* a high-powered executive. When her IT department told her they wanted to slowly migrate all of their apps over from the Java Struts framework to the Spring Framework for Java, she immediately asked, "How much will this cost? Why?" Executives care about the bottom line, but the IT department was ready for this; before Alice joined the company, they had asked the previous executive in her role and he had said no when they did not have good answers to these same questions.

The head of IT proceeded to give Alice an entire presentation on the Return on Investment (ROI) of this decision, and the plan to migrate, safely, over an 18-month period.

> **NOTE**   Struts and Spring are two popular frameworks for the Java programming language.
>
> A "zero day'" is a vulnerability in a product or software component that has been disclosed, but for which there is no known patch currently available from the software provider.

First, the IT manager explained that in 2016 there were three different serious zero-day vulnerabilities in the Struts framework,[41] which had proven very expensive for their company. They had one serious security incident as a result, which cost over $250,000, and was extremely embarrassing. It was very time-consuming, redirecting project resources for weeks while they cleaned up the mess. It also made customers upset when they were unable to access the site for almost a week while the incident response team assessed the damage. The other two Struts vulnerabilities had not resulted in a breach or any other type of security incident; however, it was still costly to investigate and create new custom signatures for the web application firewall (WAF) product, and again their projects ended up delayed. They estimated that in 2016 alone, Struts had cost them at least one million dollars and damaged their reputation as a brand that customers could trust. He didn't know how to calculate the cost of the reputation damage.

All three vulnerabilities had to do specifically with Struts, the framework, not Java, the programming language. After performing a careful option analysis process, the IT department decided they felt Spring was more secure, better maintained, and more modern than Struts, and they felt it was worth it, financially, to migrate 100% of their applications to it.

He laid out his plan to Alice; every time they added a new feature to one of their older apps, they would add three additional weeks to the project to migrate it to Struts. Also, all new development would be in Spring. They would start the project off by bringing in a trainer who specialized in Spring *and* in security, to ensure they were off to a good start. They would also create a secure coding standard for their new framework and perform code review to ensure that it was enforced.

His plan would cost $550,000, and he estimated it would save them that amount in the first year after implementation, in reduced security incidents and events. It was also an excellent investment; it would drastically reduce their technical debt.

With all of this research and evidence right in front of her, what could Alice do? She approved the project on the spot.

When you are selecting a programming language or framework for your project, you need to consider more than just security. That said, I believe that security should always be able to veto a choice if necessary (although they will be expected to offer alternative solutions). Let's look at some more programming language and framework examples with our friend Bob.

Example #1

Bob has worked in many IT shops during his time in the Canadian government. Some of them were quite modern, while others seemed to lag behind, collecting more and more technical debt as time went on. When he started his first project management position, he worked somewhere that used a programming language he had never heard of; even when he searched it online he found almost nothing. They also used .Net, and the shop was split between the two languages.

When a project came up for a new software product, Bob had assumed that they would use the newest .Net framework version, and either VB.net or C# as their programming language. When speaking to the tech lead for the project, he had been informed they were going to use the strange ancient programming language because they "need to make sure those programmers had work to do." He was told that some of the programmers were insecure in their jobs, because they didn't know .Net.

Bob was shocked. Why would you intentionally create new technical debt? That language wasn't even supported anymore. Bob spoke to upper management and came up with a compromise: they would add training for the programmers on that project to learn .Net and pair them with other programmers who already knew it, to ensure they didn't make any serious mistakes during the project. This way he updated his team's skills and got his project done, with no new technical debt! The programmers were thrilled to find out they would have paid training and on-the-job mentoring. It was a bit more expensive up front, but in the long run it was a great investment in their employees. Bob was particularly proud of how the project worked out.

Example #2

Bob worked in another IT shop, managing projects again, and found out that every app was using a different version of the .Net framework. Some were at

4.5, while others were only on version 2. They had to manage so many different SDKs that the operations folks were very frustrated with the developers, often having conflicts when they attempted to deploy two apps to the same web server. Bob hired a consultant to come in and look at the security of one of his applications, and the consultant had scanned the entire code repository with something called an "SCA" tool. The consultant found out that several of the older versions of .Net had critical security vulnerabilities in them; the security team was very upset when they found out. Bob ended up creating a grid of all the insecure versions of the framework and creating a new project to upgrade all of them to versions without critical vulnerabilities, as well as an ongoing plan to ensure they stayed within three minor versions of the current version of the framework. The security team made Bob a security champion by the end of the project, giving him a small certificate to display at his desk. Bob was so proud!

> **TIP**   SDK stands for software development kit; however, that name is not very intuitive. An SDK is the components that need to be installed on your local machine or a web server in order to make programs written in that language run properly. Some types of SDKs can have different versions installed at the same time on the same machine, while some cannot. Be aware that when you choose to upgrade one of your applications to the newest SDK version, you may be causing problems for others in your office.

> **NOTE**   SCA stands for Software Composition Analysis. This is the process (usually performed by an automated tool) of verifying that all the third-party components, libraries, or frameworks included in your application do not have any *known* vulnerabilities in them. They will also keep track of your licensing for you. More on this later in the book

Example #3

Bob briefly worked on a top-secret project, leading a team that was making a tool to dissect malware by in-house analysts. The team wanted to write it in C, rather than Rust. Bob had heard that Rust was more secure, because it was memory safe. He argued they should use Rust instead. The team explained to him that as part of their "Buy, Borrow, Build" new-tech mantra they were repurposing a tool from another government they had good relations with. That tool was already written in C; they would have to start again if their tool was in Rust. They also explained that since it would only be used in-house, by their own experts, it would be safe from external attackers. Lastly, they explained that they had no one on staff with any Rust experience, so training would be required. After weighing all of these factors, Bob agreed that they should proceed with using C instead of Rust and documented the decision as part of the project design.

Programming Languages and Frameworks: The Rule

When selecting a programming language and framework, ensure you choose one that is supported and will likely be supported for a long time. Use the latest or second-from-the-latest as your version; never start with an older version. Evaluate the security offerings it has and try to select one that has all of the security features you will want built into your product. Never select a framework that is well known for being insecure, no longer maintained, unsupported, or otherwise problematic.

> **TIP** Although it goes without saying that we should never choose a framework only because it's new, cool, or exciting, it should also be stressed that having a long-term vision for your technology stack is crucial. Having fewer types of technologies, frameworks, languages, libraries, components, moving parts, etc., makes for an easier-to-maintain set of systems and therefore less technical debt.

Verify using an SCA tool that the version you are choosing does not have any serious known vulnerabilities. Use an SCA tool to scan your repository weekly and in your pipeline on every build, to ensure you do not accidentally introduce known vulnerabilities to your product.

Untrusted Data

In the previous chapters we discussed various types of user input and why we should never trust that input. Now let's look at what we should do instead, as a plan for every type of input from now on:

1. When you receive input, from any source, you will validate that it is what you are expecting—the type, the size, the format, the source—and that it is "appropriate." By appropriate we mean that it is reasonable based on your business context. Only you and other stakeholders involved in your business can decide if input is appropriate based on your unique business context.

   a. Verification will be performed on the server side, not within your JavaScript or otherwise on the client side.

   b. If this input does not meet your requirements, reject it and issue an error message that explains clearly to the user what you are expecting (not what they have done wrong).
   Example: Social Insurance Number Format: 999 999 999

   If someone enters any characters other than numbers, reject it.

   If someone enters too many numbers, reject it.

If someone enters not enough numbers, reject it.

If someone enters special characters, reject it and log it as a potential security issue.

c. If this is a rare case where you must accept special characters, you must escape them. Do this very carefully, and if possible, use the function within your programming framework for this or a dedicated third-party component for this purpose such as the OWASP Java Encoder (github.com/OWASP/owasp-java-encoder). If escaping functionality is not available to you in your framework, test your custom escaping functionality carefully and thoroughly.

2. If this input triggers a transaction (add, delete, update, purchase, etc.), you will verify if this is not a CSRF attack by checking the proper token has been passed, a captcha has been filled, or the user has been re-authenticated in another way.

> **TIP**   Cross-Site Request Forgery (CSRF), an attack that aims at active user sessions, is explained in-depth in Chapter 5.

3. If this input will be output to the screen, perform output encoding, as detailed in Chapter 3. Ensure you apply the proper output encoding context, if applicable.

4. If this input will be used to query a database, you must use parameterized queries (called stored procedures when using MS SQL). You must never concatenate it with other text and then send it as one command to the database (sometimes known as "inline SQL"). Place the input in the appropriate parameters, then call the stored procedure; this approach will neutralize the majority of database-related injection attacks.

5. If the user input will be used to direct the app to another site, this is called a redirect or forward. It is generally considered unsafe to send users along to redirects or forwards that have not been validated. When validating a link for this purpose you will want to have a list of pre-approved links. If it is not on the list, it is unlikely you want your users redirected there, and therefore you should stop the application from using the link.

If you follow this flow chart from now on for all input to your applications, you will be eliminating a very large percentage of potential vulnerabilities, including but not limited to injection, XSS, CSRF, privilege escalation, and many types of business logic vulnerabilities. In Figure 4-1 we can see a flowchart for validating untrusted data.

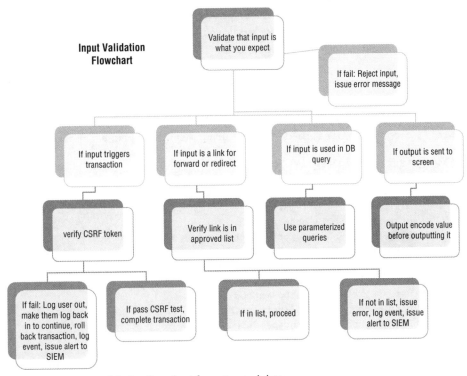

Figure 4-1: Input validation flowchart for untrusted data

HTTP Verbs

The HTTP protocol, the way applications communicate over the internet has several methods. These methods are generally referred to as "verbs" since most of them, linguistically, are verbs. These verbs are used to perform actions on your web server, on behalf of your application; for instance, you can delete something using the verb (you guessed it) DELETE. The verbs are used to talk to the web app living on the web server. Quite often most software developers, operations, and DevOps folks only think of the verbs that they *are* using and tend to forget all about the verbs that they are *not* using and thus leave all verbs active on the web server, whether they need them or not. With all verbs being enabled, but not being used, this means it's unlikely they have been properly tested to ensure they don't do anything they shouldn't do. Occasionally malicious actors will attempt to use the wrong verb, in efforts to get information or perform actions (attacks) against your application or web server. Ideally, any HTTP verb that you are not using should be disabled/blocked on the web server.

Most web applications only use GET, POST, OPTIONS, and HEAD, meaning the other HTTP verbs are usually unused and therefore unrequired. *All unused HTTP verbs should be disabled to reduce attack surface.*

WARNING   WEBDAV extends HTTP to include even more methods and *should not be enabled in production unless you are certain you need it, and have followed hardening instructions.* Avoid using WEBDAV, if possible.

The following is an example of disabling these verbs on Apache Tomcat Web Server. Note that this is just an example, so you will need to adjust it to be sure it works as desired with your custom applications. (Source: narayanatutorial.com/ tutorial-blog/owasp/disable-dangerous-http-methods-apache-tomcat-server.)

```
<security-constraint>
    <web-resource-collection>
        <web-resource-name>All JSP direct access</web-resource-name>
        <url-pattern>*</url-pattern>
        <http-method>PUT</http-method>
        <http-method>DELETE</http-method>
        <http-method>DEBUG</http-method>
        <http-method>HEAD</http-method>
        <http-method>CATS</http-method>
        <http-method>JEFF</http-method>
        <http-method>OPTIONS</http-method>
        <http-method>TRACE</http-method>
        <http-method>MKCOL</http-method>
        <http-method>LOCK</http-method>
    </web-resource-collection>
    <auth-constraint>
        <description>
          No Access
        </description>
    </auth-constraint>
</security-constraint>
```

Identity

As discussed previously, when we talk about identity in a computer system or network, we mean the way the computer recognizes who you are. When it verifies you are who you say you are, that's authentication (AuthN). When it uses your identity to figure out what you are or are not allowed to see and do, that is called authorization (AuthZ). The system of granting or denying functionality and information within your application or network is called *access control*.

If your system has users, you are going to have to figure out how to identify them. If it is a system within a network, you should *not* write your own identity functionality; you should use the pre-existing system in your network (unless you have very special business requirements). The most common network identity system is Active Directory, by Microsoft. However, some public cloud providers are offering their own identity systems and there are many other identity systems on the market that can also perform this type of functionality. I will not suggest a specific system to use; you should choose the one that works best for your business and technical requirements. Any of them will be significantly better than one you would write yourself (unless this is business you are in, meaning you are an identity or cloud provider company).

The differences between and the pros and cons of each identity system could easily fill an entire book. The purpose of this section is to get across the idea that you should never create your own system for identity. Always buy a pre-made system, unless you have special business requirements that force you to create your own—in which case, use a well-established protocol such as OAUTH.

Session Management

As discussed previously, the HTTP protocol and the web were never designed to manage a session. Pages were planned to be static (unchanging): people would visit them, read the information, and leave. As we all know, that is not what happened. As users log in to an application, as they move from page to page, that is a session that needs to be kept track of. This section will discuss strategies for session management.

> **TIP**   Remember the rule to always use the features in your framework, rather than writing your own? This applies here! If your programming framework has session management features, use them. Do not write your own from scratch.

Sessions are managed by sending something (usually called a session token) back and forth between the browser and web server, to reverify that it is the same user and the same session. Sessions when a user is logged in or not logged in are both tracked, but when a user logs in or out, that session is destroyed and a new one is created. We keep track of a session using a session ID or session token, passing it back and forth with every request (see Figure 4-2).

Session ID and session token are used interchangeably in industry. Session IDs are passed in a secure cookie (use the settings previously detailed in Chapter 3) and are never passed in the URL parameters. Session IDs are only used to manage sessions; don't use them for other information (such as an account number) in order to be efficient. Code is free; just write more.

Following is more guidance on session management, from the OWASP Cheat Sheets Team:[42]

- Session IDs should be at least 128 characters long.
- The session ID should be unpredictable (randomized) to prevent guessing attacks. Use a well-recognized random number generator; do not write custom code for this. Users should receive a new session ID each time they log in.

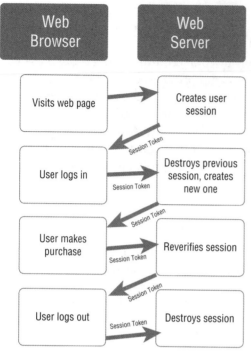

Figure 4-2: Session management flow example

- Use the built-in session management implementation in your framework, if one exists.

- The session ID should have an expiration date and/or time; it cannot last forever, even if the user is still logged in.

- The session ID should only be passed over encrypted channels.

- The session should be destroyed after a user logs out.

- Web applications must never accept a session ID they have never generated. In the case of receiving one, this scenario must be detected and logged as a suspicious activity; an alert should be generated and the IP blocked. *This constitutes a security incident.*

- Session IDs should be regenerated during authentication, re-authentication, or any other event that changes the level of privilege with the associated user.

NOTE   If you want to continue to learn more about application security after reading this book, I encourage you to join your local OWASP chapter.

Bounds Checking

In 1996, Aleph One wrote a paper called "Smashing the Stack for Fun and Profit" that shook the software world.[43] The article detailed how a user could enter an excessive amount of data into a C programming language software application, overloading the variable within memory, *overwriting the stack* with the user's input. The article explained how an attacker could then enter shell code (machine-readable computer instructions that do not require a compiler), and thus take control of the computer that the application was hosted on. This vulnerability was possible because the C programming language is not memory-safe, meaning if you declare a var of type char and give it 20 characters of space, but then a user enters 30 characters of input, the programming language would not handle this for you; you are on your own. The program would save the first 20 characters in the place you made for it in memory when you declared the variable, but the next 10 characters would overwrite the next 10 places in memory. Those 10 places in memory might be your program's next instruction, another variable, or just unused space. No matter what is stored in those 10 places in memory, it would make your application work improperly. However, an advanced attacker can use this type of situation to inject their own code to be executed, which is called Remote Code Execution (RCE). This vulnerability of overwriting memory to perform an exploit is called a *buffer overflow* and is considered a critical security vulnerability.

As programming languages evolved, all new programming languages were created to be memory-safe (providing protections against these situations); however, many non-memory-safe languages are still in use in production the world over. You may wonder why.

Many systems in production today are gigantic, extremely complex, and very fragile. This is often called technical debt; however, we cannot pre-judge every situation without more details. The cost of replacing such a complex system may be more than it is worth, the risk involved in such a large project would be quite high, and sometimes the business decides to "accept the risk" of the situation. Other times the business does not fully understand the risk, in which case it is imperative that the security team communicates clearly to upper management (like the example earlier involving Alice's decision to migrate all applications to a different Java framework). Each situation is different, and only your business can decide which is the correct way forward.

That said, there are some firm rules we apply no matter what the situation, if you are using a language that is not memory safe:

1. Perform bounds checking on every input, every single time. Test this functionality very carefully, and repeatedly.

2. If your language has a framework overlay available or dependency you can add that can test bounds for you, use it.

3. Perform type checking on every input, every time. Test this functionality carefully also.

4. If possible, create unit tests for your bounds checking to create a regressive testing system that is run on every new code check in.

5. If possible, perform code review and verify every input has proper testing.

6. If possible, hire a penetration tester and ask them to set aside a generous amount of time to test your system input bounds.

7. If available, add compilation options to detect these types of issues.

A more advanced, additional layer of protection would be to add runtime protections, such as Address Space Layout Randomization (ASLR), Data Execution Prevention (DEP), Stack Canary, and so on. All of these are protections that alter the way memory is used in hopes of preventing these types of attacks.

NOTE   As an additional precaution, consider implementing a responsible disclosure program, in case you missed something. This suggestion is not specific for only this vulnerability; it's generally good advice for any AppSec program.

TIP   An example of a memory-safe alternative to C and C++ is the Rust programming language. Examples of memory-safe languages include Java, .Net (VB and C#), and Ruby on Rails.

If you are in a situation where you are choosing the programming language for a new project, I urge you to always select a memory-safe language, if one is available.

Authentication (AuthN)

As defined previously, authentication is making sure your user is who you think they are. Not another person with the same name as Alice or who looks like Alice, but *the* Alice, as identified by your system. Authentication and authorization are often paired together as an activity, but it should be noted that authentication is always performed *first*. We do this to ensure we know who we are dealing with, before allowing them access to anything within our system (AuthZ).

In Chapter 1 we discussed the three different factors of authentication (something you have, something you are, and something you know). Now you need to figure out how to use those in your application to verify the identity of your users.

You have a few options:

1. Use a pre-existing internet identity online service from a third party to verify your users. The Canada Revenue agency uses banking login identities to verify Canadians when they do their taxes. Many social sites online allow users to verify using their credentials for Twitter, LinkedIn, Facebook, Google, or Microsoft accounts.

Pros:

- Implemented very quickly.
- You are not responsible for maintaining or testing the code.
- The teams building these systems likely have more time and resources to allocate to ensure these systems are highly secure.
- Some users may trust this approach more or find it more convenient.

Cons:

- Some users do not want to share data between companies and prefer to make a separate login for each site.
- Some users may not belong to any of these third-party sites.
- There is likely a cost associated with using such a service.
- It is likely these services will collect personal information and metadata from your users.
- If there is a breach of the third-party system, it will affect your site.

2. Purchase or find a free library or software system to become part of your system to perform the identity functionality for you.

Pros:

- Implemented more quickly than writing your own.
- You are not responsible for designing the system yourself, just implementation.
- The teams building these systems likely have more time and resources to allocate to ensure these systems are highly secure.
- You host the data, which may be preferred by some customers.

Cons:

- There is likely a cost associated with using such a system.
- If there is a vulnerability found in the third-party system, it will affect your site, and you will be required to update your system with a patch when it is available.
- You host the data, which means you are responsible.

3. Write your own authentication system from scratch.

   As mentioned previously, this is not generally recommended. A company would create a product to perform this functionality; a lone software developer on a project team should always use a tried-and-true system that already exists.

Authorization (AuthZ)

Authorization is the determination of what a user can or cannot access within your system and access control grants (or declines) that access. Is Alice allowed to see another team's documents? Can Bob delete another user on the system that he administers? Questions like this are answered by authorization and access control.

The most popular methodology for determining access is Role Based Access Control, or RBAC for short. It means "determine someone's access based on the role that they are assigned in your system." You might be someone's boss in your workplace, but in the computer system you may have only regular system access, and your employee may have admin rights, because that is the role that they perform within the system (they are the administrator).

Let's get a bit deeper into this with Alice and Bob.

When Alice was first promoted to the executive level, she was very excited to have more privileges and powers in her workplace. She had an expense account, signing authority of $50,000, and an office on the top level of her office building. However, one day Alice was using her company's document management system and she found a directory of documents that she was not allowed to access. She was confused, and annoyed. She called the IT department and they explained that they kept the Risk Register in that directory, and that only the IT Security team and the Chief Information Security Officer (CISO) had access. Not even the CEO had access; she only received briefs from the CISO. They explained that not only did Alice not have a *need to know*, her account within the document management system was not assigned the role of "Security Operations," and therefore they would not be able to give her access. She would need to gain permission from the CISO in order to add that role, since she is outside of the security organization. Alice said she was satisfied with that answer. She had only wanted to understand why one part of the system was restricted. This explanation worked for her; she told them not to bother creating a ticket for her.

> **NOTE** A *Risk Register* is a document outlining all of the known risks to your organization. The information in this document is very sensitive, and if it fell into the wrong hands, it could be quite damaging to a company. Such a document could serve as a playbook for any malicious actor, outlining all of the organization's weaknesses.

TIP   *Need to know* refers to whether someone is required to know something in order to be able to do their job. It is the application of *least privilege* applied to information.

Last year Bob managed a project to create new accounting software. On his team were Sarah (a software tester), Emily (a software developer), and Jennifer (a database administrator, the DBA). They all played different roles within the project and their company, so they needed different sets of permissions and access. Emily, the software developer, didn't need Database Owner (DBO) permissions, but the DBA definitely did. Bob, as the project manager, never needed access to the web server or database, so he didn't ask for those rights within the system.

When it came time to request access, Bob asked that he be given only regular-user access so that he could see the app running, while he requested the following for his team:

- **Software tester (Sarah):** regular access to the app, as well as the ability to run all of her testing automation tools on her PC. She also needed write-access to the DevOps Pipeline software, so she could add tests to the pipeline.

- **Software developer (Emily)**: access to the app, access to the dev environment, the ability to create and run stored procedures in the dev DB, as well as access to run the DevOps pipeline, but not make changes to it.

- **Database administrator (Jennifer)**: access to the database server at the database owner level. No access to the web server, pipeline, or even the code. Jennifer doesn't need any of that, so no request was made.

At the beginning of the project Emily had wanted more privileges on the database server, the web server, and the pipeline, because she's a software developer, and who doesn't want access to everything? But the security team had denied her, based on her role within the project. The security person had explained to her that by limiting her access to only the systems she needed, if there was ever a breach, ransomware, or any other type of malware on her machine, it would be limited to the roles and access she had to the various systems. Emily agreed, begrudgingly.

This project situation is where RBAC is extremely helpful. The system administrator can easily assign the proper roles to each of Bob's project members to ensure they are only authorized access to the things they need to get their jobs done. The sysadmin simply went into their directory system and assigned each team member their roles and applied it to the project resources.

Using roles, rather than assigning specific access for each person manually, is especially helpful in situations where someone changes teams, jobs, or leaves the organization. Simply changing their role and switching the group (team) within their organization will remove and add all the access they need.

Manually administering access is never advised; it's a recipe for errors that can lead to security incidents.

There are three other widely accepted access control models:[44]

- Discretionary Access Control (DAC)
- Mandatory Access Control (MAC)
- Permission Based Access Control (PBAC)

Discretionary Access Control (DAC) means the owner of the information/system/resources can grant and remove access, based on their discretion, to someone else using the same identity system (for instance, on the same network, members of the same photo-sharing site, etc.).

When Bob's first grandchild was born, he took hundreds of photos and added them all to his online cloud storage account. At the time, the system gave him the option to grant specific user(s) on that system access to his photos, or not. Bob gave his entire extended family access to the photos, adding them one at a time via their usernames (email addresses). Bob's entire family started using the folder to share all of their family photos with each other. A few years later, there was a divorce in the family, and Bob remembered that he had given everyone read/write access to his folder. He made an active decision to remove access to that ex-family member, just in case.

Unlike role-based access control at Bob's work, when someone changes roles, DAC systems are not updated. They are based on system identity, not role.

Mandatory Access Control (MAC) grants access to information and systems based on the sensitivity level of the resource and the approval of the user attempting access it.

For instance, Alice doesn't have top-secret clearance, but Bob does, so in a system like this Bob would be able to access everything up to and including top-secret systems and data. Alice would not be granted such access. She only has public access, meaning she can only access public records.

MAC is generally used for systems requiring an extremely high level of security assurance; for instance, for a government military system or dataset.

Permission Based Access Control (PBAC) is based upon permissions. Users are granted certain permissions over information and systems, and when a user attempts to access something within the system, the access control mechanism verifies that they have been granted the permission before providing access. Types of permissions could include READ, WRITE, CREATE, UPDATE, DELETE, PRINT, REBOOT, etc.

After the divorce in Bob's family he decided to change the access control system to his photos; he granted everyone READ and WRITE, but after that, only he had DELETE and UPDATE.

Error Handling, Logging, and Monitoring

All application errors should be caught and handled gracefully; there should never be a stack trace or database error on the screen. This is not only so that we look like the professionals that we are, but also so that attackers are not given extra information to use against us when creating their attacks.

BACKUPS AND ROLLBACKS

Bob remembers years ago receiving a call from a user of one of the applications that his team made. The web application had crashed with a stack trace on the screen, and the user had thought their entire computer was broken. Bob's team had to manually roll back the transaction, which took forever. While doing this they discovered that there had been several of these types of crashes, and they had a serious flaw in their software. If they had been logging their errors and sending this information to the SIEM, they might have noticed this problem months early. They agreed to add logging, monitoring, and alerting requirements to all new software projects.

When errors happen, an application should never fail into an unknown state; it should always roll back any transaction it was performing, and close anything it may have opened. Such a situation should also always be logged, so that if an incident were to arise incident responders would have something to work with when they investigate, and so that auditors can verify that the system is and has been working correctly. If the error is unexplained or otherwise potentially malicious, you should also trigger a security alert.

When we say "fall into an unknown state," we mean where an exception (a program error) is not caught, and the program has nowhere to go next or is unsure of what it's supposed to do. When an error happens, we "catch" it in a try/catch block, then we "handle" it by taking a specific action. Possible handling includes issuing an error message, logging the error, issuing an alert, rolling back a transaction, or logging the user out of the system. There should be a universal or global error handler in each of your applications that catches anything that is not otherwise handled (caught).

TIP   When an application falls into an unknown state, this is where malicious actors flourish. Penetration testers and security researchers are always looking for such a situation, as this is where many vulnerabilities lie. It is *vital* that your application never falls into such a state.

Rules for Errors

The following is a list of error handling rules. Follow these rules to ensure your application never falls into an unknown state.

- All application errors must be caught and handled; they can never be left unhandled or uncaught.

- Having a catch-all mechanism (global exception handling) is highly advisable, to ensure unexpected errors are always handled properly.

- Internal information, stack traces, or other crash information should never be revealed to the user or potential attackers.

- Error messages should reveal as little as possible. Ensure they do not "leak" information, such as details about the server version or patching levels.

- Do not reveal if it is the username or password that is incorrect if there is a login error, as this allows for username enumeration.

- Always "fail safe" or "fail closed," do not "fail open" or to an unknown state. If an error occurs, do not grant access or complete the transaction; always roll back.

- Security-related errors (login fails, access control failures, server-side input validation failures) should issue a system alert. Ideally, log files will feed into an intrusion prevention/detection system or an application SIEM. This can be tested by running a vulnerability scanner against your application; it should cause events that trigger logging.

- When you log an error using information coming from an external source (external system/user input, rather than from your application itself) protect your logs against attack:[45]
  - Encode the content from the external source
  - Remove all non-printable characters (CR, LF, TAB, etc.)
  - Limit the maximum length of the information logged in order to prevent an overflow attack[46]

TIP   Yes, that's right! Malicious actors will even target your logs for attack. Nothing is sacred. This form of attack is usually referred to as *log injection* or *log forging* attacks.

Logging

Logging is your application writing details about the events that occur within it, to a very, very long document (known as a log file).[47] Almost everything it will report will be very boring, and that's why most people don't sit around reading logs directly. "Wrote this record to the database as this time, for this user" and "This user successfully logged in at this time" are not riveting stories. Log files tend to be measured in gigabytes and terabytes, so it would be impossible for a human being to keep up; and that is why industry invented log readers, SIEMs, and regex.

Log reading software opens gigantic files and allows you to search them. The Unix operating system allows use of the grep command to search your logs with regex (regular expressions). This is helpful when there is an incident and you are looking at a specific time frame or for a very specific event. This is not good for everyday use.

A Security Information and Event Management (SIEM) system is software that will ingest all of your logs and then attempt to put them into a human-readable form and alert your security engineers in your Security Operations Center (SOC) of anything it thinks they should investigate. Most large companies have one. If your company has one, your app logs should be readable by the SIEM.

Monitoring

Monitoring is both the act of paying attention to what's happening in your systems, and also using an IT tool that automates the process of checking for failures, slowdowns, crashes, and any anomalies it considers potentially dangerous or problematic. We will be talking about using a monitoring tool when we say "monitoring" in this book.

Your applications should be monitored, just like your network should be monitored. If your application is down, you want your tools to tell you instantaneously; you do not want social media notifications to be the way you find out about a major issue with your application. If at all possible, as a more advanced activity, you will want to create automated responses to specific alerts within your systems. This can be done using triggers and serverless applications; we will cover serverless later in this book.

> **TIP**   Error handling, logging, and monitoring all go hand in hand. If you aren't logging, your monitoring won't work. If you don't catch errors, then you won't have complete logs. It is essential that these systems are tested periodically to ensure that they are working properly.

When and What to Log

- System logs must not contain sensitive data or personally identifiable information (PII).
- Login fails and errors should be logged, as well as successes.

- Brute-force attempts should be logged (defined in this book as 10 or more successive failed attempts to log in, in under 1 minute, or 100 or more failed attempts in a 1-hour period).

- All security-related events, such as a user being authenticated, a user being locked out after several failed login attempts, an unaccounted-for error, or input validation errors.

- Your logs should be consumable by the SIEM, and automatically delivered to it.

TIP   An advanced attacker will attempt to remove evidence of themselves in your logs. Protect your logs accordingly.

The following information must be contained in your logs:

- What type of event occurred (why this event is security-related/name for event)

- When the event occurred (timestamp)

- Where the event occurred (URL, including subdomains)

- The source of the event (IP address)

    - If the IP comes from X-Forwarded-For header, do not forget to properly validate it; it could have been tampered with[48]

- The outcome of the event

- (If possible) the identity of any individuals, users, or subjects associated with the event

You can, of course, log more than what is listed here.

WARNING   When determining if something is sensitive or personally identifiable information (PII), ensure you look at all the data together, not just field by field. Sometimes the combination of multiple data points together *becomes* PII.

Using and Protecting Your Logs

- Log files and audit trails must be protected, even the backups.

- Ideally logs are all saved into the same space, in the same format, to be easily consumable by a SIEM or other security tools.

- Only authorized individuals should have access to logs.

- All access to the logs (if someone opens them, edits them, etc.) should also be logged in your network logs.

- Logs should be monitored.

- Logs should be stored in an encrypted format.

- Logs should be accessible by your incident response team and this team should validate the log history kept to be sure that they will be able to have the expected data when they will need to do investigation on an incident.

- Logs should be stored on a secure server or other secure area.

- Log files must be incorporated into your organization's overall backup strategy.

- Log files and media must be deleted and disposed of in the same way you would dispose of any sensitive information.

WARNING Never log PII or anything else sensitive such as SIN, passwords, or dates of birth. PII is information relating to an identifiable person.[49]

For more detailed information on this and so many other application security–related topics, please check out the extremely helpful "OWASP Cheat Sheets" project.

Exercises

1. When should you use your own identity on the network (user account) versus a service account? Give two examples for each and explain your reasoning.

2. Explain possible reasons or situations why C and C++ are still widely used in our industry when RUST (a memory-safe language) exists. Try to think of two or more.

3. What is your favorite programming language and/or framework, and why?

4. Which programming language and/or framework do you think is the most secure? Why?

5. Why do we need to protect user sessions?

6. If an attacker where able to get a hold of someone else's user session while they are logged in to their online banking, what could the attacker do?

7. If you were going to explain the difference between authentication and authorization to a non-technical co-worker, how would you explain it?

8. Should C-level executives have special privileges on your network and other computer systems? If so, why? If not, why not? What types of privileges would you give them, if you gave them any?

9. Should network system administrators have special privileges on your network and other computer systems? If so, why? If not, why not? What types of privileges would you give them, if you gave them any?

10. Should help desk employees have special privileges on your network and other computer systems? If so, why? If not, why not? What types of privileges would you give them, if you gave them any?

11. Your boss tells you that turning on logging and monitoring will cost too much. How do you explain its value and importance from a security perspective? Write a paragraph to convince your boss. Remember to make sure you explain what the potential risk is to the business, in a way your boss can understand (who is a smart, but not overly technical, person). If you speak over your audience's head, you will not pass this question, nor will you convince your boss.

Common Pitfalls

This chapter will cover common pitfalls that are not otherwise covered in the previous chapters. It is my firm belief that memorization of many types of vulnerabilities or breach statistics is not the most effective use of our time when we are trying to learn to secure software; instead, we need to learn to defend against all issues.

That said, despite all of the defenses we learned in Chapters 1 through 4, a few specific situations require special attention: vulnerabilities that are common and damaging, but for which we have not yet learned specific defenses. That is what we will cover in this chapter.

OWASP

The Open Web Application Security Project, more commonly known as OWASP, is a worldwide community dedicated to helping everyone create more secure software, found online at OWASP.org. They have approximately 300 chapters around the world where they hold free monthly events to teach about application security and other helpful topics. They host several international and regional conferences per year, in-depth and unique training opportunities, project summits, and are the creators of over 100 open source projects that help to push the application security industry forward. They are the creators of the Zed Attack Proxy, the most-used web app proxy and security scanner, and several other tools, documents, and even their own free books. They are a community that is open and anyone in the world can join. Despite all of these amazing contributions to the industry by the OWASP community, they are most well-known for one single project, called the "OWASP Top Ten."

The OWASP Top Ten is a list of the ten most critical web app vulnerabilities, which is updated every few years. It details each of the vulnerabilities, the risks, and mitigations. It is not a standard, nor a complete list of all web app vulnerabilities. It is created by a team of volunteers, using data from their professional experience and industry-supplied data, to find the most harmful and most pervasive web app vulnerabilities. It is a very helpful document if you want to begin your journey to becoming a penetration tester (you will find these issues often), learn defenses against these vulnerabilities if you are a programmer, or raise awareness about web application security at work; it is quite informative. Some of the vulnerabilities can be found with automated tools, and others require a human being. Some of the items on the list are a specific issue (XSS, for example), while others are more a systemic issue or design issue (such as "not enough or improper logging").

> **WARNING** Although the OWASP Top Ten is a very helpful tool for learning, it should never be used as a checklist to ensure you are creating secure software. You want to ensure your applications don't have any of these issues, but it is far more valuable to concentrate on having a good overall defense strategy, rather than aiming to only protect against or test for these specific issues. Another project, the OWASP Proactive Controls, lists the controls used to defend against all of the Top Ten, and much, much more. The OWASP Proactive Controls are an excellent OWASP resource to start learning application security defense strategies.

As the OWASP Top Ten provides the list of most harmful and most common vulnerabilities, and this is a book to help you learn to create secure software, we will cover the Top Ten only briefly. After the list, we will dive deeper into the three list items that were not covered by previous topics in this book, as well as bonus topics that are not part of The Top Ten.

> **TIP** There are many, many more vulnerabilities that are not on the world-famous OWASP Top Ten list. Don't stop here; this is only the start of your journey.

Here is the list for version 2017, as of this printing, with my summarization of each item:

```
owasp.org/www-project-top-ten/OWASP_Top_Ten_2017
```

1. Injection

Definition	Tricking a system into running an attacker's code, instead of its own.
Mitigation	Input validation, using parameterized queries if accessing a database.
Action	Code review (SAST) and testing (DAST and/or IAST) required. Apply least privilege to all accounts and systems to minimize damage if attack is successful.

2. Broken Authentication

Definition	Errors in implementation of Session Management and/or Authentication (AuthN), allowing inappropriate access or privilege to systems, data, and/or user sessions.
Mitigation	Follow best practices as outlined in Chapter 4, in the sections "Session Management" and "Authentication (AuthN)."
Action	Code review (SAST) and testing (DAST and/or IAST) required.

3. Sensitive Data Exposure

Definition	Sensitive or private data exposed or leaked to users or systems that should not have been. Caused by broken protections, mis-labeling or other mistreatment of data.
Mitigation	Label your data's sensitivity level. Follow best practices as described in Chapter 3, in the section "Protecting Sensitive Data."
Action	Code review (SAST) and testing (DAST and/or IAST) required. Your org may require audits as well to verify you are compliant with applicable regulations such as GDPR (European Union) or ISTG (Canada).

4. XML External Entities (XXE)

Definition	Some XML processors allow the loading of entities that are defined outside the document (i.e., External Entities). An attacker taking advantage of this is able to instruct the vulnerable XML processor, via its own crafted malicious XLM file, to send requests (ex: HTTP/FTP/...) to internal or external systems in order to perform actions or read data. Essentially, this is misconfiguration of XML processors, but it is so pervasive and damaging that it has been granted its own category.

Continues

(*continued*)

Mitigation	Don't use XML (use JSON or something else more modern). If this is not an option, disable these features on all XML processors (XML external entity and DTD processing).
Action	Audit all XML parsers for this issue. Add a dedicated security unit test suite to constantly ensure that any XML parser instantiated is correctly configured.
	Manual testing looking specifically for this issue. More details will be provided in the "Deserialization" section of this chapter and in Chapter 6, "Testing and Deployment."

5. Broken Access Control

Definition	Errors in implementation of Access Control and/or Authorization (AuthZ), allowing inappropriate access or privilege to systems, and/or data.
Mitigation	Following best practices as listed in Chapter 4 in the sections "Identity" and "Authorization."
Action	Code review (SAST) and testing (DAST and/or IAST) required.

6. Security Misconfiguration

Definition	Any system that is improperly configured such that it leads to security vulnerabilities.
Mitigation	Follow the hardening guide for every product in your network. Implement a defense-in-depth strategy to minimize damage if something is missed. If possible, hire someone well-experienced with each system for implementation and/or auditing.
Action	Config audits and change management (self-documenting, preferably), and testing (DAST and/or IAST) required.

7. Cross-Site Scripting (XSS)

Definition	Tricking an application to run an attacker's JavaScript, in a user's browser.
Mitigation	Input validation, output encoding, Content Security Policy (CSP) + x-xss-protection security headers. As covered in Chapters 2, 3, and 4.
Action	Code review (SAST) and testing (DAST and/or IAST) required.

8. Insecure Deserialization

Definition	An attacker replaces a serialized object with their own, malicious, serialized object. The object is deserialized as the attack is executed.
Mitigation	Whenever possible, avoid using serialization. If unavoidable, do not accept objects from unknown sources, or only use primitive (unchangeable/basic) data classes from an approved/accepted list.
Action	This list is long and will be discussed at length in "Deserialization" section in this chapter. Code review (SAST) and testing (DAST and/or IAST) required, at a minimum.

9. Using Components with Known Vulnerabilities

Definition	Including a library, dependency, or component that contains a known security vulnerability in your application, potentially creating the same vulnerability in your application.
Mitigation	As we will discuss in Chapter 6, "Software Composition Analysis (SCA)," use a Software Composition Analysis (SCA) tool to verify if your components are known to be vulnerable.
Action	Use SCA against your code repos and in your build pipelines/processes.

10. Insufficient Logging & Monitoring

Definition	Attacks and other security events or incidents not being detected/prevented/documented due to improper, misconfigured or absent logging and/or monitoring systems.
Mitigation	Follow best practices, as described in Chapter 4, in the section "Error Handling, Logging, and Monitoring."
Action	Auditing and testing of these systems required to ensure that events are being detected properly and timely.

Defenses and Vulnerabilities Not Previously Covered

What follows are specific defenses against common vulnerabilities not covered by the previous strategies in this book. We will cover:

- CSRF

- ▪ SSRF
- ▪ Deserialization
- ▪ Race Conditions

Cross-Site Request Forgery

Cross-Site Request Forgery (CSRF), affectionately known as "Sea Surf," was briefly discussed earlier in this book, but it is an important issue and unfortunately still somewhat common, so we will revisit it in more detail. CSRF was only recently removed from the "Top Ten" after several programming frameworks built automated defenses directly into newer versions. It speaks volumes that the industry has adjusted some frameworks to help eliminate this vulnerability.

> **TIP** Building the defenses directly into programming frameworks is the absolute best way to combat insecure software. Developers already have to balance quite a bit of responsibility and knowledge in order to do their jobs well, so the more we can take off of their plate, the better the results.

Unsimilar to XSS, the goal of CSRF is to trick the user into clicking a link that performs the attacker's request/actions, against the web application the user is logged in to. It uses the code of the vulnerable application against itself, not the attacker's code. It is called "surfing" because the attacker is surfing on the victim's credentials.

That said, sometimes CSRF is confused with cross-site scripting (XSS), because they both use the word "cross." Let's discuss the differences and similarities to ensure you understand.

An *XSS attack* is when an attacker tricks a web application into executing *the attacker's code* in the user's browser (on the client side). It only works with JavaScript, and can be reflected against the web server, stored in or reflected by the document object model (DOM), or stored (saved into your database).

> **TIP** DOM-based cross-site scripting means the vulnerability is in the client-side code, rather than on the server. This can make it more difficult to test and defend against.

While the goals of CSRF are similar to XSS attacks, to control the application to the attacker's benefit, in CSRF the attack uses the application's own functionality to execute the attack. The two attacks are not at all related, despite the use of the word "cross" in both names. The CSRF flowchart is shown in Figure 5-1.

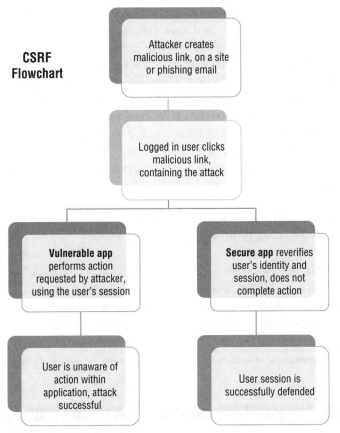

CSRF Flowchart

Attacker creates malicious link, on a site or phishing email

Logged in user clicks malicious link, containing the attack

Vulnerable app performs action requested by attacker, using the user's session

Secure app reverifies user's identity and session, does not complete action

User is unaware of action within application, attack successful

User session is successfully defended

Figure 5-1: CRSF flowchart

NOTE To summarize CSRF, it is an attacker taking over a user's active session and then performing a malicious act.

If you recall from earlier in Chapter 2 when we discussed Alice logging in to her favorite clothing site, we talked about how there are many situations where users leave their accounts logged in to a site for a very long time (hours or even days or months), and this is the type of situation that CSRF attempts to take advantage of. Although we discussed regenerating sessions in the "Session Management" section in Chapter 4, users are going to do as they please, while we refresh or destroy sessions invisibly, to ensure they remain safe while using our applications online.

The CSRF attack is an attacker tricking a user into clicking a link containing the attack, or when the attack is contained within a malicious site. The attack will attempt to perform an action against a web app, without the user's knowledge or permission. If the user is already logged in to the site (like when Alice shops for clothes online), and the site is vulnerable to such an attack, the site will perform the transaction (usually theft of some kind).

Many modern frameworks will automatically pass a token for you, in order to defend against this type of attack (Java, .Net, Ruby on Rails), while others offer it as a feature, but as a developer you must choose to use it. For details on how to implement it, visit the OWASP Cheat Sheet on this topic.[50]

That said, you have more options than just tokens for protecting against this type of attack; anything that reverifies the user and ensures they are aware of the action taking place is acceptable; re-logging in or filling out a captcha are the most commonly used options, outside of using a token.

A secondary layer of defense against this type of attack is to verify that the referrer header is from your site, and not another site or email, before performing an action. Performing both defenses is advised.

> **WARNING**   Some believe that the referrer header is easy to spoof, and it is if you can access the server, create a request there, and then send the forged request from the application. However, that situation is not CSRF, and it is a much, much larger problem than CSRF. The referrer header cannot be spoofed using JavaScript alone (which would be necessary for a CSRF attack), and thus verifying the referrer URL is a valuable second layer of defense.

INDUSTRY SUCCESS

The OWASP Top Ten truly succeeded with CSRF by raising awareness about this vulnerability; the instances of this vulnerability in the wild have reduced drastically between 2013 and 2017 (source: OWASP Top Ten 2017), and most modern frameworks now include defense functionality. I applaud OWASP for all that they do for our industry and the world.

Server-Side Request Forgery

A Server-Side Request Forgery (SSRF) attack involves a malicious actor adding or changing URL parameters, resulting in the ability to instruct the server, or gaining information or access that they should not have. Attackers can use this to call internal APIs or access databases. An application that is vulnerable to this attack is like a window directly into your network, behind your perimeter defenses; it's terrifying.

This type of attack is usually paired with other exploits in order to do even more damage, meaning we must not only work to defend against it directly, but also add other mitigations to reduce damage if we are vulnerable. The SSRF flowchart is shown in Figure 5-2.

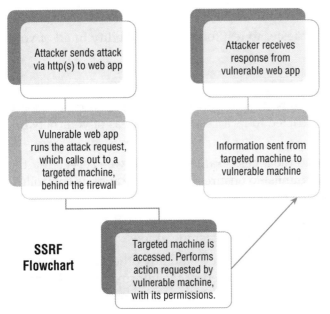

Figure 5-2: SSRF flowchart

The defenses (prevention) and mitigations (harm reduction if an attack does happen) against this attack are layered: [51]

Defenses

1. Do not use URL parameters to build calls within your application or network, as they can be manipulated easily. Avoid using them altogether if possible.

2. Perform input validation (using approved or accepted lists), as per earlier chapters.

3. If your application must call out to other sites, create an approved list of domains that are permitted. Reject all others.

4. Use request filtering, if available on your stack. Much like output encoding, this technology can ensure your HTTP responses do not contain anything damaging (such as an SSRF attack).[52] If it is not available on your stack, then ensure your responses do not contain what was sent in the request (user input), unchanged. The data should be validated before adding it to a response; there is no need to reflect that information unchanged and unvalidated.

5. Disable unused URL schemas such as file:///, dict://, ftp://, and gopher://. If you aren't using them, disable them.[53]

6. Create customized unit tests for this vulnerability.

7. Hire a skilled security tester to test for this vulnerability in all of your applications.

Mitigation

1. Use zero-trust design on both your network and applications to ensure your application is restricted in its access to other areas of your network and applications.

2. Apply least privilege to the access granted for your web server and the application service account(s) to ensure if your application is controlled, it will have less access to resources.

3. Follow the hardening guide for every web server, PaaS, or container that hosts web apps. Always follow all hardening guides.

4. Handle attempted attacks just as you would any other incorrect input: issue a vague error message. Never reflect the information of the attack on screen or in your response.

5. Ensure all internal services require authentication (for example, older versions of MongoDB did not require authentication or authorization to access the database).

Commercial products are available to help protect further against this type of attack. Speak with your security team if you are concerned that your other defenses are not enough, if you require a very high level of security assurance, or if you believe you are being targeted for this type of attack by an advanced adversary.

This attack has become more common over the past few years, as more information about it has become available. Although it is not listed on the "Top Ten," it is common and dangerous enough that it deserves its own mention.

> **NOTE**   SSRF is when an attacker is able to issue instructions to a web server (to read data or perform certain function calls), then using the web server to attack assets behind the firewall (with all of the access and power that the web server is allotted). This is also known as *pivoting* in penetration testing; gaining access to a network resource, then using that resource to gain further access.
>
> That said, this attack can also be used to gain access to data and information that is confidential, or to call internet resources such as APIs.

Deserialization

Serialization is changing data from memory (object) to a file or stream, usually so that it can be transmitted or stored. Deserialization is putting it back into its original state (memory/object) after the transmission of the data or when it is needed again. This happens most often in XML, JSON, and Java, but there are several other situations and technologies where this can occur.[54]

If an attacker can replace the serialized version of your data with something malicious, it can result in a devastating attack. Such a situation is referred to as *insecure deserialization*.

The easiest way to avoid this problem is to not use this feature. If you do not serialize anything, then you won't need to deserialize it. This may sound like a simplification, and it is. This is not always possible, but if you can, avoid any situation that is potentially risky.

If you cannot avoid the requirement for serialization, then do not use object serialization of data; instead, use a data parsing data format (JSON, XML, YAML) to load data into the object graph.

If you *absolutely must* accept serialized objects, only accept them from a trusted source and only accept objects containing primitive data types (types defined as part of your programming language by default, such as int and char).

Following are some precautions for serialized objects:

- Never accept a serialized object from an untrusted sender. That sender should be on an approved list of potential senders. Never accept a serialized object from a user.
- Use defensive deserialization with a look-ahead object input stream with a strict approved list of allowed classes.
- Only deserialize signed objects and verify the checksum *or* use HMAC with a SHA256 hash.[55]
- Only accept primitive (unchangeable) data types.

Several other steps are explained on the OWASP.org website of how to safely process serialized objects from untrusted sources; however, as this is a constantly changing landscape, they will not be outlined here.

The main lesson here is to avoid serialization/deserialization whenever possible. If you must accept serialized objects, only accept them from trusted sources. If you cannot follow this advice, proceed with extreme caution.

NOTE   To summarize deserialization, it is an attacker replacing serialized information with their own serialized information, which contains an attack against the web server or application.

Race Conditions

A race condition happens when software actions depend on timing, and the threads should be set up synchronously, but they aren't. Or it should lock a resource, but it doesn't. Or it's supposed to wait for something else to happen before it does the next step . . . but the programmer forgot to put that check in.

Imagine Alice wants to edit a file on one of the shared drives at work. She opens it, and the word processing software puts a lock on it while she has it open. If later Bob wants to open it, it will only allow him to see the document in a read-only format, so that he doesn't overwrite a colleague's changes.

But imagine if the word processing software didn't put a lock on the file? This happens more than you might realize.

As an example, suppose on the way home from work you go to the grocery store to buy food for dinner. Before you left work, you checked your checking account and saw that you had $60. While you were shopping for food, your spouse paid a few bills, leaving only $10 in the account. By the time you go to check out at the grocery store your account has updated to its new balance of $10 and your card gets declined. Although this type of situation is definitely less than ideal, it makes sense.

Now imagine someone was intentionally trying to create a race condition. They use an online shopping card, fill it up, and just as they press the Purchase button, they also attempt to transfer the money to another account. Ideally the banking software should put a lock on the account until transaction #1 is complete, then attempt transaction #2. Transaction order would be determined based on which request was received first.

Banks are expecting this situation; people have been trying to steal money since currency was invented. However, race conditions apply to every change in a system that is dependent on another:

- Competing for resources (editing a document)
- Updating values (bank balance)
- Anything where the timing of one activity depends upon another condition

The simplest mitigation is to use a lock on any record that will be changed, until the action is complete. If one transaction depends on another, verify the previous transaction has completed before starting the next one. Program in your dependencies; make it a part of your design. If a transaction does not complete, roll back the transaction, issue an error if appropriate, and fail closed (as opposed to open or into an unknown state).

The main cause of race conditions is that the existence of a dependence of one change upon another is missed in the design. Threat modeling can help you find race conditions and prevent them before they turn into a problem. Always map out any dependencies when designing your applications and other systems.

Closing Comments

Unless you are creating a presentation on the topic or going to an unnecessarily intense job interview, it is not necessary to memorize the OWASP Top Ten. It is, however, necessary that you follow the defenses listed in this book from now on when creating software.

Now that we have covered the basics, in the following chapters we will cover formal application security activities, creating an AppSec program, and how to secure more modern types of software, tech stacks, and technologies.

Exercises

1. Someone on your project team wants to accept serialized objects from an untrusted source. You know this is a bad idea. How do you explain the risk *effectively* to your teammate? Write down your answer. Be persuasive and clear.

2. The OWASP Top Ten is a standard: Yes or no.

3. Name three of the OWASP Top Ten that we already covered in this book before Chapter 5.

4. Does the XXE vulnerability apply to JSON? Does it apply to YAML? If so, why? If not, why not?

5. Name an example of a race condition (it does not need to be computer related).

6. Why do we roll back incomplete transactions? Why does that matter? Give an example of when not rolling back an incomplete transaction would be problematic.

What You Should Do to Create Very Good Code

In This Part

Testing and Deployment

This chapter will focus on testing and deployment of your application and the systems on which your application depends. This includes APIs, infrastructure, your database, etc.

The definition of "testing," for this book, is to verify the quality, reliability, and security of software. It means checking that your software does everything that the client asked for and that the project requirement document listed, but also that it *only* does those things. Testing should also ensure that the *confidentiality, integrity,* and *availability* (CIA) of your system and its data are properly protected and maintained.

The definition of deployment for this book will mean "the actions taken to release your application to production." This can mean right-click ⇨ Publish, manually copying and pasting code to a server, creating formal run books to send to an operations team for execution, or creating an entire automated Continuous Integration/Continuous Delivery (CI/CD) system.

This chapter *is not* about how to become a penetration tester. Several high-quality books are dedicated to that topic; this is not one of them.

Testing Your Code

The code within your application is the written instructions that you send to the interpreter or compiler. This section will cover how to test these written instructions. This type of testing is sometimes called *static testing* because the code is not changing or running while you look at it; it's just text. The opposite of this is *dynamic testing*, which generally refers to when your application is running on a web server or some other platform and the tester can interact with the application live. This section will cover static testing.

Code Review

The first type of testing we can do on our code is to review it for security issues. This is sometimes called "secure code review," and it entails reading over all parts of the code that perform a security function (generally referred to as a "security control"), and all integration points (because integration points should *always* have security controls). Integration points are where different pieces of the system fit together—for instance, a web app front end calling an API, an API calling a stored procedure in a database, or an application logging an error to a log file on a separate server.

When performing a secure code review, you do not necessarily need to read every line of code in your entire application; often the scope involves only the security controls/features. Each engagement is different, and it is important clarify requirements before you begin. That said, security controls will *always* be in scope.

What types of security functionality do you need to review?

- Authentication
- Authorization
- Security configurations (encryption specifics such as key-length or algorithm, and security header settings)
- Identity management/systems
- Session management
- Input validation
- Output encoding

Everything we've discussed in previous chapters needs to be reviewed to verify that it has been correctly implemented.

What are you reviewing for? First, to ensure that there is a security control in all the places that there should be. Second, to ensure that the correct security control is implemented, based on the context, and third, that it's implemented and configured correctly.

You might be thinking "What places should have a control?" Besides looking for items we've mentioned in this book, review your threat models (discussed later in this chapter), your requirements list, and any security-related user stories.

TIP Alice always has someone else review her presentations and documents before she shows her boss, as she knows that she tends to miss her own mistakes. The same is true with code. Code review is best performed by someone other than the one who wrote it.

Code review can happen in many different situations during the coding, testing, or release/maintenance phases of the System Development Life Cycle (SDLC); it can be performed on each new piece of code before it is merged into the main branch, it can be performed right before you publish version 1.0 of your application, or even after a data breach has occurred during the incident investigation. That said, usually a secure code review is performed after sending the code for quality testing if you are in a Waterfall-style software development environment, and before releasing each new feature in Agile (reviewing only new code). In a DevOps environment there are several different timings that could be used for code review: before each check in of your code (integration of your changes into the main code base), before each major release, for every single code push—it will depend on your team's needs.

To kick off a secure code review, ask a colleague or friend to review your code, and offer to review theirs. If you don't have someone to help you, review your own code; set aside time for this activity and remind yourself that you are looking for problems within the security controls and business logic of your application. If you aren't sure about something, ask the security team, a friend, or look it up on the internet.

Several useful guides are available online about how to perform code review, including language-specific advice. Using a checklist from well-known guides or creating your own will help you provide consistent results.

If you have no idea what you are doing when you start, that's okay; this is an activity that you will become better at over time. Each time you review an application you will learn more about code review, and you will become a better coder. Each new mistake you find will teach you a new lesson. You might not find code review to be the most exciting of all types of testing, but it is an easy place to start where you can safely and immediately provide value to your team.

Static Application Security Testing (SAST)

SAST stands for Static Application Security Testing, but it is often used interchangeably to refer to SAST tools, rather than the act of performing a static type of software testing. A SAST tool can analyze the code, binaries, and even byte code for potential security problems. Each tool has different functionality, so try out any tool before you commit to purchasing it. When evaluating code, a SAST tool will parse the code, just like a compiler would, but instead of breaking it down into byte code to be run on a server, it looks for potential security risks.

This can be anything from identifying a known vulnerable class or function, to alerting that security controls appear to be missing or implemented improperly, memory leaks, unused variables or functions, poor code quality, and more.

The wonderful thing about SAST tools is that they can go several layers deep from function to function; way past the point that most human beings would be able to review manually. They can and do find many, many vulnerabilities that most humans would miss, and the results can be very impressive.

That said, most SAST tools produce a very high number of results that, once investigated, turn out to be false positives.

> **NOTE** A false positive from a security testing tool means the tool has reported that something is a vulnerability, when it's not actually vulnerable. A false negative means the tool has missed a vulnerability. All tools produce both types of results, but ideally you want to receive as many as possible true positives (it reports legitimate vulnerabilities) and true negatives (it doesn't miss anything).

Yes, you read that right. SAST tools produce the highest number of false positives of any type of application security testing tool, even more than manual code review. Why is this?

The first reason is that when you configure a SAST tool you can choose to set it to be quite strict, and only have it show you what it believes to be true positives. This means it will not show you anything unless it is near certain that it is a vulnerability. If you set your SAST tool to this setting, you will miss out on most of the findings; there will be many, many false negatives. This means the tool will see things it suspects are a problem, but not tell you. It is likely you would be missing the majority of the problems within your application. This is far from ideal if you are trying to ensure that your software is secure.

> **NOTE** Some SAST tool perform "symbolic execution," a means of analyzing a program to determine what inputs cause each part of a program to execute. An interpreter follows the program, assuming symbolic values for inputs rather than obtaining actual inputs as normal execution of the program would. —Wikipedia[56]
>
> For the most complete set of potential problems, configure your SAST scanner to report anything it suspects is an issue. Then set aside quite a bit of time to investigate your results.

The findings from your SAST tool should be looked at more like a list of "hints" of where you need to do some code review, rather than a list of confirmed vulnerabilities. If you look at the SAST results like this, you will get a lot more value from the tool, and just like with manual code review, this is something you will become better at with patience and practice.

A SAST tool is not able to replace a manual code review; they provide different analyses and results. Automated code analysis is not usually able identify business logic flaws; it cannot understand such a context. It is recommended to combine the two approaches (automated plus manual review) in order to increase the coverage and find the maximum number of vulnerabilities.

A SAST tool must be configured according to your programming framework, protocols, and other technologies in order to provide the best possible results. For example, a SAST tool that is properly configured for your tech stack will recognize the security-related functions coming from the framework, such as input validation or output escaping, and be able to spot potential errors in implementation.

SAST tool effectiveness varies greatly based on supported technologies; evaluate carefully before you commit to buying a tool.

A long list of current tools, free and paid, is available at owasp.org/www-community/Source_Code_Analysis_Tools.

WARNING   It's not currently possible that an automated tool (of any kind) can give 100% accuracy when finding vulnerabilities. What this means is you *must never* forward unvalidated results from a SAST tool to a software development team and/or log bugs into your bug tracker. There will be many false positives, and when you waste the development's team with false positives, you will lose their trust. *Always validate the results from any automated tool before forwarding them to another team.*

Software Composition Analysis (SCA)

As we discussed in previous chapters, most modern applications contain many libraries, frameworks, and components made up of third-party code (code that your team did not write), and when you include them in your software, you are also including any vulnerabilities that they have. It is a best practice to limit third-party code whenever possible to reduce your attack surface, although in practice this is not a simple task.

The best way to ensure that third-party code is secure is by performing SCA.

According to several sources on the internet, *software composition analysis* (SCA) is the process of automating the visibility into open source software (OSS) use for the purpose of risk management, security, and license compliance.[57] However, SCA tools also report on propriety (closed source) libraries and frameworks as well, so this definition is not quite complete.

Most large companies with several dev teams do not have a complete inventory of web app assets (a list of all the software they have created), nor the corresponding *software bill of materials* (SBoM) (all the components and the version of each one) for each of those assets. An SCA tool can create an SBoM for your software and can automate the process of keeping the SBoM up to date. We want an SBoM so that we understand our various components, and how to protect ourselves. If a vulnerability is being exploited in the wild in version X of framework Y, we want to know as soon as humanly possible if we have framework Y anywhere in production and if any of those instances are version X. This is something an SBoM can tell you immediately.

SCA tools work based on a list of "known vulnerable" components. They can create the list they use in their tool in many ways: gathering information from public lists, purchasing lists from other companies, hiring security researchers to review popular frameworks and components, using automated tools to analyze components, and subscribing to security feeds from the creators of components. Some companies allow other tool makers, governments, or large companies to subscribe to their lists directly (usually for a cost).

SCA tools can be automated, both to point at your code repository (the place you store all of your source code) and to run when you deploy new code (ideally automated in a CI/CD pipeline). Scheduling regular scans of your code repository requires read-only access and can help you ensure that all of your applications (including older legacy applications) are given security attention. Even if you haven't released an application in a very long time, the components in your application are still potentially under scrutiny by malicious actors and may have changed from being listed as "OK" to "known vulnerable." This is why it's critical that we scan our code with an SCA tool, even if we haven't changed it in a long time; if it's currently in production, it still needs to be secure.

We should also be scanning code before we release it. We may have updated a component or added a new one, and that specific version may be "known vulnerable," even if it's very new. When a new version of anything is released, security researchers and malicious actors often review them for security issues, and therefore the first few days after release is often when new vulnerabilities are found in products, patches, and frameworks. When we use an SCA tool to check even new components, we create more secure software.

Some SCA tools also offer integration with programming IDEs (integrated development environment, the place where you write your code). The integration proxies the IDE to ensure that developers can only download packages from their repository of pre-approved packages. If this is offered as part of an SCA tool your office has purchased, take advantage of this service; it allows you to prevent security bugs (which is even better than finding and fixing them).

For an online list of various SCA tools, some free, some paid, visit `owasp.org/ www-community/Component_Analysis#tools-listing`.

Unit Tests

Unit testing is a level of software testing where individual units/components of a software are tested. The purpose is to validate that each unit of the software performs as designed. A unit is the smallest testable part of any software. It usually has one or a few inputs and usually a single output.[58]

Unit tests are often written in your IDE and stored alongside your code in your repository; they are almost as valuable as your code. Ideally, developers run all unit tests before checking their code in, and if their code fails a test, the developer must either 1) fix their code or 2) adjust the test for the new code changes. They aren't allowed to check in broken code that doesn't pass the unit tests.

> **TIP** Often when discussing unit tests people will talk about "code coverage." This means what percentage of the code has a unit test that verifies it works correctly. There is no standard amount that every organization must have. That said, every organization aims for 100 percent, but it is rare to encounter very high code coverage in the wild. Try not to be too tough on your developers if they are nowhere near 100 percent; few are.

Unit tests are generally *positive* tests; they verify that the code does what it is *supposed* to do, every time. However, unit tests can also be *negative*; verifying that your application *fails gracefully* if it receives bad input. Negative unit tests are often used for verifying not only the quality of your application, but also the security.

In order to make negative unit tests, talk with the developers where you work and make sure you have permission to touch their code. Then create a copy of several of their unit tests, add something on the end to denote that it is a negative version of the same test (for instance _abuse) and add an appropriate payload (potentially problematic code). Run the negative unit tests and find out which code passes, and which fails.

> **TIP** If you have a security champions program at work, ask a champion to help you. This is a perfect activity to teach them about security, and eventually you will be able to delegate this task. If not, don't worry; we'll talk about starting a security champions program in later chapters.

For example, if there is code that will be displayed to the screen, attempt to add a `<script>` tag, then verify that the code properly encodes it and the `<script>` tag is not executed. This is a rather extreme example; if it executes this, you are in trouble. The OWASP Cheat Sheet team created a handy "XSS Filter Evasion Cheat Sheet,"[59] which is definitely a great place to start for payloads (bad code to add to your negative unit tests). You can add logic tests, bad input, retest issues found during manual security testing, and tests for all of your threat models.

The main value that unit tests offer, negative or positive, is regression testing. Regression testing is rerunning functional and non-functional tests to ensure that previously developed and tested software still performs after a change.[64] Negative unit tests offer automated security regression testing, which is extremely high value early in the SDLC. They require up-front work and maintenance, but the outcome is quite advantageous from a security perspective.

TIP If your company has a penetration test, security, or vulnerability assessment, when you receive the report consider creating unit tests out of the results (if applicable). This way you can ensure that those same mistakes don't happen again. In fact, if you have permission, apply your learnings from the report to all of the applications where you work; create unit tests for all of the applications where it may apply. The same developers made several different applications where you work, and they may have made the same mistake in more than one place.

Infrastructure as Code (IaC) and Security as Code (SaC)

Way back in the day, when Bob actually *did* the tech work, as opposed to managing tech projects like he does now, they used to name their servers cute names after TV show characters. Each server was a separate physical machine, and he remembers having to rack them and how heavy and loud they were. He remembers having to walk from machine to machine when he needed to update the operating systems, carrying a CD (compact disc) with the updates. Eventually they could get the updates over the internet and that made life easier, but he still had to walk around and press the Next button more times than he cares to remember.

Over time they switched to virtual machines (VMs), and several operating systems could all live on one server. By then everything was network connected, and they got updates from the internet instead of CDs. They started using automated systems to deploy patches, which meant no more evenings of pressing Next or physically walking from machine to machine. Bob was thrilled at the advancement. He's aware now that they have DevOps and site reliability engineers (SREs) that do something called "Infrastructure as Code" but that's way above Bob's level of understanding so he sticks to managing projects and lets them take care of the technical details.

> *Infrastructure as Code (IaC) is the process of managing and provisioning computer data centers through machine-readable definition files, rather than physical hardware configuration or interactive configuration tools.*

> —*Wikipedia*[60]

Infrastructure as code (IaC), sometimes referred to as *configuration as code*, defines your infrastructure using written code, as opposed to a system image or install file. This code can be run to create, replace, or update your infrastructure. The code can be stored in your code repository and/or released via a CI/CD pipeline, just like the code for your application.

Using IaC leads to more uniform results, and if you store the code in a code repository, this means you can easily track (and audit) any changes (and roll back if necessary). It also means that you can apply security testing to it, just like any other code.

NOTE   IaC checks all sorts of security boxes; change management, disaster recovery, eliminating the possibility of human typing errors, and more. Although this is a book about creating secure software, our code lives on servers, and therefore it has importance. Plus, code is code; let's secure all of it!

Security as code (SaC) is the practice of building security into DevOps tools and workflows by mapping out how changes to code and infrastructure are made and finding places to add security checks, tests, and gates without introducing unnecessary costs or delays. —O'Reilly[61]

If developers are automating everything, even infrastructure, then we must automate security as well. Although there are many different ways to implement the concept of SaC, in this section we will focus on how to test IaC for security issues. We will cover the idea of automating secure checks in future chapters when we discuss DevOps and DevSecOps.

The code written for IaC can be scanned for issues, just like any other code, and should be scanned before it is released into production (at the very latest). For IaC specifically, we will want to scan to make sure not only are there no vulnerabilities within it, but we need to ensure that whoever wrote the infrastructure definitions also enabled the desirable security features and configurations for each infrastructure definition. This can mean forcing HTTPS for a web server VM, which version of TLS to use, closing ports, putting a container inside a specific V-LAN on your network, etc.

TIP   Protect your Security as Code and Infrastructure as Code just as you would your application code. Store it in a version-controlled code repository, make sure changes are tracked, be careful who has access, and always have backups.

Testing Your Application

Once your code has been compiled into byte code or interpreted into a dynamic running piece of software, this is when you can test your *application*. Tools and testers can interact with your software to learn how it responds, for better or worse, verifying how secure your application truly is. This is generally called dynamic application security testing (DAST).

When testing your application, you want to look for both security bugs (implementation errors) and flaws (design errors). You want to test the way it handles itself in regard to confidentiality, integrity, and availability (CIA) (including its data and other systems it connects to and depends on). You want to test it against any applicable policies, standards, or legal requirements, as well as industry best practices and commonly found issues. You will want to carefully examine every security feature, and every integration point for potential weakness, misconfiguration, or error. Lastly, you want to ensure that it always fails securely and gracefully, no matter the awful treatment you serve it.

While performing testing it is important that we do our best to avoid "making a mess." Be careful not to break things, destroy data, or crash systems. Even if you are able to exploit a vulnerability, or take a trophy, it isn't always necessary; you're here to verify the security of an application, not to show off your skills. Ensure you always stay within the scope of your testing agreement, no matter the temptation. As you become more experienced it will be easier to control your efforts, and to be more precise in your actions.

Before testing an application make a backup of the data, and the application itself if you do not have an automated deployment system. Ask for written permission to test any applications that you test for someone else, and ensure the person giving you permission has the authority to do so. It is rare that the person in the cubicle next to you is actually authorized to "accept the risk" for your security testing, so always make sure you are covered from a legal perspective before you begin any testing engagement.

> **TIP**   Generally, definition of scope and approval for testing is documented in a formal process when consulting or performing testing as a third party. Several books and articles are available online that explain how to formally document this process for your legal protection.

Whenever possible, test the application on a dedicated test environment, not live on production. Using a dedicated test environment will allow you to conduct your testing without risk to production systems and data.

> **TIP**   Write out a formal statement of scope for your testing, specifying the IP addresses and URLs to be tested, and whether you will test APIs, the network, the WAF, etc. List the tools you will use, how you will conduct your testing, where the security and network teams can expect you to come from (so they know if it's you or an attacker), how long and when you will be testing, and anything else you can think of that they may want to know. Have someone with authority sign this document and keep it somewhere safe. This document is usually called "The Rules of Engagement" or a testing scope document.

Manual Testing

Although much attention in our industry tends to revolve around automation, manual security testing is to this day the most accurate type of security testing (when performed by an expert). Although automated tools are able to find most issues significantly faster than manual efforts, there are many types of security bugs and flaws that only a trained human being can detect. A combined approach of manual and automated testing is used for best results.

Browsers

A modern web browser is the #1 best security testing tool for a web application, because using a browser is how we talk to web apps. A trained attacker can use a browser to find all sorts of things wrong with an application, or even with your network. Most business logic issues, which are generally design flaws, are found using nothing more than a browser; automated tools are generally unable to find such issues. A browser is the most direct way to "talk" to a web application and should be the first tool in your web app testing toolbox.

Browsers are generally used to verify whether there are business logic issues; does the application do things it is not supposed to (to its own detriment)? Can you get it to perform actions it should not? Are you able to see information that you are not supposed to? You can also use it to log in to all the different types of users and verify that none of them are seeing anything outside of the role they have in the system (for instance, can a regular user see the admin page?).

This is also a chance for you to examine the URL parameters and any other places for user input (such as input fields).

TIP   You should put a couple (two or three) different popular and modern browsers into your toolbox, because you never know when you will find something that only shows up in one specific browser. Different browsers also have different implementations of security features, configurations, and their own vulnerabilities. One browser is not enough.

Developer Tools

Always turn on "Developer Tools" in your browser when testing. If there is a built-in tool or feature that is made for developers in your browser, take advantage. You want to see everything that the developers can see; there are often security treasures to be found.

For example, you can right-click any field on the web page and choose Inspect to see everything about that field. View the Store and Network tabs to see if anything is being stored locally that you should know about and what the network settings are. The Debugger tab is also full of helpful information that should not be overlooked.

TIP   When using developer tools, always look to see if there are "hidden fields," and if they contain anything sensitive. If so, fix or report it; nothing that is valuable or sensitive should ever be put in a hidden field.

Web Proxies

We've already covered the idea of web proxies in this book. They sit between your browser and your web app, seeing communications between the browser (front end) and your server (backend of your app). What we didn't cover, however, is that web proxies make for amazing manual security testing tools.

A web proxy intercepts the HTTP requests and responses between the front end of a web application (the part running in your browser), and the backend (the part on the web server). A web proxy is software that you run on your computer that you are accessing the web application from, and you can turn the proxy function on and off.

Most web proxy software allows you to "catch" (intercept) the HTTP request before it leaves your computer and enters the network. This allows you to change the values manually. Web proxies also usually allow you to repeat requests, change them, use word lists to automate multiple requests, and often help you automate analysis of the responses.

When using a web proxy, you can test for all sorts of well-known vulnerabilities, such as injection or XSS, by putting the attacks directly into web proxy, forwarding the request, and then watching the application's behavior to see if your attack was successful or not. You will want to examine every possible input to the application while working with your web proxy.

> **WARNING**   When attacking a web application for testing, ideally you would test that it is vulnerable, without causing damage. For example, when testing for XSS you could have a message box pop up or steal the cookie or user session. When testing for blind SQL injection you could send timer "sleep" commands to the database and then time the responses to see if it is following your commands. Both of these examples exploit a vulnerability but do not cause damage or expose potentially sensitive client data. Some clients will want more than this; for instance, data from the database to prove you can read it. Check with them to see what they are comfortable with before you dig too deep.

A web proxy will also show you all of the APIs that the web application calls; you will want to examine these to ensure they are secure, as your application depends on them. Using a web proxy, you will be able to interact directly with the APIs, without the web app front end. When you first change the values in your requests, you may want to try to enumerate a web page or API (find all pages and functions of it). Perhaps there's an API called "Employees" and it has a function you can call named "Title." Perhaps you would try to call "Address" to see if it existed? Again, you will want to examine and test every possible input for each API.

An expert attacker using a web proxy and a browser can be very dangerous for your application, and this means that you can use these same tools to perform in-depth testing of your own or others' applications. This is an advanced skill, but just like anything, you can learn it if you are patient.

Fuzzing

Fuzzing or fuzz testing is an automated software testing technique that involves providing invalid, unexpected, or random data as inputs to a computer program. The program is then monitored for exceptions such as crashes, failing built-in code assertions, or potential memory leaks.

—*Wikipedia*[62]

In more casual language, fuzzing is throwing stuff at an application until something sticks.

Imagine there is an input field in your application, and you put an "a" in it, then press the Submit button. The application acts a certain way; the expected way. Then you submit "aa", and again, the results are good. Then you submit 100 "a" characters, then 200, then 1000, then 10,000, and so on. Then you submit <script> tags, single quotes, and shell code to see if your application fails or acts differently. When using a fuzzing tool, you can add more threads and put it in the background to speed up this process.

Automated tools are often really good at this; they have quite a bit of patience when compared to human beings. As soon as the tool sees something out of place, or a slightly different response, this is when a human takes over. Every anomaly needs to be thoroughly investigated to verify if it is a vulnerability. Remember, when an application falls into an unknown state, this is often where vulnerabilities live.

Fuzzing can occur on any input to your application, including URLs (APIs), input fields, files/folders, cookies, headers, discovering hidden fields, and in HTTP methods.

Dynamic Application Security Testing (DAST)

This section covers automated tools that catalog your systems (make a list of what it's looking at, sometimes called "crawling" or "spidering"), then attempt to perform automated security analysis by interacting with your running systems. You might also know this as vulnerability scanning, VA scanning, or web app scanning. There are two categories within this section: infrastructure (copies) and custom applications (unique).

Infrastructure

If you and your friend both have a copy of the Windows 10 operating system, and have both run the same updates, you are running the same *copies* of the operating system. If neither of you have applied a specific patch that resolves a certain security issue, then you both have that same security issue.

When someone says, "run a VA scan," they often mean run an automated vulnerability scan against some sort of infrastructure. The results from these tools tend to be more accurate than other tools; if you are missing an update or have a poor configuration selected, it's the same issue as it would be on any other copy of this version of this type of infrastructure. Windows 10 is Windows 10. You may have different settings enabled, but they all have the same settings, patches, and other components available. It is very different than custom software.

Reported vulnerabilities in infrastructure and frameworks are often reported and recorded in centralized repositories, along with how to find and fix them. Automated VA (vulnerability assessment) tools use the information in such repositories to know what to look for.

Custom Applications

Custom applications, though, are different; each one is *unique*. As discussed previously, this means the tools must look for patterns that may be vulnerabilities, rather than exact matches. This means lower accuracy, both in the results that are reported and the items that go unreported.

If someone asks you to scan a web application or asks you to use a DAST tool, they usually mean a pattern matching tool, looking for vulnerabilities in applications. Such tools usually perform cataloging and fuzzing, rather than pattern matching and scripted attacks.

Programming frameworks used in applications are similar to infrastructure, in that they are used widely, and vulnerabilities can be reported to centralized repositories. They are also versioned, and if you download a specific framework version that has a known vulnerability in it, automated tools will pick it up. That said, just because you are using a third-party component or framework that is known to be vulnerable, that doesn't necessarily mean your application is vulnerable. You may not call the part that has the vulnerability, and it might need to be called in order to be exploited. You may also have other code that prevents the vulnerability from being taken advantage of. You will need validate these types of results, even if they are coming from a trusted SCA tool.

TIP   Quite often web proxy, fuzzing, and automated DAST "scanning" capabilities are all combined into the same tool. For a security tester this is fantastic; you would ideally want all three capabilities when performing security testing. That said, our industry has several names for tools that have one or more of these functionalities, which can be quite confusing for newcomers. If someone asks you to use a web app scanner, DAST, or VA scanner, it is highly likely they mean a combination tool.

VA/Security Assessment/PenTest

When clients ask for a penetration test, they often *actually* want a security or vulnerability assessment (the two terms are often used interchangeably; we will say "security assessment" for the rest of the book). Let's explore this.

A *security assessment* involves a security professional trying to find every possible security vulnerability or problem, checking that every security control has been properly implemented, verifying your system is not vulnerable to your threat models, ensuring all the different roles and access settings work correctly, that your business logic cannot be manipulated, etc. The purpose is to try to find all real and potential security problems, report them, and provide information in order to fix them. The report usually also contains information about the risk that each issue presents to the business and your system.

Since the vulnerabilities reported have not been exploited, they are not fully *validated*. This means there may be false positives. The testing activity presents less immediate risk (no exploit means less potential mess), but it also means the results are less accurate. That said, the software developers can often validate the issues themselves, if need be.

> **NOTE**   When we say exploit or penetrate a system, we mean to take advantage of the system in a way that was not intended by the creators. This could be dumping the values of a table in the database, running a script that is not part of the system, escalating privilege within the system (moving from a regular user to a superuser, for example), gaining access to other adjacent systems from the one that you are testing, etc. It could also be creating a proof of concept to provide evidence that you are able to exploit a system, for instance by stealing credentials or issuing commands to the database.

A *penetration test*, on the other hand, is slightly different. A penetration tester is trying to penetrate (break into/exploit) your systems, to prove real, rather than theoretical, risks. Some penetration tests require the tester to acquire trophies (a password or screenshot, for example), or have the tester leave behind evidence of their exploits to prove they were successful, such as leaving a file or image. Quite a bit of the time allocated to such testing is spent developing the exploits, which often makes for longer engagements. Penetration testing is often called "pen testing" for short, or "ethical hacking".

A penetration test attempts to do all of the things that a security assessment involves, *with the addition of* the exploitation of vulnerabilities to prove they are valid.

Penetration testing is more well known that any other application security activity, and this is both because of the media's attention surrounding "hacking" and because, quite frankly, exploiting a system can be really exciting. When you have worked for hours toward a goal and then the data spills out of the system, it can make you feel powerful, smart, and successful. What's a better feeling than that at work? It certainly beats filling in change request forms.

Penetration tests are sometimes used to "shock and awe" management or other teams who are not on board with what the security team is trying to achieve. Nothing gets someone's buy-in faster than showing them you've broken into one of their systems.

That said, it's not always a good way to make friends and allies. It's generally best, if you work full time somewhere, to show the other team the vulnerability you have found and offer to help them fix it first, rather than show off to management how insecure their system is after you broke it. You get more flies with honey than with vinegar, and if you are an employee, rather than a consultant, this is critical for your career and relationships within your organization.

Now that we've seen the differences, let's look at the similarities of security assessments and penetration testing. Both require a trained security tester, multiple types of tools, manual and automated testing, and quite a bit of time. They both aim to find vulnerabilities within systems and report them to the client. They both pose potential risk of damage to the system being tested (with penetration testing posing more risk), and they both provide quite a bit of valuable information to the organization.

Going back to how we started this section, how does a client choose between the two types of activities? This is where you need to advise them as the trusted expert. Ask them questions about what they are trying to achieve and about their risk tolerance, and then make suggestions. Always explain in advance what you are going to do (an assessment versus penetration), and then also put it in writing. As always, ensure they back up all of their systems before you test, no matter which option they choose.

HIRING A HACKER

Years ago, Alice worked somewhere that had a serious security incident that resulted in a data breach. As an executive, she didn't understand the technical details, but she certainly understood the business consequences; their stock price plummeted and it was all they could talk about at every board meeting. Alice was tasked with "hiring a hacker," to find out where they had other potential leaks and to create a plan so this could never happen again. Alice had no idea where to start. She called some friends and one of them recommended a security firm that employed *ethical hackers*, a term she had never heard of before.

When Alice met with the consultants, they asked her what happened and what she wanted to achieve. She told them about the incident. During the discussion Alice said she needed to know any other places that an attacker could get into their five mission-critical systems, and the consultants suggested they add a quick scan of their other six public-facing web apps, just in case. They suggested that they do security assessments of the five critical applications, rather than penetration tests, because she already had buy-in that security needed to be taken seriously and they wanted to dedicate as much time as possible to finding vulnerabilities. Alice agreed on the spot; she was so relieved they had explained it all and offered options. Now she could get back to the board, explain the plan, and feel confident they were doing the best they could in the given situation.

Security Hygiene

Verifying that your applications are following your policies and standards for cryptography and other security configurations is a high-value and easily automatable security test.

The first thing we will look at in this section is cryptography. Several free and paid tools on the market will analyze your cryptography settings for the platforms your applications sit upon and the way your data is sent in transit over the internet. This includes which protocols and algorithms you are using, how long your keys are, how strong the ciphers are, and more. If you are using the public cloud, it is unlikely you will find anything you deem a serious problem, but you will find policies where you could be stricter (and therefore more secure). If you are scanning systems within a legacy data center, you are likely to be extremely surprised by some of the findings.

The second type of analysis in this section is verifying the security header and cookie settings. As discussed previously, these configurations are like seatbelts for your software; in an emergency they can save you by offering another layer of defense (but most of the time they aren't actually called upon or used). You should always add all applicable security headers and verify you have done it correctly in this step.

Sometimes these two types of tests are combined and/or covered by other tools. When selecting a toolset to test your software, one or more of your tools must verify your cryptography, security header, and cookie settings.

There are a few ways to run these tests:

- Visit one of the free websites that test for this and enter your URLs into them manually, save the reports, then make a project of following up on the results. This would be an excellent summer project for a student, recent grad, or junior employee, and it would get you great results. Some free and high-quality websites to visit would include `securityheaders.com`, hardenize.io, and SSL labs.

- Add this type of test to your CI/CD pipelines. Several products that are free or paid are available to accomplish this. The tests are fast, and the results are accurate.

- Use a SAST tool against your code base to verify cookie and security header settings.

- Use a VA scanning tool to test your Transport Layer Security (TLS) settings (encryption of information while in transit) on your infrastructure.

- Perform manual code review to verify cookie and security headers.

- Use a web proxy or DAST tool to test for cookie and security headers; most offer these features.

Security headers, secure cookie configurations, and ensuring your encryption is following best practices are easy AppSec wins.

DANGEROUS TESTING

Denial-of-service (DOS) testing is rarely performed in the wild. Generally, you purchase protection for DOS or you don't. It can be quite dangerous to perform such a test, and generally the answer will be that, eventually, you lose. If an advanced attacker (such as a nation-state) wants to perform a distributed DOS attack (DDOS) against you, no matter who is protecting you, you are likely to fall. That said, few DOS attacks are launched by such powerful groups as a nation-state, and thus these protection services are very helpful. The key here is ensuring that non-advanced attackers cannot topple you, and that you have a plan if an advanced attack is ever executed against your organization.

Stress and Performance Testing

Stress testing is finding out how much stress (number of users, traffic, etc.) an application can handle, and still work properly. It is to determine if the upper limits of the system meet the *requirements* of the system (as per your design and business needs). You want to ensure your system can handle your expected maximum load, and then some.

Performance testing is measuring responsiveness, reliability, and quality under a specific workload. For instance, if you know that 20,000 employees are all going to be on a webinar at the same time, you would want to test it with slightly above that amount to verify it performs at acceptable levels under those conditions.

Some companies offer denial-of-service testing, which is a mix of both performance and stress testing, and they will ensure they do topple your system and show you the results of such an attack.

It is quite possible to perform your own stress and performance testing in-house, with the right tools. You must be very, very careful though, as this could potentially take down other systems. You should use a pre-prod environment, not production.

If you think back to our mandate to protect the confidentiality, integrity, and availability (CIA) of the systems and data of our organizations, it is clear these tests verify the *availability* of our systems.

It is vital that stress and/or performance testing is performed on any system that will be publicly available. This includes APIs.

Integration Testing

Integration testing means putting two or more of the different pieces of your application together, and ensuring they work. It also means checking your new code into the rest of the code, to make sure it all still works. It also means connecting your entire system to another entire system, and ensuring they work together. All of these situations need to be tested for. When we connect two changed parts together, there is opportunity for bugs, including security bugs.

Integration points between components and systems often have security functionality, which you can review via the code, or test using any of the testing types previously explained in this chapter. The point of integration testing is ensuring that the two or more parts, when acting together, do not create (security) bugs.

TRUNK-BASED DEVELOPMENT

Bob remembers a junior software developer that used to work for him. The developer was really quiet during a project for around six weeks, and Bob started to suspect something was up. When he asked the developer, it turns out he made a branch of the project code for himself and had been working on his own changes for those six weeks. Bob asked him to integrate his code and it was a disaster; there were so many bugs that it took an entire week to merge it into the main branch. From then on Bob created a rule that they would do "trunk-based development," checking in their code regularly to ensure it integrated with the rest of the application.

Integration testing can be performed manually, or it can be automated.

Manual integration testing is more likely to be found in Waterfall and Agile development shops. In Waterfall, the integration would happen late in the project life cycle, during the testing phase. In Agile, it could be done with every new feature or sprint, but that is not always the case. Every shop that performs manual integration testing does it differently; there is no set standard.

In DevOps environments a Continuous Integration/Continuous Delivery/Deployment (CI/CD) pipeline is used to deploy software. CI/CD pipelines are software that integrates, tests, and deploys software for you. Generally, in DevOps environments developers and operation folks will create their own integration tests to add to the pipeline, to ensure their new code is working well with all the other code.

We will discuss CI/CD further in the "Deployment" section in this chapter.

Interactive Application Security Testing

Interactive Application Security Testing, called IAST for short, is a new type of automated tool created by multiple application security companies. IAST works as an agent deployed within your application that monitors your application and reports vulnerabilities that it finds, *as it is used*. IAST can gather information during manual tests, automated tests, and regular use, finding vulnerabilities and reporting them in real time (as they happen).[63]

IAST only tests the parts of the code base that are actually used, meaning that you must perform other testing and use the application for it to give you full value. Running IAST during a QA testing round and during a security assessment would be ideal.

IAST runs all the time, which means it can continue to find bugs as it is used or updated. It also combines looking at code (static) and the running app (dynamic). IAST is generally used to refer to the tooling, rather than an activity that a person can perform.

As with SAST, IAST tools have a strong dependency on the target technology in which it is used, because it is agent-based. Apply the same rules as you would for SAST, selecting an IAST tool that supports the technology stack (programming language, framework, and protocols) that you are using. Your application's stack must be supported in order to integrate IAST into the runtime of your application, *and* in order to find the maximum number of bugs.

Regression Testing

There's a joke in programming that goes something like this:

Question: You have an application with 10 bugs, and you submit 10 bug fixes. How many bugs do you have now?

Answer: 1 or more

The reason for this is that every time we make a change (including bug fixes) there is a potential to create a new problem. As discussed earlier in this chapter, regression testing is rerunning your tests to ensure your software still passes after a change is made.

If major changes are made to your application, you need to perform regression testing for functionality but also for security. Having someone perform a security assessment, fixing the issues, and then never testing the application again, while you continue to make changes, is a recipe for an insecure application. Our job is not done if the application continues to change, and this is why we perform regression testing.

Whenever possible, automate any tests that must be repeated. Usually unit tests are used for this purpose.

Testing Your Infrastructure

Your applications live on infrastructure; physical servers, virtual machines (VMs), containers, and even serverless applications briefly run in a container before they self-destruct. Although it is generally not the responsibility of an application security professional or software developer to patch their systems, if your application is compromised due to insecure infrastructure, you still have a problem. This book will not advise that you run your own infrastructure or conduct a network security assessment, but performing basic checks can be quite helpful.

All three types of infrastructure, physical servers, VMs, and containers, run operating systems, and those operating systems can be scanned for missing patches, poor configuration, and other anomalies that may require your (or the operation team's) attention.

If you have an automated release pipeline that releases infrastructure, add appropriate scanning software. Work with your operations people to ensure they receive the results in a timely manner and are able to action them.

For example, if you use containers to host your application, you can leverage the Center for Internet Security (CIS) benchmark guide to harden your containers. You can also use several different types of tools to scan the container to ensure its configurations are compliant with the applicable CIS benchmark (github.com/dev-sec/cis-docker-benchmark).

If you release software manually, ask your operations and security teams what they need from you to ensure the platform is secure. They might say nothing, but they may have some great ideas for you. If there is anything you can do to enable better security on the infrastructure side, it is in your best interest to do so.

Testing Your Database

Databases are infrastructure *and* they manage your data. This means they should be hardened like any other server, but we also need to secure the data itself.

You will need to scan the infrastructure with a VA scanner regularly.

You also want to verify the following:

- That each account can only access the areas and databases that it should be able to

- That you are not able to connect to any part of the server without an account

- That all ports are closed except the one(s) required for operation

- That the server is networked in a zero-trust model (everything closed/blocked except for the application(s) that it serves)

- That no other software is on the server except the database server operating system

- That all data is classified and labeled, down to the field level (is this secret, top secret, or unclassified?)

- That production data is not being used in any other environments than production; customer data should never be used for testing or development

- That access is being monitored and audited for sensitive data exposure and inappropriate access (for instance, employees should not be searching databases for information on people from their personal life)

- That unique service accounts are being used for each application, and that none of them are granted DBO (database owner) or any other excessive permissions

- That, when possible, you use a subservice account by type of operation: one account dedicated to READ operations and another for CREATE/UPDATE/DELETE operations in order to prevent data from being altered if the READ user is compromised

- That regular backups are taken, and rollbacks are practiced

- That the data is encrypted in transit (on the way to and from the DB) and at rest (the entire DB is encrypted, as a whole)

- That sensitive data fields are encrypted also within the database (a second layer of encryption)

- That every possible security control and feature is enabled as per the hardening guide, unless there is a documented business reason not to

- That error messages are not overly verbose

- That the DNS resolution settings are set to internal-only

- Anything else you can think of. This list is not exhaustive.

You can also use guides from CIS to identify which hardening measures you can apply on your database in addition of the security best practices provided by the database vendor.

Testing Your APIs and Web Services

APIs are used by web applications to talk to web services, neither of which have a graphical user interface (GUI). They still require all the same testing that a normal web application requires, except for the parts that are related to the GUI. That said, APIs and Web Services are tricky, for a few reasons.

First off, APIs are usually hiding. They don't have a front end, meaning you only see the APIs when there is a call to them from the application (you must be using a web proxy to see the call). This means you must manually attempt to enumerate them (find all of the APIs), then try to figure out all of the different functions, and *then* you can test them. That's a lot of work. Ideally, the person who asked you to perform the test will also provide you with as many details as possible (such as an API definition file). However, you still want to enumerate for yourself, as often there are more APIs than people realize.

Secondly, as of the writing of this book, there are few automated API-focused security testing tools on the market, and I have yet to find one that works as well as the current web app scanners (DAST) available on the market. With very, very little training someone can point a DAST tool at a web app and find vulnerabilities, but for APIs you usually need to do manual testing with a web proxy and/or a tool that can make API calls for you. There are newer tools that will search for your API definition files in order to make testing easier, but no completely automated solution appears to exist at this time to find vulnerabilities in APIs. This means you need someone with training to perform this task, making this task more expensive.

To test APIs, craft a request to the API to call a function. If you saw the application call an API, just copy the API call. If it's an API that you stumbled upon while performing enumeration, it might take a while to get the first request formatted properly. If you can find the definition file, it will help you form your requests. Once you have a proper request, start sending bad requests, changed requests, requests with attacks, etc. Go through each API and every function within the API. Try calling every function using different HTTP methods (GET, POST, PUT, DELETE, etc.), to see if they work. Try to test limits (how large or small a value can be, the type, the number of calls you can make, etc.). Try adding bad input and attacks, such as single quotes, `<script>` tags, and more. Try all the same things you would on a web app input field that you could tell was calling an API in the backend. This is your chance to speak directly to the API, without interference from the web app.

Just like any manual testing, there is more than discussed here, and it is a skill you will develop over time. The more valuable lesson here is that you need to test APIs just as thoroughly as you would any web application, because they are just as valuable a target.

Testing Your Integrations

Wherever two systems connect there should be a security function or security control, and that means you need to verify it is there and then test that it works properly. If your application calls an API and that API triggers a serverless app, which then updates a database, each one of those integrations needs to be tested.

First, verify that there is a security control between the connections (there should always be authentication *then* authorization, at the very least), then verify it's configured correctly.

Second, if possible, connect to the second system and "talk" to it. If it's an API, call the API, and follow the previous advice in this chapter. If it's a serverless app, trigger it via its logic app if it has one or call it yourself, send it different values, and experiment with it as best you can.

NOTE   Logic apps are triggers that call serverless apps. They trigger when certain events happen; for instance, if you hit a resource quota for an API, if someone tries to log in too many times in 24 hours, or logs in "too quickly" (a speed faster than a human could perform).

If you have logic apps, trigger them all yourself (if possible) to ensure they trigger, then make sure whatever is supposed to trigger them actually does, every time. Ensure they do not trigger when they are not supposed to.

In summary: test the limits of every piece of your application and the systems it depends on, as well as the security controls in between.

TIP   While testing logic apps always ask yourself if the trigger values seem appropriate. If your app is set to trigger if a user tries to log in 100 times in 5 seconds, perhaps that number is too high? Is it possible for a human to log in 10 times in 5 seconds? Probably not. This is a chance for you, as the tester, to suggest that an improvement on this security setting would be to lower this threshold to 10, rather than 100. Any advice you have that will help block bots will be of high value. They hired you for your expert advice, so give it to them.

Testing Your Network

As a software developer or application security professional it is well outside your job description to test your organization's network. That said, you can, and should, ensure that your system is compliant with the network security policies of your organization.

If your organization uses zoning (firewalls in between different areas of the network, assuming trust within each zone), you need to make sure that your application architecture will work properly if your app is in one zone, your API in another, and your database in a third zone. Talking to the operations and network teams to ensure that they are aware of your application's needs will mean a less painful deployment down the road.

If your organization has a zero-trust model for its network, you will want to ensure that all of the components for your application follow this policy and guidance.

All ports should be closed except those that your application requires. APIs, serverless, database calls, etc., should only be performed by a service account that is dedicated to your system (never a shared or employee account). Access lists should only include the correct service account(s) and admin(s), all other accounts blocked, and connection attempts logged and alerted upon.

Your systems should always be designed such that they follow the policies of your network security team. If you are unsure what they are, ask. Working with the other teams from the start will ensure you don't need to make architecture changes later in your project.

In summary, you should not perform network security testing yourself, but *you should* verify that your systems are compliant with network security policy, and that your design follows industry best practices. It is likely to be well-received if you follow industry best practices and are "stricter" than the current policy of your workplace; do not be concerned that you are "overdoing security." As long as your application works properly and you are not interfering with other systems, you will be fine.

Deployment

Deployment is in the same chapter as testing because deployment offers multiple opportunities for testing; the two phases within the SDLC are closely linked.

Deployment means "the act of releasing your system into an environment," usually the production environment. The terms "roll out," "release," "publish," "go live," and many others are often used in place of "deploy," but they all mean the same thing; putting all the things in the right place, turning them on, and revealing your application to the world.

> **BIAS ALERT**
>
> I am positively biased toward automating the deployment process. This is to avoid errors, save time, and ensure the process is *perfectly* repeatable. Although it is always a good feeling to be needed at work, it is even better to know that you have everything set up such that, with the press of a button, your systems can be redeployed in case of an emergency.

There are several different ways to deploy your application. Let's take a look.

Editing Code Live on a Server

You may not believe it, but many systems are still edited live, directly on the server. This is wildly dangerous; all manual work is prone to errors, and this means there is no backup of the current version of your code. If you make a mistake, there's no chance to test it first because it's already live. It also means that over time your application will change, and if for some reason your server dies or someone deletes the file or formats the machine, your application is gone. Imagine losing years of work in an instant.

It is industry best practice to use a code repository (sometimes called a code library, version control, source control, or "repo" for short). It is a place where you store all of your code, including every single change you make. It records when and who changed what and allows you to roll back at any time to any previous version. Some code repositories will also deploy your code for you, as a bonus feature, as well as record bugs and so much more. Code repositories are a software developer's best friend, and as an application security engineer you want to get to know them, too.

> **WARNING** Never store secrets in your code repository. Secrets are passwords, connection strings, hashes, and anything else that your application needs to function, but that need to remain restricted. If a secret is accidentally pushed to your repo, you must rotate it immediately and perform a postmortem to prevent it from happening again.

If you find out that anyone in your organization is editing code live on servers as a habit, this is a security incident. The fact that there is no backup of the code, the fact that they have write access to production servers, the fact that no security alert was triggered when they performed the action, and the fact that they are not following your organization's policy, are each cause enough for a security incident.

> **WARNING** You may think it is far-fetched that a production server would somehow be damaged, formatted, flooded, or otherwise destroyed, but this has happened to me on multiple occasions. As we move toward the public cloud, this problem is becoming rarer, but only a small percentage of all applications in the world are hosted in a public cloud; many companies host their own data centers (for a multitude of reasons). No matter where your application lives, you must *always* have the most recent copy in source control.

Publishing from an IDE

Many types of IDEs allow software developers to publish to various environments directly from the place they write the code. This process is sometimes affectionately referred to as "Right Click ⇨ Publish," as those are usually the commands used to perform this action. If a developer has already run their unit tests, they are publishing to a dev or test environment, and the application is just one part of a bigger system, this can work quite well. This is often the process within Waterfall or Agile shops when performing a bug fix or when a dev is pushing to the development environment so they can test, before following the rest of the process to move it to QA (Quality Assurance), UAT (User Acceptance Testing environment), Pre-prod (a copy of prod, often used for stress and/or performance testing), then finally prod. Other environments might be included in this process as well.

If at all possible, you will want to ensure that your devs are running their unit tests before they push any code, anywhere. There's no point in them pushing it to dev, running a bunch of tests, and then realizing it failed half the unit tests and they are back to the drawing board. If you work in an organization that pushes code this way, you want to work really hard to gain permission and buy in to add unit tests that focus on your security goals.

You should also add security testing activities to the other environments and testing phases, as much as you have time for and that the other teams will tolerate.

And of course, automate your tests whenever possible.

"Homemade" Deployment Systems

With developers being developers, many shops create their own custom deployment systems. The systems replicate the changes from environment to environment, ensure that various approvals are obtained, and everything is automatically documented. If you can convince them to add security testing to any of these steps, this would be a big win for your team. For instance, have the first environment trigger a software composition analysis (SCA) scan and kick it back to the developer if it has any "high" or "medium" findings. As long as you can get buy in, you can get your job done within this type of system.

That said, you should perform security testing against their custom deployment system. If someone was able to manipulate the system, they could potentially publish whatever they wanted or pollute your code base. This custom deployment system should be considered a mission-critical application for your organization.

You should also ensure they are following all the development best practices they usually would; sometimes developers forget that the tools they make to do their jobs have significant business value. All code should be saved into the code repository, systems backed up, documented, tested, follow the secure SDLC, etc., just like any other high-value application within your organization.

Run Books

Run books are instructions (with screenshots and scripts) written by the development team to hand to the operations team, so the ops team can deploy their applications for them. It sounds great, but in practice this process can be rather messy. Quite often the application works on the developer's machine, but not once it is deployed, and finger-pointing ensues. Having to manually follow written instructions for an extremely complex deployment is error-prone, slow, and tedious.

That said, if your developers and operations team are following this process, so must you. Ensure that instructions for all security features and their configurations are in the run book, with every possible detail included.

Contiguous Integration/Continuous Delivery/Continuous Deployment

Continuous integration/continuous delivery, also known as CI/CD, actually represents three different concepts within one system, as shown in Figure 6-1.

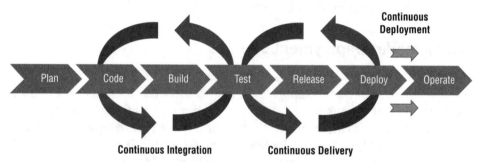

Figure 6-1: Continuous Integration/Continuous Delivery (CI/CD)

Contiguous integration is the practice of merging all developer changes back into the main branch of the code, regularly, with testing to ensure it all still works—ideally, multiple times per day. This can be done manually, but usually a tool is used for this.

Continuous delivery is ensuring that you are able to release changes very quickly. The system should always be ready to deploy, using automation (which includes everything from continuous integration, plus more testing). It requires using an automated tool, generally referred to as a pipeline, to perform the act of continuous integration. Automating this process makes it faster, eliminates human error, and allows for adding automated tests, which improves quality. This software is often called a CI/CD pipeline or DevOps pipeline, and each new release is called a build.

Continuous deployment is the practice of allowing your CI/CD pipeline to release new changes to your production environment without a manual approval step. The results of the automated tests decide if the changes are released, and if a test fails, it stops the deployment and is often referred to as "breaking the build." Continuous deployment is not mandatory for using CI/CD and is often considered the sign of an advanced DevOps organization.

CI/CD pipelines are the most well-known feature of DevOps environments, with the goal of their usage being the same as ours; reduce human-made (security) errors, faster (security) feedback, ability to implement (security) bug fixes faster, automation of (security) testing, and reducing risk by regularly releasing many small changes instead of large changes less often.

If you work in a developer organization that uses CI/CD, you want to add security activities to that CI/CD. That said, you need to be careful to respect developer and operations' wishes, and only use the allotted time and space they give you. If they tell you that you can do 8 minutes' worth of testing per build, then you should ensure your testing only takes 8 minutes.

Here are some ideas for starting out with a CI/CD pipeline:

- Scan newly checked-in code to see if it contains something that looks like a secret. This test is really fast, because it only checks the delta (the changed or new code), and if you catch a real secret, you will have provided huge value to your organization by preventing a security disaster. Ideally, block check-in if a secret is found. If this is not possible, trigger a security incident and rotate that secret immediately.

- Conduct an SCA scan to verify that new components that are known to be vulnerable have not been added to your application. This is also a very fast check; it just looks at the lists of packages for your application and then cross-references them against a known "bad" list. This type of test also has extremely high accuracy, which makes it ideal for a pipeline test.

This is not a book about DevOps, but that said, if your organization is using DevOps, then you must get on board if you want to achieve your mandate. If they are sprinting, you must do your work in sprints. If they are using a pipeline, you want to get at least one security test into every pipeline. If you don't work within the way Dev and Ops are working, *you will be left behind*.

Exercises

1. If you could only choose one type of testing to perform on your application, which type would it be and why?

2. Which type of testing do you think would be the fastest? Why?

3. Which type of testing do you think would be the slowest? Why?

4. What types of vulnerabilities would you want to look for in regression testing? Name at least two, and why you chose each one.

5. Does your workplace have a zero-trust network design? If you don't know the answer, your homework is to find out.

6. Does your workplace allow use of a CI/CD pipeline? If you don't know the answer, your homework is to find out.

7. In a CI/CD environment, should you implement a Static Application Security Testing (SAST) tool and run a complete scan of all of the code, every time there is a new build? Why? Why not?

8. Why is it critical to put all new changes into a code repository?

9. Why do we test integration points between different systems? Is it more or less valuable than testing the rest of each system?

10. Why do we test databases, even though they aren't publicly accessible?

11. Why do we test APIs, even though they aren't publicly accessible? (This might be a trick question.)

12. When does it make sense to do a penetration test versus a security assessment of a system? Explain your answer.

CHAPTER 7

An AppSec Program

This chapter will discuss application security programs, which are the formalization of AppSec activities as part of your System Development Life Cycle (SDLC). An AppSec program is not a piece of software; it's a set of related activities with a particular long-term aim.

In this case our aim is to ensure that the software we are creating and maintaining is secure. We aim for this to reduce the risk for our organization, as well as those we serve (customers, employees, citizens, etc.). We strive to protect and preserve the confidentiality, integrity, and availability of the systems and data in our care.

We create formal application security programs to improve our security posture, to ensure *all* of our applications are defended (not just some), and to be able to prove to others we have done our best to protect our organization. Without a formal program we can't be sure we are reliably producing software that is safe to put on the internet, and we would have little to defend ourselves if a large breach happens at our workplace.

A program is the activities we do: performing threat modeling on every new design, reviewing all pull requests for security issues, adding security checks to our pipeline, etc. The idea of a program is that the activities are formalized; they are officially a part of the way your organization builds software. No one can "skip" a security step in the SDLC, because the activities are mandated.

APPLICATION SECURITY PROGRAM REQUIREMENTS

➤ Ideally run by a team dedicated only to this, but at least run by one dedicated person.

➤ Security activities are added to the SDLC.

➤ The AppSec team supports developers with resources, tools, education, policy, guidance, and anything else they need.

➤ The AppSec team verifies that the secure SDLC is being followed, and that the software produced is secure (testing and tooling).

Application Security Program Goals

There is currently no industry-accepted standard for what makes up an AppSec program; almost everyone is just winging it. There are many activities that are common, but that doesn't mean they are the best ones for your organization or program. Some organizations use OWASP SAMM or BSIMM to help them figure out the best activities for their organization, while others decide for themselves. In the wild, application security programs vary greatly; some have great depth with many activities, others are cursory checks implemented solely to meet regulations or laws, and there are gems with vibrant security cultures where everyone makes it a priority.

TIP   The OWASP Self Assessment Maturity Model (SAMM) project is extremely helpful when starting an AppSec Program from scratch. Although it is not technically "industry accepted" or a recognized standard, it is maintained by a group of experts with the goal of providing a framework to create your own Secure SDLC. (Source: `owaspsamm.org/model`.)

The Building Security in Maturity Model (BSIMM) tries to help organizations find the activities that will give them their best return on investment by providing a study based on current industry practices. (Source: `www.bsimm.com/framework.html`.)

When building your own program, it is important to be as efficient and effective as possible, as you will never have the resources, budget, or time to do all the things you wish you could. Unless you work in an extremely high risk or otherwise special situation, business requests will always come before security, and this means limits for you and your team.

When choosing which activities to add to your application security program, you should create a list of goals of what you want to achieve and then select your activities and tools based upon your goals and what will work best within the current systems your organization has in place. Base your goals on the priorities of your organization to ensure you work the hardest to protect what is most important to the business.

With this in mind, let's examine some high-level program goals that we could set and work toward.

Creating and Maintaining an Application Inventory

If you don't know what you have, you can't protect it. This is why we make an inventory of all of our applications and other assets, including APIs and databases. Most large companies have many applications that they are unaware of, meaning they receive no security attention and are therefore quite likely to be an area of weakness.

You may be surprised to learn that creating and maintaining an inventory of your applications is one of the most difficult IT tasks to do well; developers are often releasing updates or APIs without documentation, old applications are lost track of, business units hire shadow IT who don't follow any of your security rules, Software as a Service (SaaS) products are operating on your network without your knowledge, etc. A surprisingly large number of organizations that you likely assume are very secure are currently tracking their applications manually in a Microsoft Excel spreadsheet as you read this.

The most important reason for you (as the AppSec professional) to take inventory of your software assets is to ensure that each application receives security attention. If all of your apps are supposed to have a secure code review performed before going live, then you need to be aware of *all of them* in order to properly implement that rule.

> **TIP**   Using a Configuration Management Database (CMDB) to hold your inventory is a great way for you to work well with the rest of IT. You want all teams to be able to find information about your applications, and vice versa. Using a common tool will create common ground for trust building and information sharing between teams.

Malicious actors will always go for your weakest link. Applications that have not received any security attention are highly likely to be your weakest link.

In big organizations, shadow IT refers to information technology (IT) systems deployed by departments other than the central IT department, (usually) to work around the shortcomings of the central information systems and/or IT department.

—*Wikipedia*[65]

Capability to Find Vulnerabilities in Written, Running, and Third-Party Code

All types of security verification tooling come down to DAST or SAST, if you examine them closely.

DAST means *dynamic* application security testing. This means interacting with the application as it is running.

SAST means *static* application security testing. This means examining the written code—the programming language as it is written or compiled.

When we (AppSec engineers and programmers) find vulnerabilities in third-party code usually we are using a Software Composition Analysis (SCA) tool, which analyzes the list of libraries, frameworks, and dependencies to see if they are on a pre-determined list of "known vulnerable" software. This would be considered *static analysis*, as SCA tools examine the libraries that are called from within our written code (the project descriptor file, specifically).

SAST tools find vulnerabilities in the custom code that you and your team wrote. SCA finds known vulnerabilities in all the code in your application that you team did not write (libraries, packages, frameworks, etc.), which is generally referred to as "third-party libraries." We must perform both in order to find vulnerabilities in all of the written code of your application.

When we discuss SCA or finding vulnerabilities in third-party code we will speak from the perspective of the consumer; a programmer or AppSec engineer. Thus, we will often lump it in with the rest of SAST, *static* application security testing.

DAST tools test all of the application, the parts your team wrote and the parts they did not, as they run together as one.

When it comes to finding bugs, we also want to perform manual analysis. Automated tools can never find everything, and a skilled tester or code reviewer can often put any tool to shame. Business logic bugs are the ones missed most often by automated tools, yet they can cause equal harm. This means we need to add time to project schedules and hire qualified security professionals in order to ensure we find the maximum number of vulnerabilities.

Back to the goal: the capability to find vulnerabilities in written, running, and third-party code. Being capable of finding flaws in these three different ways, rather than only one way, means that you will have a more complete picture of the security posture of your applications. Often companies will rely on only one of these three pillars, which can be as a result of budget limits, inadequate staffing, or lack of buy-in from management. If this is you, select the method that provides you the best return on investment and fits into your current processes.

Knowledge and Resources to Fix the Vulnerabilities

If you ever have the chance to sit down with an experienced penetration tester, they will eventually confide in you that the most frustrating part of their job is coming back to the same place a year later and finding the exact same vulnerabilities in the same systems. Nothing is fixed. Year after year. They hire a pentester to meet a regulation requirement (usually PCI), but they just want to check a box; they don't care about making the application more secure.

There is little purpose in working very hard to find vulnerabilities but not fix them. This goal is about ensuring your organization has people who have enough time, skill, and knowledge to remediate (fix) the issues that you are finding. Having someone with lots of time but no programming experience will require a lot of guidance and resources. Highly skilled and trained people who are also overworked and already near burnout will also not have the time to remediate the vulnerabilities.

NOTE Oftentimes companies have the best of intentions, but do not realize the workload that will be created by adding more security verifications to their SDLC. It is vital that we create time in our project schedules to fix issues *and* to ensure that our assigned resources have the training or knowledge required for the task at hand.

Education and Reference Materials

Software developers need support when it comes to security; the training they receive in programming bootcamps, college, and university is inadequate. If you have standards, policies, or guidelines for your organization, you will need to teach them to your developers if you want them to be able to create code that meets your requirements.

Education can be a workshop, lunch and learns, computer-based training, giving a 5-minute speech during an all-staff meeting, bringing in an instructor, etc. The point is that if you expect your developers to know a specific security control, defense, or coding method, you must teach it to them. If you don't, some of them will know it and some of them won't, and you will certainly have more security vulnerabilities in your products.

Reference materials can mean purchasing a Java security book if your developers use a lot of Java. It can mean content subscriptions, videos, blogs, secure code samples, or anything else they request to help them know how to do their jobs more securely.

TIP I created the We Hack Purple Academy and Community (`WeHackPurple.com`), an organization dedicated to teaching application security, secure coding, cloud security, and more. If you like this book, you might want to check it out!

Providing Developers with Security Tools

If you recall from the first chapter, the earlier in the SDLC that we find a security bug or flaw, the cheaper, easier, and faster it is to fix it. Starting security earlier in the SDLC is known as "shifting left" or "pushing left." When we give developers security tools, this means they will find and fix some security problems during the coding phase, which is *before* the testing phase (when we are most likely to be invited to perform security activities). This is a big win!

Another reason we would want to give software developers security tools is numbers; there are 100 or more software developers (on average) for every security professional. This means they have more time, but usually less (security-related) skill. Teaching all the developers on your team to use just one tool could yield amazing results, and not cause a large strain on the dev teams.

If we foster the developers' interest in security, we may be able to turn them into security champions who take on even more responsibilities. Giving security champions extra training so that they can perform secure code review, writing negative unit tests, performing more advanced security testing, etc., is a valuable use of your time and resources. It's win-win in anyone's book.

Software developers are builders, and most of them have great pride in their work; they *want* to create secure applications. Giving them tools, training on how to use them, and a safe place to do so, can enable them to build the high-quality software they strive to create.

> **TIP**   You can make this a fun activity for developers and create rewards and point systems for devs who find and fix more vulnerabilities. Give them recognition and/or prizes. This doesn't have to be "just another task on their plate"—it can be enjoyable, educational, *and* productive.

Having One or More Security Activities During Each Phase of Your SDLC

It is necessary to formalize (mandate/create policy to support) the security activities that you want to see become a part of your SDLC. If you want every new project to include the security requirements you created, write a policy to support this. There must also be time allocated to these activities in your project schedules as well, or they won't get done.

Following are some examples of activities you could perform during each of the phases of the SDLC (no matter which methodology you are using). Choosing any one of these per phase of the SDLC will improve the security of your final product.

- **Requirements**: Security requirements as per Chapter 2 of this book, security user stories, security evaluation and approval of proposed tech stack

- **Design**: Threat modeling, whiteboarding designs to look for security flaws in architecture, secure design evaluation as per Chapter 3 of this book

- **Coding**: Linters, writing security unit tests, SAST or SCA scanning, secure coding as per Chapter 4 of this book, using IDE plugins or web hooks to correct insecure coding, using known-secure templates and/or libraries

- **Testing**: DAST, SAST, and/or SCA scanning, security assessment or penetration test, a secure code review exercise (including a SAST tool), scanning for secrets, plus anything from Chapter 6 of this book
- **Deployment/Release/Maintenance**: DAST, RASP, or WAF, monitoring, logging, security alerts, trained and ready incident response team, and established process

This list is not exhaustive; the potential list of activities is almost endless. The key takeaway here is that you choose what your activities will be and that they happen *every time*.

> **TIP** Whenever possible, support your policy with templates, code samples, documentation, and anything else you can think of to help the other teams reach compliance.

Implementing Useful and Effective Tooling

Choosing, procuring, and implementing security tools takes time, energy, and expertise; you do not want to leave this responsibility in the developer's hands. Not every tool will create the same amount of value for your organization, and each product has unique pros and cons. This book will not suggest specific products or brands; the best way to choose is do a proof of concept (POC) with the tool and test it for yourself. If possible, include developers in the POC process to ensure they also want to work with the tool. They are, after all, the customer of our efforts.

Whenever possible, ensure the workflow for your tools is automated (often a CI/CD can help with this). Manual work means errors, unnecessary time wastage, and boredom. If this tool will be run tens, hundreds, or thousands of times, it should not be run manually.

> **TIP** Create a knowledge base to share security lessons for developers to add to and learn from. This activity is one that gains value as time goes on, and in a few years, you won't know how you ever lived without it!

An Incident Response Team That Knows When to Call You

Security incidents are the most expensive, damaging, and humiliating way to discover a vulnerability in one of your applications. A security incident means someone has attacked one of your applications. It may also mean a data breach, system failure, your systems being unavailable, your data integrity being affected, unauthorized access, or any other negative consequence as a result of the attack.

We, as IT professionals, want to prevent all types of IT security incidents, whenever possible. We also want to be ready in case we are called upon to assist in responding to an incident. Responding to a security incident is called *incident response* (IR), which involves managing the situation and communications, investigating what happened, reducing damage and cost, eradication of the problem, and recovery of your systems and data. It should also include a postmortem exercise and documentation of what happened via a security incident report.

Most large organizations have trained incident response teams, and many smaller ones do not. If you are a startup with five people, you do not need an incident response team, but if you are an enterprise organization, it's a must.

This may surprise you, but the average time to detect that a data breach has occurred is 197 days,[66] as of the writing of this book. That means you could be having one or more data breaches or incidents happening right now, and not know it. If you are not actively looking for issues, you are less likely to find them.

KNOWING IS BETTER THAN NOT KNOWING

Alice recalls the first time she hired a co-op student to the IT department. He was security obsessed. The student was the son of a friend, and hiring him had been a favor. The student ended up reporting six security incidents in the first month, which made many of the people in the IT department upset. Alice took the young man aside and told him "We never had any security incidents before YOU got here!" He responded by saying, "These have been happening for months and you didn't know. Now we can stop them from happening. We will be more secure because we know what's going on." Alice was flabbergasted. She had planned to tell him to stop whatever he was doing but realized how wrong she had been; it's much better to know than not to know.

If no one on the incident response team understands application security, or software in general, responding to and investigating such incidents will inevitably become your responsibility. Ideally, you would go introduce yourself to the IR team, tell them of your AppSec skills, and offer them assistance and training.

If you can teach the IR team to detect incidents related to your application, and when they should call you in, you will be in a much better position to help them.

In an ideal world your applications would be logging and alerting on security events (something that might be a security incident, but you're not sure), and at least one person would be checking the alerts regularly. If you have a Security Operations Center (SOC) and they are using a Security Information and Event Management (SIEM) system or other monitoring tool, you would want to have the logs from your applications fed into the system they are using, and *you want to teach them when to come to you with alerts from your apps.* If no one is reviewing the alerts, there is very little benefit to creating them in the first place. Even if you just have a serverless app that triggers an email that you receive the next morning, it is better than never receiving notice at all.

Continuously Improve Your Program Based on Metrics, Experimentation, and Feedback

This last goal might seem obvious and unnecessary to actually write out as a goal, but if we don't formalize things we often forget. There's a big deadline we need to meet, and then a new feature, and then . . .. We haven't met with the dev team for six months and they feel ignored, or we haven't looked at our metrics in a year and it turns out we're not putting our energy toward the best activities. It can slip away from us if we don't plan for it to happen.

Let's break this program goal down a bit.

Metrics

Metrics are a method of measuring something, or the results obtained from this.[67]

We need to measure the effectiveness of our activities. There is not enough time for us to do every single activity or task that we want to; we must choose the activities that make the absolute most impact in order to create a successful AppSec program.

You can take your measurements in many different ways: you can use a vulnerability management system, a database, a business intelligence SaaS, or even just MS Excel.

Here are the most important parts of gathering metrics:

- You must continue to take the measurements consistently. You can't just measure "sometimes"—your data will be incomplete.

- You must have a consistent measurement method. If you are using a DAST tool and a SAST tool, then you need to use both of them on all of your apps. You can't do DAST on half of your apps and SAST on the other half if you want to be able to compare all of the application and team results. It's okay to have partial measurements (for instance, if you measure how much coverage you have with a specific tool, i.e., 20% with SAST and 80% with DAST), but only if you analyze the data with that in mind. In this example that would mean comparing all SAST results separately from the DAST results or using your coverage statistics to help you adjust their values within your dataset.

- You must have a consistent measurement scale. You cannot compare apples and oranges. If one tool rates vulnerabilities from 1–10 and the other uses low/medium/high/critical, then you need to decide how to translate one measurement into the other form. For instance: low = 2, medium = 4, high = 8, critical = 10.

- You need to measure metrics that *matter*, not vanity metrics.

Vanity metrics are usually things that are easy to measure, but don't offer much value. An example of a *metric that matters* would be measuring your progress toward a goal. Perhaps you are using two different activities or tools to help you reach the goal; if you can measure both and see which is more effective, you may decide to drop the lower performer and double-down on the higher performer. But without metrics, you would never know.

Examples of metrics that might matter to you:

- Are you having reoccurring incidents (same cause)?
- How long does it take to fix vulnerabilities (rollback, patch, or remediate)?
- How long does it take to detect incidents?
- How many instances do you have of policy non-compliance?
- Are there errors in incident handling?
- How close are you to your security posture goal?
- Is the security team meeting their SLAs or are other teams waiting on you constantly?
- If you have performed education on specific vulnerabilities, have they reduced in number?
- Is the incident response process always being followed, every time?
- Are you seeing more vulnerabilities being reported? Is this because you have a new tool (good), or because you have new employees who are untrained (bad)?

The types of things you can choose to measure is a very long list; choose the ones that help you reach your program goals, not the ones that make you look good.

PUTTING YOUR EFFORTS IN THE RIGHT PLACE

Years ago, when Alice did content development, she worked somewhere that measured everything—every click, every social media post, every employee's performance. Alice was in charge of writing articles that helped people use their products better, and she loved it; she produced twice as much content as anyone else. She knew this because they had dashboards where she could see everyone else's performance, which was both encouraging and stressful; Alice always wants to be "the best" at whatever she does. She noticed a colleague was getting around 5,000 clicks per link he was posting on social media, but she was only averaging 300–400. Alice didn't understand what she was doing wrong; she was trying so hard. She decided to take some more measurements of her own, including how long people stayed on the page. It turns out her colleague's readers were averaging 1–2 seconds per click, meaning no one was reading any of his posts. Alice's readers were staying on average 1.5 minutes! This meant they

> were reading the entire article, almost every time! She was ecstatic. She told her boss, and they changed the way they released their content and where, so her colleague could attract people who would stay to read the whole article, and so that Alice could have more readers. Win-win, all thanks to *metrics that matter*!

Experimentation

When you first set your eyes on a goal, you may not know how to achieve it. This is where experimentation comes in. It could be creating a proof of concept for three different Runtime Application Security Protection (RASP) products to see which is best for your org; giving different types of training to small groups of developers, evaluating their learning, and then giving everyone the "best" training; or adding your own script to one pipeline and measuring the results for a few weeks, improving it over and over until it meets your expectations, then rolling it out to the rest of the pipelines in your organization. It's okay to try something out and decide it's not good; you just learned something and that has value. You also likely saved yourself a lot of time and money.

The DevOps and startup cultures are really big on experimentation, learning, and constantly striving for improvement. And they have structured ways and repeatable processes to do it. With this in mind, I highly recommend the following two books:

- *The DevOps Handbook: How to Create World-Class Agility, Reliability, & Security in Technology Organizations* by Gene Kim, Jez Humble, John Willis, and Patrick Debois, published by IT Revolution Press, LLC

  itrevolution.com/book/the-devops-handbook[68]

- *The Lean Startup: How Today's Entrepreneurs Use Continuous Innovation to Create Radically Successful Businesses* by Eric Ries, published by Crown Business

  theleanstartup.com/book[69]

Feedback from Any and All Stakeholders

All feedback is important. The software developers, product owners, project managers, other security teams, and the rest of IT are all your customers; they consume your application security program and services. Their feedback *matters*.

It is crucial that you ask for feedback, and that doesn't mean an automated survey once a year. Meet with your security champions regularly, ask during project meetings if they need anything more from you, ask people to come to you and tell you what they like and what they don't like, and always tell you if you broke something.

If you are going to release a standard or policy, hold a consultation. Ask the developers what support they need to be able to meet the new standard you are trying to set. Ask if they understand it, agree with it, or object to parts of it. Even if only very few people show up, those are generally the people who have the most to say. You can even hold more than one. The purpose is not to ensure that 100 percent of people agree to it, but to ensure the most vocal developers are on board and that you haven't made any grave errors.

When receiving feedback, try hard not to take it personally; not every person is graceful or skilled in telling someone how they feel about something. If you take the feedback poorly, people are unlikely to confide in you again, and then you are planning your program blind. Try your best to remain open.

A Special Note on DevOps and Agile

It doesn't matter which SDLC methodology our programmers are following when we set our AppSec target; DevOps people still have requirements and code from Agile teams still need testing. It's the activities and tooling that will need to change, not our end goals.

If software developers are doing their work in sprints, we must learn to do our work in sprints as well. If DevOps teams are using CI/CD pipelines to release their code, then we will figure out which tools work best in their pipelines.

It is critical that we adjust our own methods, as it is our responsibility to enable the developers to create secure software, not the other way around.

Application Security Activities

The list of application security activities is very, very long. It is, essentially, anything you do to try to ensure the software you are creating is secure. With a definition that broad, it could be easy to get lost. Look at Figure 7-1 see how security activities could be added to the SDLC. Here is a list of well-known and widespread practices:

Running vulnerability (VA) scans is likely the most-common AppSec activity; running an automated tool to perform DAST (*dynamic* app testing). It can find quite a few things, quickly, with decent accuracy; it misses a lot, though. It can be automated to run in a pipeline, run on its own on a schedule, or be run manually.

Security/vulnerability assessments are often used on high-value or otherwise significant applications, to find as many vulnerabilities as possible.

Threat modeling can range from an "evil brainstorming" session to more formal pursuits such as developing attack trees or following the STRIDE or PASTA models. Identifying all possible threats to your system, and then mitigating them, is a manual process.

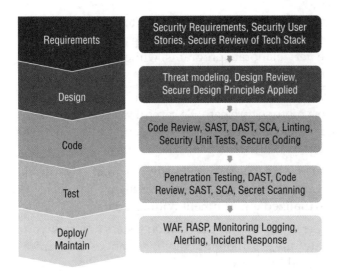

Figure 7-1: Security activities added to the SDLC

Secure code reviews are reviews of the security controls, within the code, for errors. They can be performed manually, but they can also be performed with the help of a SAST tool (*static* application security testing).

Software composition analysis (SCA) is verifying the security posture of your third-party components (code you did not write) and is simplest to perform using a tool or pre-approved list. Performing such a task manually would be too large of an undertaking, unless developers are limited to an extremely small subset of potential components.

Penetration tests (PenTests) are often performed by external resources, for intensive security testing and/or to grab management's attention. Finding and then exploiting vulnerabilities is a great way to get buy-in from teams that aren't on board the AppSec train.

Responsible/coordinated disclosure is a process for allowing security researchers and others to safely report security issues about your products to you. Currently Google and a few other large software companies are pushing for an industry standard for the information to become public knowledge within 90 days, assuming 3 months as enough time to mitigate the issue and deliver a patch. Unfortunately, the actual timing for this process varies greatly from organization to organization. This process was originally known as "responsible" disclosure and has been steadily migrating toward "coordinated" disclosure, as this industry-recognized process has matured.

Bug bounty programs are pre-planned, managed activities between security researchers and companies to enable security testing of products by either any researcher or approved/invited researchers. The idea of a bounty is that only researchers that find a unique and valid bug are rewarded, and this creates competition.

Developer education and advocacy programs are designed to teach and enable developers to create secure software through teaching and other support. Some companies have very elaborate programs, while others may settle for throwing this book at you.

Policies, guidelines, and standards are tools that you can create to mandate, guide, and lead developers to a more secure path. Be careful when writing them to ensure they are understandable, reasonable, and accurate. Passing them by your favorite developers is always a good idea.

Giving developers security tools, as discussed previously, is a great way to scale your team. Just make sure you train them and give them a safe place to use them (such as a virtualized environment with test data).

Red Teaming is allowing a team of trained penetration testers to attack your production systems (carefully), to find vulnerabilities and test how gracefully your systems respond to attack.

Reviewing all new tools, frameworks, components, platforms, and other tech that the devs want to approve and/or offer security guidance on using them. This will likely consume a lot of your time, but is a highly valuable activity.

Providing IDE tools to ensure/reinforce secure coding and package management.

Adding security tooling to developers' CI/CD pipelines.

Application Security Tools

Just like the list of AppSec activities, this list of tooling could never be complete. People build their own tools and open-source or share them. There are currently countless startups inventing cool new tech, and well-established security companies re-inventing themselves and their products. There will always be more. That said, here is a list of tools that you may want to explore.

Standards

- DAST (dynamic application security testing).
- SAST (static application security analysis).
- Software composition analysis (SCA)—verifying if your third-party dependencies are known to be vulnerable.
- Web proxies for manual testing of applications and APIs.
- Fuzzers for finding holes in your input validation.
- Web application firewalls (WAFs) are a shield of regular expressions used to verify user input. They block HTTP(S) traffic to and from your web application based on approve/block lists and regular expressions. Some WAFs also use artificial intelligence/ machine learning (AI/ML).

Newer Tooling

- RASP (runtime application security protection; also known as a reverse proxy) is a runtime stub (binary file) that is placed inside your application, which acts as a shield against application attacks. It usually uses artificial intelligence and machine learning to detect threats, rather than only regular expressions and approve/block lists.

- Vulnerability management tools for gathering metrics and measuring your progress.

- IDE tools and hooks for helping developers correct insecure coding decisions.

- Interactive application security testing (IAST) is a tool that is a binary placed inside your application that performs a mix of SAST and DAST, live, as users interact with your app.

- Service mesh is an infrastructure layer that encrypts and manages the communications of your APIs.

- Amalgamation tools for pipelines that allow you to add only one security tool to your pipeline, plug several security tools into the amalgamation tool, then receive the results of all your tools in one dashboard. It runs multiple tools for you, concurrently.

- API gateways handle authentication and authorization for APIs, protecting them from unauthorized calls and other abuse.

- Least privilege automation tools verify which permissions are actually required, then remove the rest, minimizing your attack surface. This is also referred to as "policy automation."

- Standard AppSec tools that are optimized for pipelines. Be careful with these—many vendors market that they are ready for pipelines, but they are the same old tool. Always perform a proof of concept to verify that it performs how you need it to.

- Package management proxies, with only secure packages available for developers to download.

- Application and asset inventory tools, to help you create an inventory of public-facing web assets.

- Creating your own custom tools, for when you need something very specific, and it doesn't already exist.

Your Application Security Program

If you are ever in the situation where you are able to make decisions about direction for an application security program, set goals. Then choose the activities and tools that will help you reach those goals. Constantly measure your progress toward your goals and strive for constant improvement. It will lead not only to more secure software, but a highly effective program.

Exercises

1. Give one reason why maintaining an up-to-date application inventory is valuable for any organization.

2. Give one example of an alert that your application could give. What type of behavior would cause such an alert, and why is it a problem?

3. Is testing the most important part of an AppSec program? If so, why? If not, why not?

4. Is it more valuable to buy a RASP or WAF tool (a shield for your application) or to spend that money on ensuring your code is secure? Explain your choice.

5. Describe a type of security incident that would require the assistance of developer. What would be needed of the developer?

6. If you could give software developers one tool to help them, what would it be? Explain your choice.

7. If you could give developers one learning resource, what would it be? Explain your choice.

8. What is the difference between SAST and SCA?

9. What is the difference between SAST and DAST?

10. Set a potential goal for your application security program at your office, a school project, or in a made-up place that you hope to work at some day. What goal did you set? Why did you choose this? How will you measure your progress?

11. Do you have current roadblocks stopping you from starting your first AppSec program where you work? If so, what are they? And better yet, how can you overcome them?

Securing Modern Applications and Systems

As developers and operations folks continue to bring new technologies into your IT shop, you will have to modernize your strategies and tactics in order to keep pace. This chapter provides high-level explanations of security tactics for the following:

- APIs and microservices
- Online storage
- Containers and orchestration
- Cloud workflows
- Serverless
- Infrastructure as Code (IaC)
- Security as Code (SaC)
- Platform as a Service (PaaS)
- Infrastructure as a Service (IaaS)
- CI/CD
- DevSecOps
- Cloud
- Cloud workflows

This chapter is a look at modern and new application security tools, as well as modern and new tactics for AppSec.

For some reason, whenever a new type of technology comes out, we tend to throw security out the window. We rush to release something new and shiny, and somehow, we forget all of the lessons we already know. It is essential that when we introduce new and exciting technologies into our production environments that they have been properly secured. In a sandbox (an environment separated from production and the internet), you can be free to run new tools and experiments, without the need to secure anything. However, when technologies are pushed into prod, they must be first evaluated for security weaknesses and properly hardened. *Every time.*

> **TIP**   If you are an application security specialist, always try to be a part of the evaluation process for new technologies. It's time consuming, but you may be able to help steer your peers in more secure directions and save yourself some serious headaches in the future.

APIs and Microservices

API stands for *application programming interface*; however, that description isn't entirely helpful or accurate. It sounds like the software (interface) you use to write the code (program) of an application, but that is an Integrated Development Environment (IDE), not an API.

APIs are the code between two pieces of software that allows them to talk; it also defines the protocol (the *way* they talk). There is never a front end to an API, as they are just the code in the middle of two applications. APIs let applications send and receive requests and data to and from each other.

Web APIs often return data and can function just like web applications with no front end. They serve data and have no GUI. They are made up of code running on a server, with nothing visible to the end user in the browser.

Mobile applications and web applications call APIs often to ask for data or to perform/initiate actions for them. In the Windows operating system there are Windows APIs communicating and performing services in the background. There are several types of APIs, but the ones we are talking about in this section are *web APIs*.

When people say "microservices" they often mean "microservice architecture," an application built of many small services, called from the same front end. Figure 8-1 shows a simplified microservice architecture. Having a suite of several services, all running independently, means that if one goes down, the rest of your app still (mostly) functions. Services, like APIs, have no front end.

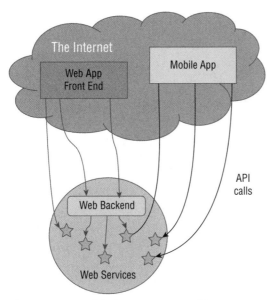

Figure 8-1: Simplified microservice architecture

APIs and microservice architecture tend to go hand-in-hand, so we will discuss securing them together. Both are generally called from web applications, mobile apps, or from other APIs or serverless applications. Both also require protecting.

APIs should use an API gateway in order to protect them against DOS-style abuse (resources being over-requested, over-consumed, or inappropriately called to force excessive errors) and in order to perform the security functions of authorization, authentication, and even input validation. API gateways also offer throttling and resource quota functionality, which are quite helpful to protect your APIs from abuse. Both features should always be enabled if your API is public-facing and often enabled for internal use. See Figure 8-2 for an example of a problematic microservice architecture. One call does not go through the gateway or the application backend; that call should be forced through the gateway.

As stated previously, even though we are using new technology, it is still critical to practice application security best practices. In the case of APIs and microservices it is crucial that we continue to code excellent input validation, use parameterized queries, and all the other secure coding best practices that we would normally use.

An excellent tool for protecting microservices is *service mesh*. Service mesh is a layer of infrastructure that helps microservices talk to each other, quickly and reliably. Service mesh is needed only in the cloud and for microservice architectures. Imgine having a thousand different services for your application and then having hundreds of instances of each service running at the same time. This requires organization, speed, and reliability. This is what service mesh manages.

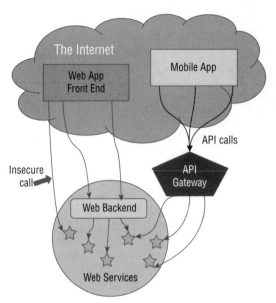

Figure 8.2: Microservice architecture with API gateway

Using a service mesh does not require changes to your code; it is an infrastructure layer. All public cloud providers have their own service mesh offerings, but agnostic service mesh offerings are also available on the market.

When creating APIs or services of any kind, it is necessary that each organization has standards for how they will be written—teams should not re-invent the wheel. This also ensures that testing is less difficult. Whenever possible, also provide templates to teams newly working with APIs and services to ensure they follow the standard.

Another method of defense for APIs is to ensure they follow the protocol and definition of the API as strictly as possible (test to verify). This ensures that the API calls are never ambiguous and that the API never falls into an unknown state due to the way it is called.

It is mandatory when creating APIs (and all applications) that we authenticate users first and then we authorize them. The reason for this is that when you authenticate someone you are figuring out who they are on your network (what their identity is). If they don't have a proper identity on your network, they might be dangerous. If you authorize them first (give them access), then perform authentication after (figure out who they are) this leaves you in a bad situation from an access perspective.

When creating error messages for APIs, it is critical that you do not share any extra information that you do not absolutely need to. Computers talk to APIs, not humans, and computers do not make typos. If there is a poorly formed request, most often this is an attempted attack. If you send back verbose error information that assists the attacker with creating a properly formatted request to your API, this puts you, your application, and your organization in danger. Ensure that your error messages do not give away any information that could potentially assist attackers in learning how to call your APIs, for instance, instructions of how to call the API properly.

Lastly, another item that applies to all applications is to only allow HTTP methods that are used by your application to be called. Block all unused HTTP methods on your servers.

Online Storage

Your data is the most valuable technical asset that your organization owns. Your organization should create secure defaults for online storage to ensure that every person using online storage has to follow the security precautions. No exceptions.

When you put your data into online storage, it is paramount that you classify your data's sensitivity level. In fact, *all* of your data should always be classified and labeled. When an incident responder comes across a data breach, it invokes a very different protocol if that information is labeled as "unclassified" versus "secret." When data is not labeled or classified for its sensitivity level, an incident responder has no idea where to start, and unfortunately must assume the worst. This is, essentially, an incident response nightmare.

Further layers of security for online storage include monitoring access to your online storage, file integrity monitoring, monitoring for port sniffing, adding alerts to the monitoring that alert the security operations center (SOC), and customized automated responses via cloud workflows.

> **TIP** Not everyone is so lucky to work at a place that has a security operations center. If you do not have one, alerts should be sent to the AppSec team, help desk, and/or business owners. The important part is that alerts can never go "nowhere" or to an unmonitored inbox.

It is necessary that online storage containers are accessed by IT personnel only after providing clear authorization by several parties. Online storage should normally only be accessed by service accounts, which are network accounts that are created for computers to talk to other computers. This way if there is an alert that Alice is accessing online storage in the middle of the night, we know that it is highly likely that she has had her credentials compromised and that we need to launch an incident investigation immediately.

> **TIP**   Service accounts are used by operating system/network/database services to conduct their activities and should never be used by IT personnel. Services accounts force the segregation between human and machine identities and activities. This segregation allows for detection of potentially malicious or dangerous patterns and behavior in order to automate defensive measures.

You can use cloud security controls as well to protect your online storage, including traffic profiling tools, Access and Identity Management (AIM), and least privilege automation tools to ensure your storage does not have excessive permissions.[73]

Lastly, it is vital that you protect your cloud management dashboard. Any cloud accounts that have the ability to change the permissions on your online storage should have multi-factor authentication (MFA) enabled, as well as long, unique passwords that are stored in a password manager.

Containers and Orchestration

When data centers first started, we had *servers*. Servers took up a lot of space and required lot of power; they were very loud and required constant air conditioning. Each server could hold only one application.

Eventually virtualization was created. This allowed us to have multiple operating systems running on the same physical machine, using *virtual machines* (VMs). This meant, for the first time, that we could host several applications on the same machine.

Next came *containers*. Containers are significantly smaller than virtual machines; instead of hosting an entire operating system, they only host the parts of the operating system that you require in order to run your application. This makes containers a fraction of the size of a virtual machine, which allows them to be hosted by the hundreds on only a single server. This is a huge increase in efficiency, which is why containers are being widely adopted so quickly.

With containers often comes something called *orchestration*. Orchestration is the management of containers. An orchestration system can start, stop, add, or remove memory, etc., for any container within its management. The idea of orchestration is that it would be too painstaking to manage hundreds or thousands of containers manually, so you use a management system to do all of the work.

That said, new technologies bring new risk. It is crucial that you follow the same best practices in regard to network security and/or cloud security that you always do for virtual machines or bare metal, including designing them with "assume breach" and "zero trust" in mind.

It is key that we limit the resources of containers, and have alerts set up if resources reach a certain quota to ensure that we are aware if they're being attacked.[74]

It is imperative that we do not run our containers as "root." The root user can do literally anything, and thus if someone is able to take over our container as root, this means they have unlimited powers over our resources. Although life is easier as a software developer, or any IT person, to have superpowers when performing their duties, it is almost never actually necessary. Prohibiting the use of root for containers would be an implementation of the least privilege concept applied to containers.[75]

Container images are often stored in registries and these registries must be secured. If your organization has its own registry, it is critical that you guard its permissions diligently. If a malicious actor were able to upload an intentionally insecure image, your colleagues could unknowingly download it, install it in production, and create a vulnerability ready for that malicious actor to exploit.

It is essential that your software developers do not download images from just anywhere; they should only be downloaded from trusted sources. You should create a policy to forbid downloading images from untrusted sources unless it is to a sandboxed environment, cordoned off from the rest of your organization's network and resources.

WARNING Supply chain security applies to images, not just web frameworks and libraries. Comparing your downloads to the checksum or hash would be a good first step. If you plan to run your own image registry, create a project to ensure that it is safe from manipulation by threat actors.

Containers and orchestration mean that we need to learn new configuration rules, new types of scanning tools, and learn about the new types of vulnerabilities and risks that they face. On top of this we must protect the accounts of those who can create or edit containers and for the orchestration systems, as those are the most valuable of accounts for a malicious actor. Those accounts should always have long, unique, random passwords, stored in a password manager, with multi-factor authentication enabled. But similar to virtual machines, we should scan all that can be scanned, verify our configurations are hardened according to guides provided by the vendor by using a linter, that we patch regularly or replace our containers with updated containers that are more secure, and apply zero trust to all of our designs.

TIP A great place to start for standards on securing almost any operating system are the CIS benchmarks. The Center for Internet Security (CIS) provides pre-hardened images and shares their knowledge freely and widely.

Serverless

Serverless is software that is *not* hosted/running all the time on a server; it is only available when it is invoked. When a serverless application is called it opens a container, runs its code to completion, then self-destructs, releasing all of the resources back into the ecosystem to be used by another process. Being ephemeral (short-lived) means that serverless software creates a smaller attack surface, as it is rarely in the running state (which is often required in order to be attacked) and there is no server available to be attacked either. The key advantage to using serverless applications is that you don't have to pay for them unless they're running, which means they could cost much, much less than a regular application. If you only have to pay for nine minutes per month of runtime, that can greatly reduce your cloud bills. However, the same application security principles still apply as any other application, plus a few more. Let's dive in, shall we?

Just like any other application, you still need to monitor and log your serverless applications. Ideally, those logs would be fed into your Security and Information Management System (SIEM) so that your SOC will see your alerts and take action if necessary.

> **TIP**   If you do not have a SIEM or SOC in your workplace, that is okay. Set up your systems to email you, your team, a business stakeholder, or the help desk. Someone needs to be alerted—figure out who the best person is and automate it.

As you might have suspected, the secure coding requirements and best practices that you know and love still apply; you still need to validate your input, and you still need to authenticate and authorize. Your data must also continue to be encrypted in transit and at rest. This does not change just because the application is short-lived.

Some differences in securing serverless include the possibility of using an API gateway as a security buffer. An API gateway enforces authentication and authorization and ensures that no one can call or access your serverless apps without going through its layer of security. An API gateway can also be used to enforce throttling (slowing down of requests) and resource quotas (cutting off users after a certain number of requests), which are both key for protecting serverless applications against DOS-style abuse.

Serverless applications should also be deployed with minimal granularity, and by that we mean that they should only do one thing and do it well. A serverless application should not be an entire full-sized application, because otherwise it does not make sense for it to be serverless. If a serverless application is being called such that it is almost always running, it should be changed into a regular application that is hosted on a server or PaaS.

It is crucial when creating serverless applications that we maintain isolated parameters. What we mean by this is that each serverless application needs to be authenticated and authorized to every other serverless application; there is no implied trust. Often, when using a microservice architecture to create applications, software developers do not employ all of the same security defenses that they would for a regular application, assuming trust between their services, serverless, and other applications. Be careful not to do this, because a malicious attacker would be able to take advantage of this by calling serverless applications they should not be able to. There is no authentication to stop them.[70]

Although this goes for every application, it is imperative that secrets from serverless applications are stored in a secret store. They should not be saved in your code library or your database.

Since serverless applications are also infrastructure, it is necessary to ensure that you apply least privilege when you are configuring your serverless app and positioning it within your network.[71]

If you are using a CI/CD pipeline, consider adding security scanning to verify the configuration of your serverless applications.[72]

Lastly, although this applies to all applications, it is essential that you ensure that all of the dependencies that your serverless application is depending on have been patched and/or verified not to be known to be insecure.[70]

Infrastructure as Code (IaC)

Infrastructure as Code (IaC), sometimes known as Configuration as Code, is creating scripts or configuration files written as code, to allow for automation of rollout. It is part of DevOps to use IaC to ensure that you can release your infrastructure via a CI/CD pipeline. From a security perspective this means that we are able to add security hardening to the infrastructure in code format, ensuring that all new infrastructure created by these scripts are already hardened when they are created. It also means that we are able to add security scanning to test the infrastructure as code as it moves throughout the release pipeline. IaC not only allows for faster deployment of patches and infrastructure changes, but it allows for faster deployment of security fixes and infrastructure hardening changes to production systems. Win! The workflow is shown in Figure 8-3.

Before the invention of IaC, operation engineers were tasked with manually installing applications and operating systems. They would have to sit at multiple machines pressing the Next button, installing software via a CD (compact disc), or using software that would help them automate some of this process such as system center. This type of work did not scale very well and was often error-ridden. It also did not make for extremely enjoyable work. This type of work—work that is devoid of enduring value, that scales linearly, that is automatable—is often referred to as *toil*.[76]

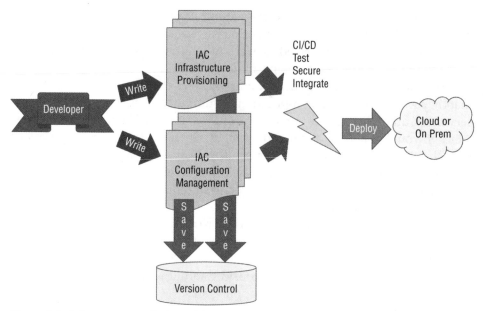

Figure 8-3: Infrastructure as Code workflow

One of the biggest advantages to IaC is that it is repeatable. When we perform tasks manually, it is possible for us to make errors, and if we perform the task enough times, statistically we *will* make errors. When we use infrastructure as code, we can guarantee that we will continue to make perfect copies, and if we create processes and policies that support ensuring that the Infrastructure as Code is secure, this is both a giant win for the application security team and the organization as a whole.

GRANT PERMISSIONS CAREFULLY

Bob remembers when they first implemented Infrastructure as Code at his old office. They had all been very excited to use this new way of deploying infrastructure, and everyone wanted to be a part of it. Unfortunately, they were very permissive with who had the ability to create infrastructure as code, and a novice employee accidentally deployed 1000 storage containers instead of 100, which ended up being *very* expensive. Bob decided they would all take training on best practices to ensure that they never had an accident like that happen again. In summary, only give this type of responsibility and access to someone who is properly trained.

Another big advantage of infrastructure as code is that it automatically documents itself when you check new versions into your code repository. Generally, configuration setting changes are not recorded very well, or at all, by most organizations. By checking all of your Infrastructure as Code into a code repository whenever you make a change, then have security testing and other testing performed on it in your CI/CD pipeline, then pushing it into prod, you have not only automated your documentation, but also your change management process. It is a beautiful thing.

When working with Infrastructure as Code, it is absolutely imperative that you ensure that all changes are made via your IaC process. You cannot log in to a production machine and make a bunch of configuration changes manually, because then you break the entire process. It also means that you are much more likely to accidentally introduce errors, vulnerabilities, or weak points in your infrastructure, because you aren't running all of the security tests and other necessary testing that is part of your CI/CD pipeline.[77]

TIP   You should not be writing manual documentation alongside your infrastructure as code. Your code should speak for itself, and manually written documentation will always be behind whatever is currently checked into source control. Generally, written documentation is almost always out of date, is a lot of work to maintain, and is therefore not a good investment of your time. Every file in source code should start with comments explaining exactly what they are for, and bug fixes should have a comment upon check-in starting which bug was fixed with a ticket number.[78]

Another item to discuss when it comes to Infrastructure as Code is *immutable infrastructure*. Immutable means you do not add patches or change it while it is in place; it means you replace it with something new that already has the new configuration, security update, or whatever other change(s) you wanted to apply. The advantage to this is that you can't accidentally corrupt your infrastructure images or break something while it is in production. By replacing your infrastructure with something new, you must have already ensured that it works properly via your CI/CD testing. Occasionally, not all patches apply properly when deploying them. This is also something that you would avoid if you are using immutable infrastructure. In summary, it reduces risk.[79]

Security as Code (SaC)

Security as Code is weaving security through DevOps, specifically, using code. While some say SaC is the same as DevSecOps, most agree they are different, where DevSecOps embodies all security activities that happen within a DevOps SDLC, and Security as Code being only the codified portions.

Examples of SoC include adding code to your Infrastructure as Code to enforce your security policies, writing code to implement and/or automate your security requirements, creating negative unit tests (unit tests that ensure you fail gracefully—also known as security regression testing), and adding security testing scripts to your pipelines.[80]

One other item to note in this section is "Security User Stories." If you create user stories where you work, there should also be stories for security situations, such as an XSS, brute force, or injection attack. Creating the security user stories ensures that all other testing efforts based upon the user stories will include security.

User Security Stories should be based off of; ensuring your CIA are intact, preventing threat models, enforcing any security-related standards or policies, and implementing your project's security requirements.

User story examples:

USER STORY	ACCEPTANCE CRITERIA
As users of product XYZ enter private information into the system, the information is protected from other users and the public. (Confidentiality)	■ Product is tested to ensure that users are unable to see other users' data ■ Product implements strong password policy and allows MFA ■ *Paste all other applicable requirements here*
Users of product XYZ are able to use the product 99.9% of the time, as per SLA. (Availability)	■ Product is tested for stress and performance ■ Product is hosted in a cloud instance with guaranteed 99.99% up time ■ *Paste all other applicable requirements here*
Users of product XYZ enter data into the system, and it is not able to be changed by administrators or any other user. (Integrity)	■ Verify all changes are logged ■ Verify authorization before every change ■ *Paste all other applicable requirements here*

Platform as a Service (PaaS)

Platform as a Service is infrastructure created and provided by public cloud vendors for hosting applications and APIs. The cloud provider takes on the responsibility of securing the platform, including patching and most configuration settings. To use a platform as a service you purchase a PaaS, select your desired size, operating system (OS), etc., and then put your application on top. You can put a container or code on to a platform as a service, and it just runs. The great thing about platform as a service is that maintenance and most of security is not your problem; however, *some* of the security is still your responsibility. Ensure that you are aware of which parts of the security configurations of your PaaS are your responsibility and then harden them accordingly.

> Although this is not specific for PaaS, turning on monitoring and logging when using cloud services is advisable, albeit not an inexpensive decision. The main cost associated with monitoring is the space taken up by the logs; logs are *huge*. That said, without logging and monitoring you will be unaware if attacks have taken place against your PaaS and other web resources.

All public-facing web assets should be available only over encrypted channels, and this means TLS/HTTPS. It is also essential that you ensure your security headers are in place and any other security configurations that are under your control are enabled and properly configured. Lastly, it is 100% your responsibility as the consumer of PaaS to create secure software that you host on this platform. It does not matter that PaaS and public cloud use a shared responsibility model; the cloud provider is not responsible for any resulting damage or losses if you create an insecure application and host it within their cloud. That is your responsibility.

> **TIP**   No matter which public cloud provider you decide to use, you will need to review and agree to their policies on *shared responsibility*. Shared responsibility policies state which security configurations and tasks fall under the client's or vendor's responsibility. Vendor responsibilities include patching, TLS certificate rotation, managing encryption keys, and more. Client responsibilities include securing applications hosted on your PaaS, deciding if you will force HTTPS or not, deciding if you will enable older versions of TLS (all versions of SSL will be blocked), and more.

Infrastructure as a Service (IaaS)

Infrastructure as a Service is another service offered by public cloud vendors. Essentially, you select the operating system, hardware, and any other specifications you desire, and then they automatically create it for you within your cloud instance. For example, if you want a Linux virtual machine created that has 4 gigs of hard drive space and 8 gigs of memory, you fill out the web form, press the purchase button, and before you know it you will have a virtual machine matching that description.

As with Platform as a Service (PaaS), Infrastructure as a Service (IaaS) follows the shared responsibility model. Unlike PaaS, IaaS requires the end user (that's you) to do all patching and other maintenance of the infrastructure that they have provided for you. The cloud provider will protect the physical data center and will ensure that the physical machines behind your virtual machine are well cared for, but they will not maintain the virtual machine they have provided for you. That is your responsibility. It is crucial to understand this differentiation between PaaS and IaaS.

Best practices for protecting IaaS are similar to all infrastructure resources: apply least privilege, use strong identity, authentication, and authorization, add them as part of your network using zero trust and assume breach designs, patch them regularly, follow the hardening guide, and do every other thing you would normally do to secure your infrastructure.

Continuous Integration/Delivery/Deployment

Continuous integration is trunk-based development. This means that you are continuously (regularly) checking your code back into your code repository alongside the other code that your teammates have written, to integrate it into the project/product as a whole. This means verifying constantly that the code that you have created does not break anyone else's code. Continuous integration removes risk by making smaller changes, more often.[81]

Continuous delivery is using an automated system to perform your continuous integration, rather than doing it manually (which would be extremely time consuming and error prone). Continuous delivery is generally considered to be the act of using pipeline software to integrate and deploy your code throughout your SDLC. The pipeline software, also known as CI/CD, integrates your code into the trunk of your code base, verifies that it compiles, publishes it to various test environments, performs various automated tests, and gives you feedback every step of the way. Continuous delivery systems are fantastic for efficiency, repeatability, and quality. It would be impossible to run hundreds of manual tests each time if you are checking your code 10 times a day. CI/CD pipeline software makes this possible.[81]

Continuous deployment is allowing your CI/CD pipeline software to release your code to production, without manual human intervention or approval. Continuous deployment happens when you have so many tests for quality, security, reliability, etc., that you trust the results enough that you no longer feel that a human is needed to intervene.[81] Although continuous deployment is a goal for many software development shops, in practice it is not often seen in the wild. It is an advanced activity and is not necessary in order to say that you are doing DevOps or using a CI/CD pipeline.

> **TIP** Using a CI/CD pipeline is not the only activity that you need to do in order to be doing DevOps properly. DevOps is a lot more than just pipeline software, as you will learn later on in this chapter.

Dev(Sec)Ops

To talk about DevSecOps, first we must discuss *DevOps*.

Although in our industry there are many definitions of DevOps, I always follow the definition stated in the *DevOps Handbook* (as previously referenced in this book in Chapter 7) and The Phoenix Project.[82]

DevOps is both a methodology for creating software and a specific culture that can exist within a software development shop. It requires a mixture of processes and products, used by people, to create rugged software. DevOps is the combination of development and operations responsibilities being performed by the same team and breaking down the silos that previously existed. It is also a much more effective and efficient way to create reliable, high-quality software. Years ago, we taught the Waterfall SDLC method in schools, then Agile, and now we are moving toward teaching DevOps because the results are so much better, and the projects succeed more often.

In order to "do" DevOps in your workplace you must follow *The Three Ways* of DevOps, as stated in The Phoenix Project.[82]

The First Way of DevOps is to ensure the efficiency of the entire system. This means not just concentrating on your part of the system, but looking at the entire SDLC as a whole and making improvements to the whole thing to ensure fast, reliable results. This often means the use of automation (including CI/CD software) and other processes and tools to ensure you are releasing code very quickly.

The Second Way of DevOps is fast feedback. The downfall of the Waterfall method was that you did not get feedback for months at a time, and that often led project teams down the incorrect path, creating a project that the client did not actually want or did not meet their needs. It also resulted in security testing and other security feedback being delayed until very late in the SDLC, when it is the most expensive, the most difficult, and there is the least amount of time available to fix things. Fast feedback means the automation of various types of testing, including security. This is also where CI/CD pipeline software is very useful. However, any automation of your security testing or feedback process will meet the requirements of The Second Way even if you are not using pipeline software.

TIP   Adding security tests to your unit testing is one way of getting very fast feedback to your software developers. Another way to get fast feedback is to use wrapper libraries to rename insecure functions to names such as "insecureMD5Hash-DoNotUse" or "ThisIsWhyWeCantHaveNiceThings" is another way to give your developers very fast feedback.[83]

The Third Way of DevOps is continuous learning, experimentation, and risk taking. The Third Way emphasizes working regularly to improve the quality and efficiency of your everyday work. This includes taking metrics and other measurements to ensure that you are moving in the correct direction. You can keep yourself and your team up to date with technologies trends such as lunch and learn sessions, formal training, books, and other ways to teach your software developers about security. Running proof of concept (POC) activities on various tools or technologies to find out which one meets the needs of your organization the best is one way to ensure you are using the best tool for the job. It is vital that you reserve a certain amount of time each week or each month to improve your daily work, in order to ensure that you are meeting The Third Way.

There are books dedicated to the sole purpose of explaining DevOps; by contrast this definition is very fast and very short. There are most certainly ideas, processes, and concepts that are missing from the preceding explanation, and there is much, much more to learn on this topic. Read the books suggested in Chapter 7 to learn more about DevOps.

DevSecOps

> **"It's what we've always done as application security professionals; DevSecOps is just application security, adjusted for a DevOps environment."**
>
> — *Imran A. Mohamed*[84]

When working in a DevOps environment, security professionals must adjust their activities so that they fit into the processes that the DevOps engineers are following. If the DevOps team is doing their work in sprints, then we (Security) must fit our work and projects into sprints. If they are using CI/CD pipelines to automate testing, then we want to have some of our security testing in their pipelines. Whatever way they are performing their SDLC functions, we want to weave ourselves and our security goals throughout. There are several strategies for this, and again there are entire books dedicated to this topic so we cannot cover all of them, but let's discuss a few.

The first and most critical item for security teams to concentrate on when trying to work within a DevOps environment is to ensure that the dev teams and the Ops teams are not waiting on them. We (Security) cannot be a bottleneck. This means that we can only break the build if it is a true emergency or a very serious risk. It means that we no longer function as a gate; we become enablers.

Another very noteworthy item for all application security professionals is that we must tune our tools in order to ensure that they are not producing false positives. Quite often the responsibility of validating the results from AppSec tools is thrust upon the software development team, because they have greater numbers. However, they do not have the same expertise, knowledge, or mandate, and this type of situation is unlikely to produce high-quality results.

The last item we will mention here is that you must provide quick and timely feedback to your software development and operations teams when working in a DevOps environment. You must also elicit feedback from these teams about your work, then integrate that feedback into your processes, projects, and policies for best results.

The Cloud

Many people have differing definitions of *cloud security*, but for this book we will talk about cloud *native* security. When discussing cloud security some people might think of it as almost the same as data center security, or network security, but that's not what we mean here. We mean, specifically, taking advantage of all of the new amazing features, services, tools, and opportunities that are available from the cloud that are not available in a regular legacy data center, and the security surrounding those new technology offerings.

Cloud Computing

> **Cloud computing is the on-demand availability of computer system resources, especially data storage and computing power, without direct active management by the user.**
>
> *—Wikipedia[85]*

Let's dissect that definition. Cloud computing is the "on-demand availability": you are able to request anything that they offer as a service, including infrastructure, Platform as a Service, cloud native security tools, etc., at any moment. You can always add more, which is both amazing and potentially dangerous.

Imagine that you are a software developer, and you are going to scale the infrastructure that your web application is sitting on. Let's say you think that the amount of traffic you will have is quite small, so you sign up for the smallest offering that your cloud provider has. However, you understand that your site may grow over time and you may have more customers as your business is more successful, so you check the box to allow it to auto-scale. Three months from then, you suffer a denial-of-service attack (DOS), which creates a giant cloud bill that you were not expecting. This is a potential risk of such an offering.

However, if you have already thought ahead and realized this was a potential risk, you would check the auto-scaling button, but you would also add a maximum (resource quota) and/or alerting. Another way to defend against such a situation would be to add denial-of-service protection, which is usually an offering from most public cloud providers.

It is extremely convenient as a technologist to be able to request resources whenever you need them or want them. Being able to automatically deploy hundreds of machines at a time or being able to handle gigantic amounts of data using the cloud's amazing processing power makes so many more things possible for IT professionals than ever before. This is what we mean by on-demand availability of resources in the cloud.

Let's go back to our definition of cloud computing and re-examine the end of the definition: "without direct active management by the user."

When we talked about Platform as a Service (PaaS) a few pages ago, this is an example of allowing your cloud provider to take over the management of your systems. By trusting your cloud provider to apply the patches and harden your PaaS, you are allowing the cloud provider to take on this responsibility. You do not need to actively manage your PaaS, leaving you more time to perform other work.

For the cloud data center, you do not need to provision extra servers, worry about air conditioning, or install software from a compact disc. They handle all of it for you; no direct management is required by the end user. This is cloud computing.

Cloud Native

Cloud Native: Applications and services that automate and integrate the concepts of continuous delivery/ integration/ deployment, DevOps, microservices, serverless, and containers. [86, 87, 88]

This definition was created by combining the best parts of many different definitions. Shall we dissect it together?

Let's start with "applications and services." By this we mean any service or software (including APIs) offered by your cloud provider, as well as any third-party services provided by vendors whose products you have purchased to use in your cloud instance. This essentially means all of the infrastructure, services, and software that you have in your cloud instance available to you. This includes Software as a Service (SaaS), which is not installed in your cloud but made available to your cloud, with the workload mostly run somewhere else.

Up next in our definition is "automate and integrate." The cloud is all about automation; reducing tedious manual workloads for IT professionals and ensuring accuracy. Not only does the cloud automate every possible activity, but it ensures that each of the moving pieces work well together, often referred to as integration. It is necessary that the various services, software, infrastructure, and networks are able to work properly together and integrate cleanly, otherwise your cloud instance will be a painful and expensive mess.

So now that we understand we want to make sure that all the software and the services work well together and that everything possible is automated, we add in the following ingredients: CI/CD, DevOps, microservices, serverless, and containers (which we defined already in this chapter).

All of these features together create a cloud native environment. Having access to all of these tools and services, having an infrastructure environment provided by your cloud vendor that is capable of supporting all of these concepts, and adding additional third-party tooling to assist you creates an amazing possibility for the security team if it is well architected and maintained.

However, if it is not planned out and designed with security in mind (following the concepts we defined earlier in this book), it can also create an insecure online target for malicious actors.

Cloud Native Security

Like many other topics within this chapter, cloud security is covered in several books already. This is merely an overview of significant topics that you need to consider when working in the cloud.

When designing or architecting for the cloud, it is imperative that you design with "zero trust" and "assume breach" ideologies in mind. It is vital that you provide secure defaults for the end user. Ensure that "the most secure way" to do something is always "the easiest way" to do it. Providing secure templates (of configurations, infrastructure, code, etc.), if possible, is an excellent way to do this.

Always use the security features that are included from your cloud provider with your purchases; for instance, if there is a dashboard with security features, take full advantage of it. You are paying for these services already when you pay for the other parts of your cloud services, so you might as well make full use of them.

As with all networks and applications, monitor all that can be monitored, scan all that can be scanned, and set up alerts on anything that you want to ensure you remain on top of. Turn on logging, and protect those logs from malicious actors with monitoring, access control, and alerting.

In the cloud, many say that "identity is the new perimeter." Whether you agree with this statement or not, using identity within your cloud environment (with role-based access control, of course) is a fantastic way to protect your resources and services within the cloud.

The key with cloud is planning in advance, ensuring there is clear guidance for your users, and automating secure defaults, policy enforcement, and other security features whenever possible. If you allow the developers or operations teams to start in the cloud before you have had a chance to create secure defaults, you will have problems in the cloud. Instead, try to lead the way by providing as much guidance and support as you possibly can.

Cloud Workflows

A cloud workflow is also known as "step functions," "logic apps," and "cloud dataflows," depending upon which public cloud vendor you prefer. Cloud workflows are triggered by cloud events, then run a predetermined workflow (set of actions). Logic applications are part of public cloud instances and each cloud vendor has a different name for it, but they all do the same thing: they trigger workflows based on events in the cloud. Cloud workflows can be triggered when someone tries to log in to an application too many times, when it appears someone is scanning your ports, when someone with an employee account is attempting to access something that the policy states they should not, etc. You set up what event(s) triggers the logic app, and it performs the corresponding workflow.

Cloud workflows need to be tested to ensure they trigger when they should, and *only* perform the actions you programmed them to do. You may have trouble testing them for security as they function differently than other applications, but as you might have guessed, it is very important that you do so anyway.

TIP   Cloud workflows are excellent for defending your systems! Every time you have a new type of security incident or detect an anomaly, create a cloud workflow to handle it or at least alert you.

Modern Tooling

Tooling for application security has changed over time, with many of the same concepts being re-invented or re-examined with new types of tooling. In this section we will discuss new types of security tooling as of this writing. This list is not exhaustive; it is meant to give you an idea of the many different types of tools available to you as an application security professional.

IAST Interactive Application Security Testing

IAST is a combination of static and dynamic application security testing that runs from within your application, while your application is being used. These tools are installed via a binary inside of your application that runs live and delivers results in close to real time. These tools only work if you use your application; you cannot just turn them on and then have them produce results—you must provide interaction with the application, even if it is an automated testing tool. These tools only test the parts of the code or parts of the application that are interacted with by your users, hence the name (interactive). This means they do not provide complete code coverage, even if they do cover all of the parts of the application that are used by end users.

Ideal situations for use are during quality assurance testing, during a penetration test or security assessment, when using a DAST automated scanning tool, and if you feel that you can accept the level of latency that they create, during production use. Latency varies from product to product and from application to application.

Runtime Application Security Protection

Runtime Application Security Protection (RASP) tools are also binaries that are installed in your applications; however, they are usually only installed in production environments. They act as a shield for your application, analyzing all of the input to your application for potential malicious activity. Many of them boast using artificial intelligence (AI) and machine learning (ML) to analyze the input to your application for malformed or potentially malicious requests, then block bad input before it reaches your application.

RASP is also often referred to as a "reverse proxy" or "next-generation WAF." WAF stands for web application firewall, another type of application shielding tool.

Latency varies from product to product, and from application to application. All tools that provide shielding for your application create latency of some kind.

File Integrity Monitoring

File integrity monitoring (Figure 8-4) ensures that your system files are not changed by another source, unless it is approved by the administrator. The idea of file integrity monitoring is to ensure that malware or other malicious software does not rename itself to the same name as a system file in order to get past application control tooling.

Application Control Tools (Approved Software Lists)

Application control tooling is used to ensure that only the software on the approved list, plus the operating system software, is able to run on a server or host computer. Application control tools are used to create a list of approved software for your organization, and they can be used for all host computers across your enterprise or used just for your server machines. All software that is not on the approved list will be blocked. This can be quite inconvenient if your organization does not pre-approve software to be used on your servers or host machines.

When malware is downloaded onto a computer, the first thing it does is try to start itself. If you have application control tooling installed, it will immediately see that the malware is not on the approved list and block it from running. The next thing that malware does is attempt to rename itself to the same name as a system file, in order to trick the application control tooling. If you are using file integrity monitoring (explained in the preceding section), this will also stop the malware in its tracks. Using file integrity monitoring and application control tooling together will ensure that your systems are safe from all but the most advanced types of malware.

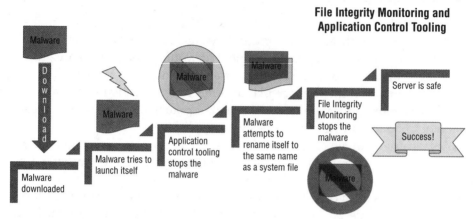

Figure 8-4: File integrity monitoring and application control tooling at work

NOTE   These tools require quite a bit of administration in order to install correctly and maintain, but they reduce an organization's risk to ransomware and other malware exponentially.

Security Tools Created for DevOps Pipelines

There are several new types of security tools being developed or on the market, specifically and only, to work in CI/CD pipelines. Some of these tools are rehashes on original ideas, such as SAST and DAST, but some are completely new and rather inventive.

Brand new types of tooling include tools that amalgamate several tools together and run them at the same time to reduce pipeline time taken for security tasks, tools that amalgamate all of your results so that you can see all of your security information for all of your applications in only one dashboard, secret stores that integrate with your pipelines, and tools that analyze your test results across applications using AI/ML and then create risk projections and/or priority lists for you.

Application Inventory Tools

Creating and keeping current a complete list of all of your applications, APIs, and SaaS software is a daunting task for any application security professional.

There are new products coming out as of this writing that help find your applications across your network and/or across the internet for you. Performing this work manually ensures that you will never have a complete list, and that your list will almost never be current. These new types of application inventory tools are very exciting for those of us who are trying to ensure we have the complete picture available to us (and our incident responders) of all of the software living within our network.

Least Privilege and Other Policy Automation

Being able to automate the enforcement, auditing, and verification of policies within your cloud environment makes policy enforcement work more accurate, scalable, and even (possibly) enjoyable. This is done by setting up agents within your environment that monitor systems to ensure they comply with your policies. This is generally only done in cloud environments, rarely in on-premises (legacy) data centers.

Tools that automate least privilege watch your instances to see which privileges they use, then remove the privileges that have not been used in quite some time in order to implement the concept of least privilege without breaking anything. Other types of policy automation include enforcement of secure communication protocols (e.g., HTTPS only), enforcement of the use of security headers, enforcement of turning on logging, monitoring, auditing and/or other defensive tooling, alerting if certain types of accounts attempt to escalate privileges or access areas of the network that they should not, ensuring that multifactor authentication is turned on for all owner accounts, etc. Policy automation is extremely handy when hardening your cloud instance.

Previously auditors had to try to find out if your systems were following your policies based on questionnaires and honesty, which was never a good recipe for efficiency or accuracy. Manually attempting to verify and enforce policy tends to be inaccurate, time consuming, and error prone (also known as toil). The automation of policy enforcement is game-changing when it comes to ensuring people are actually following the security policies that you have set forth (also known as compliance).

Modern Tactics

Several corporations, governments, and non-profits have shared their winning strategies and tactics for modernizing their security activities via conferences, books, whitepapers, and open source projects. The very long list includes Netflix, Microsoft, Intuit, and the Communication Security Establishment Canada (CSEC).

Unfortunately, it is much more common to *not* share good ideas in our industry, as some groups feel that revealing their methods for successful security programs is not to their advantage. This leads to many technologists having to rely on trial and error, rather than learning from other people's successes and failures, which hurts our industry. In this section we will discuss a handful of ideas that have been shared via social media, conference talks, and informal conversations.

While adding security tools to your DevOps pipeline is an idea that is well known in our industry, some have been creating asynchronous pipelines and run their long-running tests in those, in order to not interrupt the build process. This way you can put your critical security tests in the release pipeline, but then your long, slow, intense tests that you will review the results of yourself long after the code has been pushed to production, can run in the asynchronous pipeline.

Several technologists have taken the test results from a penetration test or security assessment and turned them into unit tests, in order to ensure that those same errors in coding do not return after the test engagement is complete. To gain further mileage you can also look for those same test results in the rest of your applications. Those same software developers that made that mistake in application A probably also made that mistake in application B or C. By taking those test results and evaluating the rest of your applications against them, you can get more value from your test engagement, which was most likely not an inexpensive venture.

Another activity that is not spoken of very often, but has great efficiency opportunity, is to run automated scanning on your code repository, rather than only on the code in your pipeline that is being sent for release. You can create "pre-commit hooks" to run various security tests, which then can block the pipeline release if it needs to. However, you can *also* run tests that do not block pipeline releases, such as weekly SCA or SAST scanning, against your entire repository. The code in your repository is just sitting there; you might as well make use of it.

Creating a secure code library with templates and known good code for software developers to grab from is another way that you could increase efficiency in creating secure code. Although this idea may seem rather simplistic, it's rarely implemented due to the amount of effort required to maintain it. However, if you can find a software developer who is also a security champion, you can name them as your Secure Code Librarian, and assign them the duty of caring for and growing the secure code library. This activity takes time to produce results, but the results can be quite stunning over time.

As more and more organizations become brave and share the best practices that they use internally, there will be more and more amazing ideas for you to evaluate for potential adoption in your workplace. Consider attending conferences, watching recorded conference talks, following various members of the information security community who share ideas online, and other ways of keeping up with our industry's creative new application security strategies and tactics.

Summary

In this chapter we covered a lot; we went a mile wide but only an inch deep. The key thing to take away from this chapter is to continue to apply all the same AppSec lessons when using new technologies that we covered earlier in the book. All software input requires validation, whether it is a car or a web application. All technology needs security testing, because it is our duty to protect our users, data, and systems. New technologies may have new potential vulnerabilities, but they are for certain going to be subject to several of the concepts already detailed here.

Exercises

1. What does the term "shared responsibility" mean?
2. What is the difference between Infrastructure as a Service (IaaS) and Platform as a Service (PaaS)? Which one(s) do you have to patch and maintain yourself?
3. Why is there (or is there not) more risk to online storage? Which of the CIA Triad can apply to online storage?
4. Name one new risk that the cloud has that a traditional or on-premises data center does not have.
5. What is the difference between a container, a virtual machine, and a physical server?
6. Name one advantage of Infrastructure as Code.
7. Name one advantage of DevOps over Waterfall SDLC.
8. Which of the modern tooling options sounded most interesting to you? Why?
9. Which of the modern tactics sounded most interesting to you? Why?
10. After reading this chapter, what do you see missing in your organization? What can you improve, and how can you do it?

Helpful Information on How to Continue to Create Very Good Code

In This Part

Good Habits

Software developers, system administrators, help desk professionals, and all other IT professionals who have special privileges on technology systems are prime targets for malicious actors. The superpowers that you have on your network and systems are much sought after by those looking to harm your organization, and it is your responsibility to protect them to the best of your ability. In this chapter we will talk about good habits for ensuring you keep your data, code, and systems safe.

The very first habit that you will want to form may sound like clickbait, but it is not. Whenever you search online about how to code something, look for *the most secure way* to do whatever it is you need to do, and your code quality will improve immediately. Generally, when people search for how to do something online, they go to the same handful of websites, and they pick whatever item has been voted to the top. They copy and paste from that top post directly into their application, try to compile it, and if it compiles, they continue their day, not thinking twice about whether they have just pasted a vulnerability into their application.

Unfortunately, whatever is in the topmost post is generally also the most insecure way to do whatever it is that you are trying to do.[89] This is because removing security features (also known as *unhardening*) often makes things "work," because everything is set to "open." This is extremely dangerous for those who are copying and pasting without evaluating the security implications of their actions.

From now on when you search online for how to do something, ensure that you are searching how to do it in *the most secure way possible*. If you prioritize security every step of the way, you *will* create more secure software.

Password Management

Information technology professionals are expected to remember an absolutely impossible number of passwords. Even the average consumer is expected to remember so many passwords that they are usually unable to keep up. On top of this, the cybersecurity industry has preached password complexity (using special characters, numbers, and upper/lowercase letters) for so long that the average person has an extremely complex password, which they make very short, in order to try to remember it and/or make it easier to type out. This has led to people creating strategies in order to remember all of their passwords, including writing them down, saving them into a file on their computer, saving them into their browser, and/or reusing the same password over and over again.

Remove Password Complexity Rules

Very short passwords are extremely easy to crack in a short period of time using password cracking software. Password cracking software guesses based on dictionary words and then applies derivation patterns (tries different variations) until it hits a match. The shorter the password, the faster the match. With the average person having trouble remembering extremely complex passwords, this has led to undersized, and therefore less secure, passwords. This means that when we add password complexity rules to the software that we create, we end up *reducing* the security of most passwords for our end users.

The keys to ensuring that your password is extremely difficult to crack by an automated tool are entropy and length.[90] The longer your password is, the longer it will take a cracking tool to break it, and thus using the maximum 64 characters that are often allowed for password fields means that you have made it the most difficult to crack. Note: *this assumes that your password also has entropy*. If you repeat the same character over and over, your 64-character password will not be very secure.

Entropy means randomness. Creating random values using a computerized system is actually quite difficult; it is a problem that computer scientists have struggled with for decades. That said, computers are way better at it than humans are.

If the values you are using for your passwords are ones you made up, the chances are they are not actually very random. Generally, human-made passwords contain or are based off of words, which is much easier for an automated system to guess. This is why using randomly generated values from a password manager ensures that your passwords are *even more* secure.

Always use your password manager to create random, maximum-length passwords for all your accounts.

PASSWORD REUSE

Bob used to use the same password for every single site, until he had his credentials stolen as part of a data breach. Bob had signed up for a service called HaveIBeenPwned, which sent him an email and told him to reset his password because his credentials had been compromised. It also advised him to get a password manager. At that moment, Bob realized that almost all of his accounts had been compromised, because he used the same credentials (username and password) for so many sites. He spent the next couple of days resetting everything, using the random values generated by his password manager, storing them one by one. This was not a fun experience for Bob.

Use a Password Manager

Password managers are software that manage, encrypt, and protect all your passwords for you. They integrate with most modern browsers, and can be used on your phone, your computer, your tablet, and most other devices. When you save a password into your browser you are not using a password manager—a password manager is a separate piece of software that is designed for the sole purpose of protecting your passwords.

Password managers will not only keep track of the credentials (username and password combinations) of all of your online accounts, but most of them are also able to handle multi-factor authentication challenges for you by auto-generating your codes. They can save your backup codes, sensitive information such as your social insurance number, credit card numbers, and anything else that you want to keep secret. Password managers are also quite good for when you accidentally click a phishing link that brings you to a lookalike site meant to steal your credentials. When you go to a site that you do not have a password saved for, your password manager will show a blank, which should tip you off and save you from this attack vector.

Password managers also create randomly generated, extremely long, complex passwords. If you have unique passwords for every single site that are all 64 characters long, this means that if someone was trying to crack your password it would take an extremely long period of time. It will also ensure that if there is a data breach on one of the sites that you have an account on (and credentials are part of the breach) only that one account that you have on that site will be compromised, as the attacker will only have that one set of credentials. All of your other online accounts will remain safe.

For most people it would be impossible to remember 64-character passwords that are random for 100 or more online sites, but for a password manager this is quite simple. You only need to remember the one password that you use to get into the password manager.

Next let's talk about that one password that you use to get into your password manager: a passphrase.

Passphrases

Passwords for computer systems were first created at the Massachusetts Institute of Technology and Bell Laboratories in the 1960s to gain access to Unix systems.[91] Back then, passwords were a single word; they were inventing security as they went.

A passphrase is a sentence; one that is easy to remember, that is long, and that no one would guess. Generally, if you are going to use a password manager you will use a passphrase to access the manager. This is to ensure that you remember it without writing it down.

Examples of effective passphrases are:

- Lyrics to songs
- A line from a joke or poem
- A sentence that expresses something that is special to you:
    - I have two daughters, and I love them both dearly.
    - My dog's name is Spotty, and he is cute as can be!
    - This is Ground Control to Major Tom. You've really made the grade.
    - Why do I have SO MANY PASSWORDS? Way too many!

Most password managers will allow you extremely long passphrases, meaning you don't have to keep them at 64 characters or less like the preceding examples. Make the passphrase for your password manager as long as possible.

Don't Reuse Passwords

Many end users reuse passwords for simplicity; it *does* make it easier to manage so many accounts, and this is why people do it. However, password reuse is taken advantage of when threat actors perform *credential stuffing attacks*.

Online criminals purchase breached credentials for pennies per account, then use scripts to try the credentials against various popular online platforms. This is called a *credential stuffing attack*. When a set of credentials works, they steal from that person. This could be in the form of ordering products for themselves, ordering things then returning them for cash or credit, stealing online data or images and then ransoming them back to the person who owns the account, etc. When someone has your credentials, and those credentials work on many different websites (password reuse), this person has a lot of power over you and your online identity.

Do Not Implement Password Rotation

Many organizations still implement password rotation policies, forcing users to change their passwords every 90 days. This led to many users adding numbers to the end of their passwords to make them easy to remember but still comply with the policy (think "Password1," "Password2," "Password3").

If you add the name of the current season plus the year together to form a password, that is likely to be the most common password on the planet at that exact moment (e.g., "Winter2021").

PASSWORD ROTATION

Alice used to work in an office with a 90-day password rotation policy; it was so frustrating. Every 90 days she would come in and spend two hours changing all of her passwords, and inevitably forgetting half of them the next day, resulting in another two hours on the phone with help desk. She started writing them down on sticky notes and putting them in her desk to save time, even though she knew she shouldn't.

Don't be cruel to your users; stop password rotation.

Unfortunately for the average user, organized crime is becoming more advanced in their use of technology for online theft and other nefarious activities, and they have figured out how to use password rotation policies against the average user. *Rainbow credential stuffing attacks* involve using scripts to not only test your known credentials against popular platforms, but to also increment values at the beginning or end of your password, then use the variations to gain access to your online accounts.

For example, many users create passwords such as "Fall2020" or "MyPassword6." It is very likely that the same user would have their next password be "Winter2021" or "MyPassword7." Rainbow credential stuffing attacks account for this and use it to their advantage.

Multi-Factor Authentication

Using multi-factor authentication (MFA) is the number-one way that an end user can protect their online accounts. As discussed in Chapter 1, factors of authentication include something you *have*, something you *are*, and something you *know*. Using two factors means that an attacker would have to compromise both in order to get into your accounts. That is *a lot* of work.

As an end user, you have no power over how your username and password is stored when you create an account on an online platform. Ideally, all passwords should be stored using a password-hashing function (PHF), which adds entropy to the password by prepending a salt and creating a hash out of the result. Unfortunately, this is not always the case, and not every company follows best practices when creating custom software. Any quick internet search will reveal that you are able to buy compromised credentials on the dark web for pennies, with countless articles detailing just how long it takes for the end users to be notified. Some end users are never made aware that their credentials have been breached.

If you have an account on a site that is not protecting users' passwords properly, a malicious actor will have the clear-text credentials that you use to access this site if the site has a data breach that includes the passwords and usernames of their users. If you have a second factor of authentication enabled, malicious actors would not be able to get into your account without it. Unless someone is attempting to spearfish you specifically, it is highly unlikely an attacker will take the time to attempt to compromise whatever your second factor of authentication is. Two-factor authentication generally stops credential-related crime in its tracks.

You should enable MFA on every account that is valuable to you or your employer.

Incident Response

Even if you are not on the incident response team for your organization, it is critical that you know what your duties are during an incident. You do not want to learn this when the emergency is *actually happening*; it's best to know these things and prepare for them in advance. Introduce yourself to the security team and ask them what you need to know when there is an incident, and they will likely be very surprised and happy to hear from you. Quite often security teams forget to communicate what they expect from everyone else in the organization.

If you are on the security team, even better. You should create a short training session for everyone where you work. It could be 5 minutes during an all staff meeting to explain to everyone what you need from them and what a security incident is. Explain to them:

- What "need to know" is, and not to share info about incidents unless they are told it's okay to do so.

- Who might be required to be available, and who should be on call.

- When there is a security incident happening, you have permission to take their time, even if they are working on another task or have deadlines.

- Security incidents are *emergencies*. And the security team needs their help in order to do a good job and protect your organization.

- Then thank them.

It doesn't need to be extremely complex, but you need them to know what they should and shouldn't do. Telling them will get you much better results than assuming they will know. Communicating this widely will not only help to ensure that "security is everybody's job," but will also help people be calmer during an emergency because they know what to do and who to call.

Fire Drills

Performing security incident simulations of other vital business activities is a very good use of your time; similar to holding a fire drill to prepare for a fire, a security simulation prepares you for IT security emergencies. It helps highlight where you may have issues in your processes, but not during the actual event. If you have a problem in your incident response process, finding out *before* an incident actually happens is ideal, so you can fix it in advance. Other types of fire drills could be red teaming, testing your defenses and alerting systems to make sure they are still active and functioning correctly, testing that your access to various systems that you don't use very often is still active, testing your disaster recovery plan, verifying your business continuity plan is effective, etc. If there is something that you are counting on, you should be testing it on a regular basis to ensure that it is always there.

> ## DISASTER RECOVERY (DR) AND BUSINESS CONTINUITY PLANNING (BCP)
>
> Five years ago, Bob was leading a huge project to provide technology services during an election. They wanted him to have not only a Disaster Recovery (DR) plan, but also a Business Continuity Plan (BCP). They took democracy and the right to vote very seriously, and absolutely nothing would stand in the way of them delivering the results to the public on election day. He ended up making a plan A, B, C, D, and E for them as part of the BCP. Plan A was to use the tech his main project was building. Plan B was to use the backup live servers they had if the first ones went down, with an entirely different internet connection and internet provider. Plan C was to use cellular signals to manually send the election results. Plan D was to use a satellite phone. Plan E was to drive a car with the results to the closest town that had connectivity and send it from there. They were not messing around.
>
> For the Disaster Recovery Plan (DR), they had
>
> - All of the app rollouts automated using a CI/CD system
>
> - A hot-hot data center setup, with two separate data centers that each ran the exact same systems, with constant syncing

- ▪ Practiced all of their rollbacks of databases and application servers

- ▪ A separate site for if there was a flood or any other physical reason that they could not enter their regular Security Operations Center (SOC) and Network Operations Center (NOC). This was expensive, but worth it for them; nothing could get in the way of democracy.

There was a lot more, but they made it clear to Bob: business would continue no matter what, and they wanted him to make a plan that would ensure that (the BCP). They also had him plan the Disaster Recovery so that if a true disaster happened, they could get back up and running, with all mission-critical systems, ASAP.

Continuous Scanning

Continuous scanning is a promise that many products make, but few are able to deliver on. This section is not meant to instruct you to purchase a tool, but to tell you should *continue* to scan everything.

If you are able to set up automated scanning of your infrastructure, network, databases, and/or applications, this is fantastic. If you are not able to schedule or automate this type of activity, ensure that you are doing it manually, *on a regular basis*, whenever possible.

If you are a software developer (and you are unable to automate this), you should use a DAST tool to find as much as you can, then fix it before sending it to Quality Assurance or whatever other team is down the line.

Although scanning tools are not perfect, anything that they pick up is usually pretty easy for a malicious actor to also find, meaning you should definitely take the time to fix it.

The key takeaway here is that you should *continue* to scan; don't stop.

Technical Debt

Technical debt is a decision. It is a decision to put upgrading, fixing, and improving last. Although management is often the one making these decisions, if you are not in management, you can still influence it. Upgrading frameworks, ensuring that all of your environments are perfect copies/mirrors, refactoring old code that seems dangerous or unreliable, masking production data that is used in other environments, are all things that you can suggest to management to add to upcoming projects, schedules, or in between other tasks.

Although we discussed this already in this book, *technical debt is security debt*. Even if your organization is not willing to prevent technical debt across the board, you can attempt to do this within your own projects as best as you can by making it a personal priority.

Inventory

Sometimes as part of "application portfolio management," creating a list of all of your applications is a crucial security exercise. Without a complete and current list, you will not be able to respond to incidents or other problems quickly and effectively. It also means that you have no idea if you have complete coverage with your SAST/DAST/IAST monitoring and all your other security activities. By definition, your security tooling coverage is incomplete if your inventory is incomplete.

Taking inventory is not a sexy job; it's not exciting or fun. That said, it is actually extremely *challenging*. Ensuring that you have continuous visibility and/or automating the process for keeping a current list of all of your web assets is an elusive goal that no one in our industry has yet to perfect.

Your inventory should include the following information:

- Application or API name
- Type of application, API, web app, SaaS product, etc.
- URL to production
- URL to dev
- Link to where the code is located
- Contact information for the team that is responsible for this application
- Data sensitivity level
- Specifics of tech stack (language, framework)
- Location (cloud/on prem/VM or container name if appropriate)
- Anything else you think might be valuable

INVENTORY

Bob was in charge of an application portfolio management project when he learned how hard it was to take inventory of software and other types of applications. He really struggled with this project, and they even hired a high-priced consultant to help them. They did lots of interviews, filled out checklists and surveys, but at the end Bob couldn't help but feel that this process should have been automated. They paid the consultant a small fortune to interview all the software developers, and at the end all they had was a fancy Excel spreadsheet. Bob had thought that they had over 200 applications, but at the end the consultant explained to him that they actually only found evidence of 72 applications.

Bob has always wondered how many they *actually* had. . .

Other Good Habits

What follows are several other good habits you should consider in order to be a security-minded IT professional.

Policies

Although this probably goes without saying, you should not break the security policies of your workplace. If you are in a situation where you feel that you must break policy in order to complete your job duties, this means there is a problem with that policy, or whatever task you have been asked to do. Quite often, when policies are created, the policy writers are not able to think of every single situation they may apply to, and therefore there may be errors. If there is a problem with the policy, you should report it to your manager so that it can be updated.

Downloads and Devices

Don't download random software, code, music, or other random files from the internet and then put them on your work computer. Also, don't bring your own devices to work and plug them into the network, unless there is a policy that says you are allowed. Only devices, software, and everything else that has been approved should be on your work network.

> **UNKNOWN CODE**
>
> Bob remembers when one of his colleagues had copied some code off of a website to use in one of his applications. The colleague had not reviewed the code properly, and it called out to a library that was malicious. It caused a security incident when it called out to a command-and-control website on the internet, but luckily the security team noticed and blocked it. Bob's colleague was in big trouble.

We all think that the items we are bringing into the workplace are safe; however, we all make mistakes.

Lock Your Machine

Always lock your machine when you walk away from your desk if you are working anywhere other than your own private home office. You should never be signed into all of your systems and then leave it all open for anyone to access while you are not there. You may think that you can trust your colleagues, but insider threats are dangerous and should be taken seriously.

MORE THAN JUST PRACTICAL JOKES

Even though it's a bit immature, Alice still sends an email to the whole team with the subject "Free Beer!" every time she sees an employee's computer unlocked. She sends it from the unlocked computer, as though it is from that person. Then she smiles to herself as she hears giggles and laughs from her team's cubicles. They all know what happened.

Privacy

With the advent of social media, many say that privacy is dead; however, it does not need to be that way.

It is important that you keep the information about yourself that is private away from the internet because information that you share on the internet can be used against you in social engineering attacks. For instance, if you have put your date of birth, your mother's maiden name, and your home address on the internet someone could easily use that information to access your online banking, change the SIM associated with your phone number, and so much more. The public (people who don't work in InfoSec) often underestimate the value of the private information they share on the internet. The following is a list of various pieces of personal information that you should not share online:

- Your mother's maiden name
- Your date of birth
- A picture of your ID/pass from work
- Your home address
- Your home phone number
- A picture of your driver's license, birth certificate, or any other form of identification
- Your Social Security number
- Any information related to your bank account or credit card numbers
- Any information that you would use to create a password, or to answer a security question for an online account
- A picture of your license plate
- A picture of the front of your house (this will give away your home address)
- Pictures from inside your office, especially those that contain anything proprietary or that are intellectual property

Quite often we don't think twice before sharing a post on social media. Taking an extra second before hitting the Tweet button to think whether this information could be used against you or your employer will reduce your risk drastically.

When it comes to anything related to security, if you aren't sure, ask the security team. They are there to advise you; it's literally their job.

Summary

It is extremely important that you manage your passwords and the passwords of others very carefully (that is, until we get rid of passwords entirely). Good practices include using a password manager (which requires only one passphrase in order to access all your passwords), removing complexity rules and password rotation requirements, and never reusing passwords. Use a passphrase for passwords that you *must* remember.

Enable multi-factor authentication on every account that is important to you or your employer. This second layer of defense is absolutely worth the extra effort it requires.

Talk to your incident response team at work, and ask them if they need anything of you. Practice fire drills on anything important, such as if a server melts down or how long it takes to restore backups of your database.

Scan all that can be scanned. Then fix the things you find.

Do your best to stop your team from accruing too much technical debt, even if you have to roll it into an upcoming project. And keep your application inventory up to date, so you know what you are protecting.

Lock your machine whenever you step away, and care for your work devices as if they are your very own. Also, respect your own privacy online because you never know when that photo may come back to haunt you. Think twice before you post.

Creating good habits doesn't take very much effort, and it will yield great results. Be a security advocate by making these small changes to your work routine.

Exercises

1. What are some of the risks of technical debt?

2. Should you post private information on social media if you only have friends following you?

3. Why are multi-factor authentication adoption rates so low? Name three ways we could increase adoption.

4. Which password manager do you use? (Note: "I don't use one" is the wrong answer here.)

5. Which security policy at your office makes it hard to get your job done? Have you spoken to the security team about updating it? Is there a potential compromise that could be made?

6. Name an activity you think might make a good "fire drill."

Continuous Learning

Continuous learning is the concept of constant skill and knowledge
development in response to changes in the workplace.[92]

Keeping yourself up to date with security industry changes and trends will
result in more effective use of your time on projects. It will give you something
very attractive to add to your resume, as well as impress your boss and co-workers,
and enable you to consistently create higher quality and more secure products.
Teaching yourself new things is also fun and challenging, making your work
life more interesting. There are only positive outcomes to continuous learning.

If you are a manager and you are creating a training program for your
employees, you will be happy to learn that regular training results in better
employee retention and high employee satisfaction. They will not only produce
better work, but they will keep working for you![92]

Continuous learning is the concept of always expanding your knowledge
to gain new skills and expertise. For businesses, continuous learning is
about encouraging employees to steadily learn by providing them with
the tools that facilitate this learning.[93]

What to Learn

You are already reading a book about application security, so I am going to assume that you want to learn more about this topic. When learning, it is critical that you focus your efforts because there are so many different resources that you will never be able to consume all of them.

First off, have you decided which area of application security interests you the most? Threat modeling? Security testing? Developer education? All of this will shape what you choose to concentrate on in your learning plan.

Offensive = Defensive

Quite often, our industry tends to focus on offensive security. You can find countless courses on how to "hack this" or "break that." This is strange, considering there are significantly more jobs in defense than in offense. Keep this in mind when you are choosing what to learn. Unless you are specializing in security testing, security research, or bug hunting, you do not need to memorize all of the different types of vulnerabilities, or how to do multiple types of exploits. If you want to learn those things, awesome! However, it is not necessary to memorize how to exploit 100 different types of security flaws in order to do most of the jobs within the field of application security.

You are able to focus your career and learning more or less on either defensive or offensive techniques if one interests you more than the other. There is no harm in favoring the one you prefer. That said, a *great* AppSec program covers both sides thoroughly.

Don't Forget Soft Skills

If you are going to work in application security, it is absolutely essential that you are able to communicate clearly and be able to see other people's viewpoints. If you are unable to understand that the developers have needs, deadlines, and policies to follow, you will not be their ally but their adversary. The same goes the other way: we must have empathy for the security team and their mandate if we are to work well together.

Also, get used to reading and writing reports. You will need to interpret the results of many different tools, summarize complex information, then communicate it to others. Being able to write clearly and understand the results from various tools and reports is a requirement to excel in this industry.

Perform a self-evaluation: do you feel there are areas that you are lacking in that you need to work on from a social- or soft-skill perspective? Add them to your learning plan. Learning these new skills will improve other areas of your life as well; you won't regret it!

THE VALUE OF SOFT SKILLS

After having worked with software developers and other IT professionals for over 25 years, Bob has seen his fair share of people who need to work on their soft skills. He's always found it annoying that some people seem to think if they have great technical skills, that they don't need to be polite or act professional in the workplace. Whenever he has been in a position where he is working with someone who just can't get along with others, he sends them on soft skills and communication training. Although at first the employee is usually upset with him, when they come back and they start making small improvements, bit by bit, Bob knows it was worth it. He's even had some of them tell him years later that it really improved their life and their interpersonal relationships outside of work. Sometimes being a project manager has been hard for Bob, but this decision has always proved a good one in his experience.

Make a list of all the different subjects that you want to learn for when you create your learning plan later in this chapter. Write them down.

Leadership != Management

Leadership training can help you in every aspect of your life. It teaches you how to take charge when you need to, as opposed to in every possible instance that you *could* or *just because you can*. It also teaches you how to effectively convince people to follow you, and help you achieve your missions. Leadership training is a worthwhile venture for almost anyone.

Leadership is not the same as management. Management is about how to supervise employees in a professional setting: how to be a boss. It will teach you how to track sick days, deal with employees who are insubordinate, and how to assign tasks. These are also valuable skills that you need to have if you want to have a management job someday.

Learning Options

There are many different ways to learn and many different resources, so this list will be extremely long.[94] It is crucial that you are selective, however, so that you don't waste your time. Think about the ways that you learn best, and that you enjoy, then choose those. Do not try to do all of these; you will exhaust yourself.

LUNCH AND LEARNS

Alice remembers when she was a policy analyst; she was promoted to team lead and instantly became frustrated with her team. They were behind the curve in her industry and she wanted them to learn new things, but she had no budget for training. She started a lunch and learn program and got people she knew from other companies (her friends) to come and speak to her team. They would show up at lunch and give a presentation while her team ate and learned. Most boardrooms were empty at lunch so it wasn't hard to find space. It ended up being really fun, and her team showed obvious improvement after only a few months. On top of that, Alice won an award for her workplace, *and* it was added to her performance review as a way that she went "above and beyond her duties" as an employee. She was overjoyed with the results, and so was her team.

ACTIVITIES YOU CAN DO ON YOUR OWN

Reading books, like *this one*

Follow blogs and/or authors on topics that interest you

Dive down rabbit holes with your favorite search engine when a topic strikes your fancy

Join an open source project to learn the tech they are using

Consider getting a certification and following the study program

Become involved in the InfoSec community: join a meetup, make friends, connect

Build stuff, attack it, then secure it again to improve your defenses

Participate in gamification; for instance, sign up for CTFs (Capture the Flag) or cyber range contests

Prepare podcasts or audiobooks to listen to during your commute to work or exercise routine

Develop your own network with others who are learning and share info within your group

Watch conference talks online, for free

Join discord or slack channels on topics that interest you

Follow prominent leaders in information security on social media, such as the author of this book (@shehackspurple)

Re-do previous tech training that you found effective; repeating it will likely teach you several new things that you forgot or missed

Complete courses from learning platforms such as Coursera, Udemy, and WeHackPurple.com

Create your own content (blogs, videos, workshops); the best way to cement your understanding of a topic is to teach someone else

Use #CyberMentoringMonday to find a professional mentor

Volunteer to help with a conference, then get in free

Subscribe to free newsletters on topics that interest you

Subscribe to paid content memberships platforms (like safari books online, plurralsight, `lynda.com`, and `wehackpurple.com`)

Use #AskInfoSec to find answers from the community

Don't forget your soft skills!

TEACHING OTHERS ON YOUR TEAM

Bob was in a meeting once with a bunch of software developers. The most senior software developer found out that a junior developer had been changing their code live on the server for over a year, without checking any of the changes into source control. The senior developer was very angry with the junior, explaining that using a cope repository was *necessary*, while the junior said they didn't understand and thought it was a waste of time. The discussion became heated. Bob told them all to stop yelling and told the senior developer to come back the next week with a full explanation as to why everyone had to use source control, and the value it provided. "Yelling that it's 'industry best practice' is not the way to convince your team." Although the senior employee seemed rather angry, the next week she came back with a full presentation about the value that source control provides, the risks involved of not using it, and persuaded all of the employees that it was in their best interest to use it. From then on, no one ever edited code live on the server.

ACTIVITIES YOU CAN DO AT WORK OR ASK YOUR BOSS ABOUT

Job-specific training via formal training at your workplace

Create a knowledgebase at work of all the tips and tricks you want to share with others, ask everyone to contribute

Attend conferences, ask for your boss to pay

Learn by teaching all the new people who join your team

Volunteer to give a talk to your team on something you want to learn, then you will *have* to go learn it. Teaching will teach it to you inside and out. Setting a date will put pressure on you. Some people really need the pressure.

Ask for the learning resources you want from your office training budget, such as books, subscriptions, and online courses

Create regular self-learning calendar blocks, perhaps two hours every week, then try to honor that time and use it for learning. Get your boss's permission.

Create your own learning plan and present it to your boss. Ask them to hold you accountable.

If your office has a Security Champions program, ask to become a champion

Volunteer for tasks at work to get experience with tech and activities that interest you

Ask if you are allowed to do job shadowing in your office of people in roles that interest you, or people in the same role as you who you want to learn from

Start a lunch and learn program at work, inviting experts who know about topics you are curious about

Join a mentoring program or start one, you will learn both by being mentored or being a mentor

Always ask questions. Always.

ACTIVITIES YOU CAN DO FOR YOUR EMPLOYEES

Hold open discussions or debates about various technologies or tech decisions with your team at work

Create rewards at for learning—include it as part of your performance reviews

Ask to have team building activities that are off site, to learn together

Share with the rest of your team when you solve a tough problem or learn something new

Some workplaces have programs that allow employees to work somewhere else for a short period of time, then come back with new lessons they've learned. If you have one, sign up!

Openly encourage your employees and teammates to learn more, and congratulate/compliment them when they do

Buy employees the learning resources that they want if you are a manager/able to do so

Create a learning plan with your employees, encourage them and check in on them every quarter

Create a chat group just for employees or your team to chat about the learning they are doing and encourage each other

Implement your own learning management system (LMS) at your office if you don't have one

Create a training team and program based off of your policies, standards, guidelines, and your business

Create onboarding training for new employees or team members

Accountability

A big obstacle for many people when it comes to learning is motivation. Only you can know what motivates you and the reason why you've decided to learn. That said, assigning yourself some accountability can definitely help ensure you stay on track to meet the goals that are important to you.

Some options for ensuring that you have accountability include:

- Finding a professional mentor. This will take career to the next level. If possible, find more than one.

- Having a friend agree to be your accountability partner, then having them prompt you and ask you about your studies.

- Making it a part of your official learning plan for work, so you *know* that you have to do it.

- Asking your boss to hold you accountable and check up on you.

- Giving yourself rewards when you reach milestones—for instance, "I get to have ice cream tonight only if I finish reading Chapter 10 of my book."

- Creating penalties for yourself if you do not reach your milestones—for instance, "If I do not finish reading chapter 10 by the end of the week, I will donate $50 to charity."

- Adding automated reminders—for instance adding a calendar reminder to "nag" you into doing the work.

Be creative with your ideas. Anything goes, as long as it works for you.

ACCOUNTABILITY

Whenever Alice creates a goal, she announces it on social media, tells all of her friends, and tells her parents. She does this because she knows she would be too embarrassed not to complete her goal if everyone knows about it. Whenever she feels tired, or she doesn't feel like doing her learning lesson for the day, she thinks about how embarrassed she would be to tell her mom that she never actually finished. She thinks about people on social media knowing that she said she would do it, but then she failed. Then she continues. She knows they won't actually get upset with her for not finishing, but telling them makes her feel *accountable*. This trick has worked wonders for Alice; she always reaches her goals. It's the motivation that always keeps her going.

Create Your Plan

The most vital step when creating a plan for learning is that you reserve time to do it regularly. If you cram everything you can into the first week, it is likely that you will be tired and less motivated by the second week, and potentially not interested at all by the third week. Planning for realistic and regular learning sessions will ensure you are successful. Put it in your calendar if you have one!

How do you learn best? There are several different learning styles, but the most obvious ones are reading, listening, watching, writing, and doing. Does one (or more) of these stand out to you as the "right" way for you? Plan your training resources around what works best for you.

Identify what you already know, and where you need improvement. This can help set your direction as well.

At the end of this chapter is a learning plan that you can copy and fill out as many times as you wish. It will help you shape your learning and make a plan that you can stick to.

WE ALL NEED DIRECTION

At one point Bob decided that he wanted to become an ethical hacker. He had no idea where to start, so he read every book he could find. He read all the blogs, he watched random videos, he had no direction. He spent countless hours and discovered that he didn't even qualify as a script kiddie yet. He gave up. When he was older, he learned a lot about how he learns, and also that it's valuable to create a plan before you start out, which he used when he became a project manager. He knew what his goal was, he gathered a list of all the things he needed to learn, obtained a certification that he wanted to get, then made his plan. He executed the plan, passed the exam, and now works full time as a project manager! If only it had been that easy when he wanted to become a penetration tester...

Take Action

Now that you have learned a lot about studying, it is time to take some *action*. Start with doing the exercises in the next section of this chapter, then *actually* photocopy and fill out the learning plan. Then *do* the learning plan. Print copies of the learning plan and sign it, then show it to someone who will hold you accountable for best results.

You will never regret learning a new skill. You will never feel your time is wasted if you have reached your goal. If you've picked up this book and read this far, you are clearly very serious about learning. Fill out the learning plan and *start now*.

Exercises

1. Get ready to create a learning plan for yourself for the next year.
   - Which books will you read?
   - Will you attend a conference? Name the one you want.
   - Will you join a professional organization or other professional community? Name it.
   - Will you listen to podcasts? Which ones?
   - Attend meetups? Which ones?

- Will you create your own project for learning or do a CTF or other hands-on activity? Which ones?
- Will you attend formal training?

2. How will you make time for this in your life? Will your boss give you time? Will you carve our personal time? What priority will you give this in your life?

3. List three new things you want to learn this year and why.

4. Name three things that if you learned would make you better at your job.

5. How do you learn best? Reading? Listening? Doing? Watching? Another way? Explain your learning style as best you can.

6. What motivates you to learn? Rewards? Recognition? Extra leisure time? Sweet desserts? Think of what motivates you and how you can use this to ensure you keep learning, all year round.

7. What format works best for you to absorb information? Class time? Job shadowing? Mentoring? Contests? Name your favorite formats.

8. Where will you do your learning? At home? At work? At a café near your house on Saturdays? Will you use your work laptop or home PC? What equipment do you need? Where will you carve out space for this? You need to know when and where you will do your learning.

9. How will you get access to the resources you need to learn? Are they free (podcasts)? Will you be able to convince your workplace to pay? Are there ways that you can pay on your own? Create a budget at the end of your learning plan (next page).

Learning Plan

Name: _____

Subject/topics to learn/event to attend:_____

Resources required: _____

Time/schedule for learning: _____

Format(s) of learning: _____

Budget required and how you will get it: _____

Accountability plan: _____

    I, _____ (your name), pledge to learn this subject/topic by _____ (date you will reach your goal).

_____ (signature)

Closing Thoughts

"Security is everybody's job."
—Tanya Janca

It is every person's responsibility to perform their job functions in the most secure way they know how; otherwise we are breaking the trust of our employer. If there are security policies in our workplace, just like any other policy of our organization, we *must* abide by them. When we are hired, our employers trust us to do the best work we can, in good faith, and this includes security-related work.

If you work in a security role, you know better than anyone else that we cannot possibly perform all of the security work on behalf of everyone in our organization. We cannot be there every moment when security work needs to be performed. For instance, we can't be there every time an employee decides if they will allow someone to tailgate them into the building; we can't be there when they choose weak or strong passwords; we aren't watching over their shoulders as they code to make sure they follow our guidelines. It's impossible to verify every single action taken that applies to security, no matter how hard we try. This means we have to educate and then trust that employees have honest intentions and do their best to perform their jobs in the safest and most secure way possible. We trust them to help secure our organization, systems, data, customers, and employees.

Some argue that "if security is everybody's job, then it's nobody's job," but this could not be further from the truth. Someone on the security team will make the office badges, implement the SCA tool, or write a security policy. The average employee does the corresponding security work: using the badge to get into the building, fixing the code by using the results of the SCA scans, obeying the security policy. The security team provides leadership, guidance, and tools;

the employees use these to get their jobs done securely. The security team also sometimes has to pick up the slack (helping to complete the security work), react to feedback (adjusting policy or processes), and do their best to ensure they support the entire organization in meeting their policies and guidelines. It's a team effort.

When writing software, this rule becomes even more exaggerated. Every developer is relied upon to write the best code they can, to participate in security activities when required, to act upon the results of various tools, and to alert the security team to issues they see that they would never see on their own. If your code is not part of the protection of your organization, then it is most likely a weakness that endangers it.

The work of securing your establishment is in the everyday decisions and actions made by all employees, not just the ones on the security team. We all work together to protect our organization; the security team is just providing tools, resources, and leadership toward that end goal, enabling everyone else.

We cannot succeed unless most or all employees are on board; we *must* work together. Adopting the attitude that security is everyone's responsibility and a part of every person's job is the best way to do this.

Lingering Questions

After reading this book you may be left with some aching questions:

- When have you done *enough*?
- How do you get management on board?
- How do you get developers on board?
- Where do you start?
- Where do you get help?

Let's go through these questions one at a time before we send you on your way to fight the world's AppSec battles.

When Have You Done *Enough*?

If you work in an organization that has no security program or very poor security hygiene, anything you do is an improvement. It's very easy to look good for your bosses, as there are countless opportunities for progress.

What happens when you are at an organization with a very advanced security program? When everyone is on board, has been for years, and all the process are working well? How do you know when to stop?

The least satisfying but most correct answer is "it depends."

> **TIP** An organization's "risk appetite" is how much risk they are willing to accept as an organization. For instance, a small startup might be okay with taking big risks, while a very large or bureaucratic organization is more likely to shy away from dicey decisions.

It depends on the value of the assets that you are protecting; you probably don't want to spend a million dollars protecting something worth a hundred thousand dollars.

It depends on the level of risk that the organization is comfortable with. Are they okay with making big technology changes, or do they wait until the rest of industry has adopted it first? Do they make decisions fast, or slow? Do they have heavy processes with multiple layers of approval, or is it a trust-based culture? The answers to these questions and more can help you understand how much risk they are comfortable with, and that will help you know how many more layers of defense are required.

It depends on the sensitivity level of the data and systems you are protecting. For instance, if the system contains valuable intellectual property or government secrets, or if the system itself is keeping a person alive (such as Bob's pacemaker).

It depends on budget. Any company can write on their website "We take your security seriously," but if they only give you a tiny budget and no staff, their prioritization of security is *not* serious.

It depends on how much buy-in you have from upper management and other teams' leaders. If upper management says they want to be PCI compliant, then you need to get them there. If they say they want you to present a plan and budget for launching a new AppSec program, then you need to re-read Chapter 7. If they say they want security testing on the new TV they have designed, but then give you almost no time to do the testing, this also speaks volumes. Talk to upper management and ask them what they need from you before you decide that you've "done enough."

RISK ADVERSE

Alice used to work for a bank. They were terrified of making any changes, to the point where it was actually causing risk. They would wait and wait to upgrade frameworks, try new technologies, or update their security controls, sometimes until it was too late. They still had mainframes for their most critical systems, and they were held back from modernizing their banking systems as a result. It didn't matter how many advantages Alice told them about. . .They were too afraid of change.

A SPECIAL NOTE FOR CONSULTANTS

If you are performing a security audit, assessment, or penetration test as a consultant, you likely have limited time to complete the deliverables for your contract. Many consultants say they've "done enough when the contract is over"; that's all the client paid for, so that's all they get.

As an alternative, you could make a list of all the items that you feel need to be done in order to secure their systems, and which parts you were unable to complete during your contract. This might be a suggestion that security testing is required on the APIs that were not in scope of the test, that a code review is required for certain security functions, or that a stress test is advised as this is a huge risk for their specific business model. It could be that they should consider creating an AppSec team and launching a program. Even work that you would not be able to provide to the client should be on the list. Then allow your client to decide if they choose to ignore your recommendations or not. You don't have to do the entire list, but at least you've communicated what you feel "done" would truly look like. This is often referred to as a "gap assessment."

When deciding what items you want to add to your gap assessment you can use checklists such as ASVS (OWASP Application Security Verification Standard), MASVS (Mobile ASVS from OWASP), WSTG (OWASP Web Security Testing Guide), MSTG (Mobile version of WSTG), etc., to ensure you haven't missed anything important for your client. Creating a template in advance will make this a low-effort activity that would provide excellent value to your clients.

It may also result in more contracts.

How Do You Get Management on Board?

If you work in a place where no one takes security seriously, it can be an extremely frustrating experience. Spending 50 percent of your time negotiating, begging, and pleading to get your work done is not going to lead to high job satisfaction.

There are a few options for trying to get management and/or other teams on board the application security train if you are finding their lack of cooperation a problem.

First, try to attract bees with honey. Hold lunch and learns, give presentations, and share reports about the security issues your org is facing. Educating others is an excellent way to draw people to your cause. Also, showing up to meetings and just "being there" can let people know they have help if they need it. You will often add value to discussions whether you mean to or not.

Second, explain risk in ways that anyone can understand. Don't say "It's a CVE with the highest risk score!" Instead say "This vulnerability in the Java Struts framework allows attackers to take over web servers with only one line of code if they are vulnerable. This means a malicious actor would be inside of our network, past the firewall, and be able to attack our resources directly. We *are* vulnerable, I checked. I need permission to create a virtual patch using our

RASP to block attacks that look like this, and I need your help to test it to make sure I get it right. Are you with me?" Who could possibly say no to that? If you feel the sky is falling, but you aren't getting buy-in, it's often a communication issue.

Another option to get buy-in is to create a proof of concept (POC) of the problem you are concerned about. Not using security headers? Let me show you our website, framed, making it simple for an attacker to steal credentials of our users. Creating a proof of concept of an exploit for a vulnerability that no one wants to fix is a great way to get that issues back to the top of the list in the bug tracker. That said, this is a rather time-consuming approach and you need to ensure that you have approval before you do it, so use it sparingly.

The last idea that we will present here is the Risk Sign Off Sheet, which I invented it out of frustration of not having my PenTest reports actioned. The Risk Sign Off document details all of the outstanding vulnerabilities from security testing engagements, what the related business risk is, then asks the highest ranking security leader for the organization—usually the Chief Information Security Officer (CISO) or the Chief Security Officer (CSO)—to sign that they "accept the risk." The purpose of the document is to make it clear they have been informed of what's happening, and that their inaction is acceptance of these risks. You will not take the fall if a breach happens, they will. Or they can give you the authority to force other teams to fix the issues.

As far as I know, no one has ever signed such a document; everyone who I know of who has used this tactic has always given authority to push through the required changes.

> **TIP** Only use this last method if you are in dire need. You can only pull this type of stunt once.

How Do You Get Developers on Board?

Software developers are builders; they literally make something out of nothing, every day. Most of them are proud of what they create, and they *want* their apps to be secure. Developers do not write insecure code on purpose; they either don't know any better or they aren't given the time and resources to do it right.

Since programmers want to create high-quality software, and you can't have high quality if an app is insecure, getting them on board isn't that difficult. There are three areas you need to address—knowledge, understanding, and resources:

- **Knowledge**: As discussed earlier, most programming courses and training don't teach developers how to create secure software. This is where you come in; teach them! Educate them on what they need to know in order to do their jobs. Send them on training. Buy them books (like this one, yes, buy them this one). Do everything you can to give them the knowledge they need to create the most secure software possible.

- **Understanding**: All of IT needs to understand security's priorities, needs, and mandate. If a software developer understands the importance of what you ask, they are much more likely to adopt it as part of their priorities. Don't tell them what to do, show them why it's necessary and then teach them how.

- **Resources**: Bugs aren't fixed in a scheduling vacuum. Software developers need time allotted in project schedules to perform security activities, otherwise they don't get done. They also need tools, reference materials, and sometimes an extra set of hands. It is your job to enable developers to create secure software, and sometimes this means rolling up your sleeves and spending a few days fixing security bugs in order to help them meet a deadline. Give them what they need, then sit back and watch them transform.

Where Do You Start?

You've just read a book about application security, so you have already started down the path toward more secure software.

If you are a software developer, at this point you will want to start making changes at work, implementing what you've learned. Apply the secure coding guide, secure design, and security requirements to every project going forward. Introduce yourself to the security team and ask if they need a new champion. Always search how to code things in the most secure way possible, rather than copying and pasting the top search result.

If you are an application security professional, use what you've learned to reevaluate your current AppSec program. What are your goals? Are you reaching them? What new activities or tools do you want to add? Are you taking measurements regularly? If not, start now, and update your program. Also, share what you've learned with your security champions; they would likely appreciate new lessons from you.

If you are hoping to work in application security, this is the start of your journey. To help you figure out which specific job interests you most in our field, and the steps to get there, I have created an ongoing live stream series, every Thursday at 6 p.m. Pacific time on YouTube, called "We Hack Purple: Finding your career in Information Security." All episodes are saved to the We Hack Purple YouTube channel permanently. Watch any of the episodes based on job titles that you might be interested in to see interviews with various industry experts about what it's like to do that job, the education required, and how to get started.

You will also want to check out the various security communities, make friends, and join the fun. There's always something new to learn, and the InfoSec community always needs new members.

Where Do You Get Help?

When you are stuck, there are several options in information security.

First off, you will want to try to solve the problem yourself. Always ask your favorite search engine before asking someone else. Next ask people on your team at work if the issue is work related. You always want to try to work on the problem yourself first; troubleshoot all your ideas.

The second step is to expand your search to a larger circle. Ask your professional mentor and/or others in your network that you know and trust. If you are part of a meetup, message someone from the group or ask during their next event. You should also try asking your favorite search engine in new ways, since you likely have more information by this point.

The third step is to further expand your search by asking the community. Post a question on Twitter using #askinfosec or put a post on LinkedIn and tag trusted friends to expand your reach. Reach out to communities like OWASP, We Hack Purple, DevOpsDays, and others that run online chats and other events you can learn from or network in.

If you still can't find the answer, at this point it might become a research project. If you eventually find the answer, make sure you share the information online with others. This helps everyone.

Conclusion

Thank you for reading this book; you are now ready to fight the good fight. All of the lessons that you have learned will most certainly ensure you are now able to create much, much more secure software from now on. Spending the time to consume the knowledge in this book shows your commitment to learning, and your prioritization of this topic. Please use this information to help others, so that we can all live in a more secure world.

We, the security team, are depending on each and every one of you. Don't let us down.

Resources

Introduction

1. Verizon Breach Report 2016, 2017, 2018

Chapter 1: Security Fundamentals

2. "There are two types of companies: those that have been breached and those that don't know they've been breached yet." `time.com/3404330/home-depot-hack`

3. "Between 30 percent to 70 percent of the code in applications come from third parties." `www.infoworld.com/article/2626167/third-party-code-putting-companies-at-risk.html`

4. Supply chain attack example: `www.trendmicro.com/vinfo/hk-en/security/news/cybercrime-and-digital-threats/hacker-infects-node-js-package-to-steal-from-bitcoin-wallets`

Chapter 2: Security Requirements

5. "Injection" vulnerability and has been widely recognized by security professionals as the #1 threat to secure software:

    `www.owasp.org/index.php/Top_10-2017_A1-Injection`

    `www.owasp.org/index.php/Top_10_2013-A1-Injection`

    `www.owasp.org/index.php/Top_10_2010-A1-Injection`

6. Output encoding and preventing XSS: `portswigger.net/web-security/cross-site-scripting/preventing`

7. Bounds Checking: `en.wikipedia.org/wiki/Bounds_checking`

8. Integer Overflow: `en.wikipedia.org/wiki/Integer_overflow`

9. Buffer Overflow: `en.wikipedia.org/wiki/Buffer_overflow`

10. XSS Prevention Cheat Sheet: `owasp.org/www-project-cheat-sheets/cheatsheets/Cross_Site_Scripting_Prevention_Cheat_Sheet.html`

11. Rust is memory-safe: `acks.mozilla.org/2019/02/rewriting-a-browser-component-in-rust`

12. OWASP Top Ten 2017: 77% of apps have XSS in them. `www.ptsecurity.com/ww-en/analytics/web-application-vulnerabilities-statistics-2019`

13. Mitre's CVE database: `cve.mitre.org`

14. POST requests are still vulnerable to this type of attack, although significantly more difficult to exploit: `developer.mozilla.org/en-US/docs/Web/HTTP/Headers/X-XSS-Protection`

15. Clickjacking: `portswigger.net/web-security/clickjacking`

16. Preload HSTS Suffix: `developer.mozilla.org/en-US/docs/Web/HTTP/Headers/Strict-Transport-Security#Preloading_Strict_Transport_Security`

17. Feature-Policy allow lists: `developer.mozilla.org/en-US/docs/Web/HTTP/Headers/Feature-Policy`

18. Nugget Package: `www.nuget.org/packages/NWebsec.AspNetCore.Middleware`

19. Same-Site 'Lax' Defaults:

    a. `web.dev/samesite-cookies-explained/#changes-to-the-default-behavior-without-samesite`

    b. `tools.ietf.org/html/draft-west-cookie-incrementalism-00`

20. Work Factor & Pepper: `cheatsheetseries.owasp.org/cheatsheets/Password_Storage_Cheat_Sheet.html#work-factors`

21. Deep Packet Inspection: `en.wikipedia.org/wiki/Deep_packet_inspection`

22. Technical debt: `en.wikipedia.org/wiki/Technical_debt`

Chapter 3: Secure Design

23. "Secure by Design": `Wikipedia.org`

24. Article from Slashdot; bug cost $1 to fix, while in design $10, coding $100, and in testing $1000: `developers.slashdot.org/story/03/10/21/0141215/software-defects---do-late-bugs-really-cost-more`

25. Canadian Center for Cyber Security: `cyber.gc.ca`

26. Luxemburg: `www.circl.lu`

27. Japan: `www.jpcert.or.jp/english/at/2020.html`

28. United Kingdom (Threat Reports): `www.ncsc.gov.uk`

29. United State of America: `www.us-cert.gov/ncas/alerts`

30. New Zealand (Advisories): `www.cert.govt.nz/it-specialists`

31. `ITSG-33`: `www.cse-cst.gc.ca/sites/default/files/itsg33-ann4a-eng.xls`

32. NIST's Special Publication 800-53 S-3: `nvd.nist.gov/800-53/Rev4/control/SC-3`

33. NIST's Special Publication 800-53 S-2: `nvd.nist.gov/800-53/Rev4/control/SC-2`

34. Cross Site Request Forgery (CSRF): `www.owasp.org/index.php/Cross-Site_Request_Forgery_(CSRF)`

35. Open VS close source: `www.researchgate.net/publication/220891308_Security_of_Open_Source_and_Closed_Source_Software_An_Empirical_Comparison_of_Published_Vulnerabilities`

36. Shortage of InfoSec People: `www.infosecurity-magazine.com/news/cybersecurity-skills-shortage-tops`

37. High Paying: `www.mondo.com/blog-highest-paid-cybersecurity-jobs`

38. Attack trees: `en.wikipedia.org/wiki/Attack_tree`

39. STRIDE: `en.wikipedia.org/wiki/STRIDE_%28security%29`

40. PASTA: `www.owasp.org/images/a/aa/AppSecEU2012_PASTA.pdf`

Chapter 4: Secure Code

41. Struts vulnerabilities 2016: `www.securitymetrics.com/blog/apache-struts-vulnerability-what-you-should-do`

42. OWASP Cheat Sheets Session Management: `owasp.org/www-project-cheat-sheets/cheatsheets/Session_Management_Cheat_Sheet`

43. "Smashing The Stack For Fun And Profit": `www-inst.eecs.berkeley.edu/~cs161/fa08/ papers/stack_smashing.pdf`

44. Types of Access Control, OWASP Cheat Sheet: `cheatsheetseries.owasp.org/cheatsheets/Access_Control_Cheat_Sheet.html`

45. Logging attacks (3 sources):
    a. `owasp.org/www-community/attacks/Log_Injection`
    b. `www.sans.org/blog/what-works-in-appsec-log-forging`
    c. `github.com/votd/vulnerability-of-the-day/wiki/Log-Overflow`

46. OWASP Cheat Sheet Error Handling: `cheatsheetseries.owasp.org/cheatsheets/Error_Handling_Cheat_Sheet.html`

47. OWASP Cheat Sheet Logging: `cheatsheetseries.owasp.org/cheatsheets/Logging_Cheat_Sheet.html`

48. X-Forwarded-For header: Dominique Righetto provided evidence

49. PII: `en.wikipedia.org/wiki/Personal_data`

Chapter 5: Common Pitfalls

50. OWASP Cheat Sheet CSRF: `cheatsheetseries.owasp.org/cheatsheets/Cross-Site_Request_Forgery_Prevention_Cheat_Sheet.html`

51. SSRF:
    a. `owasp.org/www-community/attacks/Server_Side_Request_Forgery`
    b. `portswigger.net/web-security/ssrf`

52. SSRF: `www.darkreading.com/edge/theedge/ssrf-101-how-server-side-request-forgery-sneaks-past-your-web-apps-/b/d-id/1337121`

53. SSRF: `www.acunetix.com/blog/articles/server-side-request-forgery-vulnerability`

54. Deserialization: `cheatsheetseries.owasp.org/cheatsheets/Deserialization_Cheat_Sheet.html`

55. HMAC SHA256: `cryptobook.nakov.com/mac-and-key-derivation`

Chapter 6: Testing and Deployment

56. Symbolic Execution: `en.wikipedia.org/wiki/Symbolic_execution`

57. SCA definition: `www.flexerasoftware.com/blog/what-is-software-composition-analysis`

58. Unit Testing: `softwaretestingfundamentals.com/unit-testing`

59. XSS Evasion Cheat Sheet: `owasp.org/www-community/xss-filter-evasion-cheatsheet`

60. IaC: `en.wikipedia.org/wiki/Infrastructure_as_code`

61. SaC: `www.oreilly.com/library/view/devopssec/9781491971413/ch04.html`

62. Fuzzing: `en.wikipedia.org/wiki/Fuzzing`

63. IAST:
    a. `www.veracode.com/security/interactive-application-security-testing-iast`

    b. `www.contrastsecurity.com/knowledge-hub/glossary/interactive-application-security-testing`

64. Regression Testing: `en.wikipedia.org/wiki/Regression_testing`

Chapter 7: An AppSec Program

65. Shadow IT: `en.wikipedia.org/wiki/Shadow_IT`

66. Time to detect breach: `www.varonis.com/blog/data-breach-response-times`

67. Metrics definition: `www.lexico.com/en/definition/metrics`

68. DevOps Handbook, purchase direct from the authors: `itrevolution.com/book/the-devops-handbook`

69. The Lean Startup: `theleanstartup.com/book`

Chapter 8: Securing Modern Applications and Systems

70. Isolated function perimeters: Reference: Snyk: `snyk.io/blog/10-serverless-security-best-practices`

71. Apply least privilege to serverless config: `www.serverless.com/blog/serverless-deployment-best-practices`

72. CI/CD scans: `blog.checkpoint.com/2020/04/29/9-serverless-security-best-practices-you-must-read`

73. Traffic profiling tools: `www.esecurityplanet.com/cloud/data-storage-security.html`

74. Resource limiting and alerting for containers: `kubernetes.io/docs/concepts/policy/resource-quotas`

75. Don't run containers as root: `resources.whitesourcesoftware.com/blog-whitesource/docker-container-security-challenges-and-best-practices`

76. Definition of 'Toil': Steven Murawski Microsoft Ignite the Tour 2019: talk "Infrastructure as Code"

77. Code is single source of truth: `stackify.com/what-is-infrastructure-as-code-how-it-works-best-practices-tutorials`

78. Be careful who you allow to create IaC: `techbeacon.com/enterprise-it/infrastructure-code-engine-heart-devops`

79. Immutable: `www.thorntech.com/2018/02/infrastructure-as-code-best-practices`

80. Security As Code: `www.bmc.com/blogs/security-as-code`

81. CI/CD definition: Steven Murawski, Microsoft Ignite the Tour 2019

82. The Three Ways of DevOps: `itrevolution.com/wp-content/uploads/files/PhoenixProjectExcerpt.pdf`

83. Wrapper Libraries: Justine Osborne, Zane Lackey, Clint Gibler and Doug DePerry on panel at DevSecCon Virtual 2020. "ThisIsWhyWe CantHaveNiceThings" joke by Justine.

84. Definition of DevSecOps: Imran A Mohammed of Practical DevSecOps

85. Cloud Computing: `en.wikipedia.org/wiki/Cloud_computing`

86. Part of Cloud Native Definition: `www.infoworld.com/article/3281046/what-is-cloud-native-the-modern-way-to-develop-software.html`

87. Part of Cloud Native Definition: `thenewstack.io/10-key-attributes-of-cloud-native-applications`

88. Part of Cloud Native Definition: David Blank-Edelman & Jennifer Davis, Microsoft Ignite the Tour 2019

Chapter 9: Good Habits

89. Topmost voted solution is least secure: example `stackoverflow.com/a/14968272/451455`

90. Length and Entropy: `en.wikibooks.org/wiki/Cryptography/Key_Lengths`

91. Origin of passwords: `theconversation.com/the-long-history-and-short-future-of-the-password-76690`

Chapter 10: Continuous Learning

92. Continuous learning definition #1: `www.ispringsolutions.com/blog/continuous-learning`

93. Continuous learning definition #2: `www.learnupon.com/blog/continuous-learning`

94. List of learning resources partially from @shehackspurple Twitter feed

Answer Key

You can participate live in open dialogue online or view the videos afterward to discuss all of the exercises from this book. We don't want to leave you hanging!

Subscribe to the SheHacksPurple Newsletter for invites to the live discussions, `newsletter.shehackspurple.ca`, and subscribe to the SheHacksPurple YouTube channel to view the videos afterward: `youtube.com/shehackspurple`.

Chapter 1: Security Fundamentals

1. Bob sets the Wi-Fi setting on his pacemaker to not broadcast the name of his Wi-Fi. What is this defensive strategy called?

   Security by obscurity

2. Name an example of a value that could be hardcoded and why. (What would be the motivation for the programmer to do that?)

   Back in the day, the author used to hardcode connection strings for dev, QA, and prod environments so she could switch them when testing. She had no idea the security problems she caused as a dev so many years ago.

3. Is a captcha *usable* security? Why or why not?

No, it is not. Captchas are very difficult for people who are visually disabled to use, and even for fully abled people at times. They are annoying and bothersome as well; users detest them.

4. Give one example of a good implementation of usable security.

The password manager called 1Password can also be used as an MFA authenticator, meaning it will generate that code you get and need to enter into a site as an MFA challenge. It automatically copies it to your clipboard as soon as you have entered your username and password, so you can paste it directly in. After you've pasted it and have logged in to the site successfully, it replaces what was previously on the clipboard, in case you needed it. *That* is usable security. They are trying (and in the author's opinion succeeding) to make MFA challenges less time consuming, less unpleasant, and less error prone. It's still very secure, but much easier for the user.

5. When using information from the URL parameters do you need to validate that data? Why or why not?

Data in the URL parameters can easily be changed by the user and is therefore not trustworthy. If the user happens to be in a public café, and your website is not available over HTTPS, an attacker could easily change the parameters in an MITM attack (Man-In-The-Middle or Manipulator-In-The-Middle). There are many other situations that could lead to those inputs being changed, maliciously or even accidentally, that could cause those values to be dangerous to your application. Always validate *all* input.

6. If an employee learns a trade secret at work and then sells it to a competitor, this breaks which part(s) of CIA?

Confidentiality. They will most certainly have violated their terms of employment, any non-disclosure documents they have signed, and very likely the law.

7. If you buy a "smart" refrigerator and connect it to your home network, then have a malicious actor connect to it and change the settings so that it's slightly warmer and your milk goes bad, which part(s) of CIA did they break?

Integrity, because the data is still available, and the data may still have remained confidential (and likely the setting was not considered a secret), but changing the setting to an incorrect/damaging setting breaks the pillar of Integrity.

8. If someone hacks your smart thermostat and turns off your heat, which part(s) of CIA did they break?

Availability, because your heat is not available to you. Hopefully you don't live in Ottawa, Canada, and if you do, that it's not February!

9. If a programmer adds an Easter egg (extra code that does undocumented functionality, as a "surprise" for users, which is unknown to management and the security team), does this qualify as an insider threat? If so, why? If not, why not?

    Yes, this is an insider threat. Practical jokes that happen inside your company and only affect those who work there can be fun and playful. Unapproved features or "surprise" functionality is a security team's worst nightmare.

10. When connecting to a public Wi-Fi, what are some of the precautions that you could take to ensure you are doing "defense in depth"?

    You can ensure you only visit websites via HTTPS, so that your traffic is encrypted. You can use a VPN (virtual private network), which creates a "tunnel" to either a safe network or your work network (usually). You can install antivirus or antimalware on your machine. You could decide to just use your cellular data instead, if you feel the network you are joining may be particularly dangerous (for instance, if the café was in Las Vegas during Def Con).

11. If you live in an apartment with several roommates and you all have a key to the door, is one of the keys considered to be a "factor of authentication"?

    No. The key identifies you as someone who lives at the apartment, but not which one of you it is. Authentication needs to identify an individual, not a member of a group.

Chapter 2: Security Requirements

1. List two more potential security requirements for a web application (which are not already listed).

    1) Password resets for users cannot be done more than one time in a 24-hour period.

    2) Each API must connect using its own service account; they cannot share.

2. List two more potential security requirements for an operating system in a car.

    1) If brakes, airbag, or any engine functionality has been tampered with, send an alert to the user and their designated garage immediately. Do not allow the car to drive until an authorized mechanic has issued an override command.

2) Each driver of the car must have their own key to identify them, plus another factor of authentication (specifically a thumb print) in order to start the car. All other potential drivers are rejected.

3. List two more potential security requirements for a "smart" toaster.

    1) Toaster cannot go over X degrees in temperature, if so, issue an alert and issue a shutdown override.

    2) Toaster admin module requires a second factor of authentication in order to override temperature settings to above manufacturer's recommended guidance.

4. List two more potential security requirements for an application that handles credit cards.

    1) Application must be PCI (Payment Card Industry) compliant.

    2) The database that contains the credit card information must be labeled "confidential," only one service account (the application's) can access it, unauthorized access attempts are logged and alerted upon, and access to this database is audited manually on a monthly basis.

5. Which security requirement is the most valuable? Why is it the most valuable one to you and/or your organization?

    I would select **"Trust no one: validate (and sanitize if special circumstances apply) all data, even from your own database."** I firmly believe that if every application performed strict input validation, the internet would instantly be a much safer place.

6. If you had to remove one of the requirements from this chapter from a web app project, which one would it be? Why?

    I would remove HTTPS, because I know the business would put it back in. Browsers will stop users from visiting sites that do not have HTTPS on their sites, and from a business perspective that just will not fly. Thus, I would choose that one.

Chapter 3: Secure Design

1. When should data be encrypted? (Select all that apply.)

    A) When an API sends data to another API

    B) On a virtual machine that is powered off

    C) When stored in a database

    D) When sent from the server to the browser

    All of them

2. What are some possible ways that we can ensure the third-party components we use are secure? How can we minimize risk in this area?

We can either review each one of them manually or use a software composition analysis tool.

3. Where should you store your application's secrets? How should your
application access your secrets?

Using a secret store to hold your application's secrets is the best way to
access and store your secrets safely (credentials, passwords, hashes, connection strings, etc.).

4. Name three types of "secrets."

Credentials (username and password), connection strings, passwords,
hashes.

5. What are some of the potential threats that a mobile banking application
would face? Name three threats and rate how likely they are to occur and
how damaging they are based on a scale of low, medium, and high.

1) People will try to log in as someone else by brute forcing credentials.

Likelihood: High

Risk: High

Mitigation to make the risk low: Block after 10 attempts.

2) Credential stuffing attacks (using stolen/breached credentials).

Likelihood: High

Risk: Critical

Mitigation: Enforce MFA for users, sign up for a service that will alert
your company when your user's credentials on other sites have been
breached so you can force reset, allow use of password managers and
"copy and paste" on password fields, do not force password rotation or
security questions.

3) Users attempting to create race conditions so they can "multiply" their
money.

Likelihood: Low

Risk: Medium

Mitigation: Test thoroughly for race conditions and implement "locking"
on bank balances while performing such transactions.

6. Name three threats that could apply to a "smart" car. Rate the threats (low,
medium or high) in terms of likelihood and potential damage.

1) Car operating system crashes, causing the owner to be unable to use their car. Threat to availability.

Likelihood: Low

Potential Damage: Very angry users who need to go somewhere but cannot. This would cause harm to the company's reputation.

2) Car operating system contracts a virus or malware.

Likelihood: Low

Potential Damage: Very angry users who need to go somewhere but cannot. Could potentially attempt to ransom the control of the car to the user. This would cause harm to the company's reputation.

3) Car's GPS data and other data is stolen. Threat to confidentiality.

Likelihood: Low

Potential Damage: Harm to company's reputation, potential great harm to the user. If the owner of the car goes to secret military bases, or has a stalker, their whereabouts could be very sensitive information.

7. Name five different types of security functionality that would potentially be offered in a modern framework.

1) Authorization

2) Authentication

3) Access Control

4) Anti-CSRF token passing

5) Input validation functions

Chapter 4: Secure Code

1. When should you use your own identity on the network (user account) versus a service account? Give two examples for each and explain your reasoning.

User Account:

1) To read your email

2) To access company files and log in to systems to use as an employee

Service Account:

1) To access the database from a web application

2) To access online storage from an API

2. Explain possible reasons or situations why C and C++ are still widely used in our industry when Rust (a memory-safe language) exists. Try to think of two or more.

   1) Companies don't have the money to re-write everything into a brand-new language just because it will be better for security. Budgets exist for a reason.

   2) Hiring Rust programmers may be more difficult than C/C++.

   3) Not everyone has heard of Rust and its benefits.

   4) "Because that's the way we've always done it." Which is *always* the wrong answer, no matter the question.

3. What is your favorite programming language and/or framework, and why?

   I prefer .Net, because I had the most experience with it, it's well supported, there is tons of documentation available, and it's a very secure framework.

4. Which programming language and/or framework do you think is the most secure? Why?

   I would select .Net, because 1) I used to work at Microsoft and have first-hand knowledge of how seriously they take security, 2) because it is maintained by a company (rather than volunteers), there is more time and attention dedicated to it and it will never be "dropped" or left unmaintained, and 3) because it is proprietary, which means no one but a Microsoft employee could work on it, unlike open source frameworks. Each employee passes background checks and is given ethics and security training on a regular basis, ensuring the best possible outcome. People working on open source projects are rarely under such scrutiny before they are given access to the code.

   That said, you can still use lots of open source.

5. Why do we need to protect user sessions?

   An unprotected user session can be "hijacked," meaning a malicious actor could take it over and use the system as though they are you. With that power they could empty your bank account, order ugly shoes that you don't approve of, or use your Twitter account to ask people to send you bitcoin (but the bitcoin wallet, of course, is theirs, not yours). The possibilities are endless.

6. If an attacker were able to get a hold of someone else's user session while they are logged in to their online banking, what could the attacker do?

They can send your money anywhere they want, including to a terrorist group in order to frame you for a crime. A creative malicious actor can do quite a bit of damage in a short amount of time, with your user session.

7. If you were going to explain the difference between authentication and authorization to a non-technical co-worker, how would you explain it?

   Authentication is a computer verifying you are the real you (and not someone else pretending to be you). Authorization is a computer deciding what you can and cannot do in its systems.

8. Should C-level executives have special privileges on your network and other computer systems? If so, why? If not, why not? What types of privileges would you give them, if you gave them any?

   C-level executives will often argue that they "deserve" special systems and network access, but often there is no technical reason that they need them. As they are often the targets of spear-phishing campaigns, it is extremely important you apply least privilege to their access. That said, they have the power to fire you, so do the best you can to protect your organization, without getting fired. Explaining the risks to them will definitely help.

9. Should network system administrators have special privileges on your network and other computer systems? If so, why? If not, why not? What types of privileges would you give them, if you gave them any?

   Network administrators need special privileges in order to perform their job duties. Ideally, they would log in to their email and use the internet with a regular set of credentials (no admin powers) and then use their account(s) with special powers separately. Either by logging in again or using the feature in Windows OS where you can right-click something and say "run as administrator." They will need access to all network settings and systems, as a bare minimum.

10. Should help desk employees have special privileges on your network and other computer systems? If so, why? If not, why not? What types of privileges would you give them, if you gave them any?

   Help Desk personnel need special privileges in order to perform their job duties. Ideally, they would log in to their email and use the internet with a regular (non-admin) set of credentials and then use their account(s) with special powers separately. Either by logging in again or using the features in Windows OS where you can right-click something and say "run as administrator." They would need access to reset user passwords, access control, and quite a bit more in order to perform their job functions.

11. Your boss tells you that turning on logging and monitoring will cost too much. How do you explain its value and importance from a security perspective? Write a paragraph to convince your boss. Remember to make sure you explain what the potential risk is to the business, in a way your boss can understand (who is a smart, but not overly technical, person). If you speak over your audience's head, you will not pass this question, nor will you convince your boss.

Dear Boss,

When we had an incident last month and you asked me to investigate, I could not. There were no logs to look at, and I was unable to explain how our data got onto the dark web; we only knew that it was there. I had received an alert from my application, saying something was wrong, but having no logs, I could not further our investigation. It was very frustrating to not be able to provide you an answer. I want to protect our organization the best I can, and to do that I need to know what happens during an incident, so I can prevent it from ever happening again. With this in mind, I ask you to help me find the budget so that we can turn on logging.

Thank you,

The AppSec Team

Chapter 5: Common Pitfalls

1. Someone on your project team wants to accept serialized objects from an untrusted source. You know this is a bad idea. How do you explain the risk *effectively* to your teammate? Write down your answer. Be persuasive and clear.

Dear Teammate,

I was reviewing your design document and noticed you are going to accept serialized objects from the public and this has me concerned, from a security perspective. Usually when we accept data or anything else from the public, we validate it, scan it, and treat it as though it's radioactive, until proven otherwise. If something is in a serialized state, that means we need to deserialize it in order to start that process. When we deserialize an object it could easily contain an attack within it, and we would have let them right into our network. Insecure deserialization is so scary it's on the OWASP Top Ten; it's very serious. Could we plan a meeting to find a less risky way to get you the data you need? I'm sure we can find a compromise that works for both of us.

Cheers,

The AppSec Team

2. Is the OWASP Top Ten a standard? Yes or no.

   No. It is a great awareness document, a place to start, and an excellent lesson to teach, but it is not a standard.

3. Name three of the OWASP Top Ten that we already covered in this book, before Chapter 5.

   Cross-Site Scripting, Injection, and Logging. (There are more than three.)

4. Does the XXE vulnerability apply to JSON? Does it apply to YAML? If so, why? If not, why not?

   No, it only applies to XML. That said, deserialization *does* apply to JSON, YAML, and even my beloved .Net.

5. Name an example of a race condition (it does not need to be computer related).

   Starbucks had a great race condition reported to their bug bounty. The security researcher (Egor Homakov) could get unlimited fancy coffee doing several transfers from one card to a second card, at almost the same time. The verification did not create a "lock" on the account balance, so when they all checked at the same time the money had not yet been removed from card #1, allowing many transfers to happen despite the balance on the first card being zero.

6. Why do we roll back incomplete transactions? Why does that matter? Give an example of when not rolling back an incomplete transaction would be problematic.

   Alice is trying to buy a coffee on a mobile app, but part way through, her cellular signal dies. The steps are: she presses "buy," it removes the money from her account, it sends the order to the local coffee shop, then it sends a confirmation to her. If she lost signal after it took her money, but before it sent the order, Alice has paid for a coffee but 1) doesn't get the coffee and 2) is unaware they took her money. She only knows that she did not get the coffee. Rolling everything back means the app can tell Alice to order again, and she will only be charged once.

Chapter 6: Testing and Deployment

1. If you could only choose one type of testing to perform on your application, which type would it be and why?

User Acceptance Testing. Although this is a book about security, we cannot ignore the fact that the app has to *work*. Next up would be a security assessment or penetration test, but, ideally, we are able to perform all sorts of testing to ensure the app is in good shape.

2. Which type of testing do you think would be the fastest? Why?

   Unit testing, because it's automated and made to run fast.

3. Which type of testing do you think would be the slowest? Why?

   Penetration testing, because it must be thorough.

4. What types of vulnerabilities would you want to look for in regression testing? Name at least two, and why you chose each one.

   Injection, because it is the most dangerous. XSS, because it is the most pervasive.

5. Does your workplace have a zero-trust network design? If you don't know the answer, your homework is to find out.

   Only you can answer this.

6. Does your workplace allow use of a CI/CD pipeline? If you don't know the answer, your homework is to find out.

   Only you can answer this.

7. In a CI/CD environment, should you implement a Static Application Security Testing (SAST) tool and run a complete scan of all of the code, every time there is a new build? Why? Why not?

   No! SAST is very slow and produces many false positives. Instead choose one of the following: run SAST only on the brand new code or 2) run SAST outside the pipeline, analyze the results yourself, and then put the results into the bug tracker. Try putting secret scanning, SCA, or passive DAST scans into your pipeline instead.

8. Why is it critical to put all new changes into a code repository?

   If you do not check your code changes into version control, eventually someone else will check in their changes and push to prod and copy over your changes. All your hard work disappears in an instant. Talk about a bad day.

9. Why do we test integration points between different systems? Is it more or less valuable than testing the rest of each system?

   I believe that integration testing is equally important as testing the system itself. This is because if the systems don't work together, then it will appear to the end user as though it is broken. The end user doesn't usually care why they can't use a system, just that it's broken.

10. Why do we test databases, even though they aren't publicly accessible?

Your data is extremely valuable, so of course you need to protect it. Also, your app touches your database, and if your app is not secure your database could still defend itself.

11. Why do we test APIs, even though they aren't publicly accessible? (This might be a trick question.)

You need to secure all of your tech, even if it is not public facing, due to insider threats, the possibility of someone getting into the network from the outside, or an insecure system reaching inside the network and contacting your system.

12. When does it make sense to do a penetration test versus a security assessment of a system? Explain your answer.

If you have less time, doing a security assessment makes sense. If the system is very delicate, a security assessment might make more sense. If you need to have full validation of your results, if you need to get management's attention, a penetration test is better.

Chapter 7: An AppSec Program

1. Give one reason why maintaining an up-to-date application inventory is valuable for any organization.

When an incident happens and the application that was attacked is on the inventory page (in the configuration management DB), you have all the information possible to help you investigate in a timely manner.

2. Give one example of an alert that your application could give. What type of behavior would cause such an alert, and why is it a problem?

If a call to an API has a <script> tag in it, you issue an alert because someone is attempting to inject code into your system.

3. Is testing the most important part of an AppSec program? If so, why? If not, why not?

Testing is the verification that your efforts to secure your application have been effective (or not). I do not feel it is the most important part to ensure you software is secure, but it *does* provide evidence that your efforts were effective. It also catches all the things you have missed.

4. Is it more valuable to buy a RASP or WAF tool (a shield for your application) or to spend that money on ensuring your code is secure? Explain your choice.

Ensuring your code is secure is always #1. A WAF or RASP is an *additional* layer of defense.

5. Describe a type of security incident that would require the assistance of developer. What would be needed of the developer?

   If an application has had an SQL injection attack, we would need to developer to help us fix the bug, get access to the correct logs, and understand what happened.

6. If you could give software developers one tool to help them, what would it be? Explain your choice.

   DAST, because it's easy to use and finds low-hanging fruit. Specifically, I would choose OWASP Zap because it's free and a great tool.

7. If you could give developers one learning resource, what would it be? Explain your choice.

   I would give them this book! ;-D

8. What is the difference between SAST and SCA?

   SAST analyzes the code your team wrote for security issues. SCA looks only at the third-party components (the code you did not write).

9. What is the difference between SAST and DAST?

   SAST is a static analysis of your *code*, while DAST is dynamic analysis of your running *application*.

10. Set a potential goal for your application security program at your office, a school project, or in a made-up place that you hope to work at some day. What goal did you set? Why did you choose this? How will you measure your progress?

    Only you can answer this.

Chapter 8: Securing Modern Applications and Systems

1. What does the term *shared responsibility* mean?

   It means that some of the responsibility in ensuring your cloud instance is yours, and some is your provider/vendor's. It's about who has to do what, so that nothing gets missed.

2. What is the difference between Infrastructure as a Service (IaaS) and Platform as a Service (PaaS)? Which one(s) do you have to patch and maintain yourself?

IaaS is a VM provided by a cloud provider that you need to patch and maintain. PaaS is a platform provided by a cloud provider that hosts your app, that you do not need to patch.

3. Why is there (or is there not) more risk to online storage? Which of the CIA Triad can apply to online storage?

   If you are using online storage, it is likely that it's always Available (CIA). But if it's online, there is more risk that if it's been misconfigured that it could be more easily found in order to be broken into.

4. Name one new risk that the cloud has that a traditional or on-premises data center does not have.

   You are risking external resources having access and/or control over your systems (the cloud provider employees).

5. What is the difference between a container, a virtual machine, and a physical server?

   A container is a virtualized, bare-minimum operating system for running one application. A virtual machine is a complete, virtualized operating system, to run one or more applications. A physical server is a machine that can hold one operating system, many operating systems (via virtualization), or many containers.

6. Name one advantage of Infrastructure as Code.

   If there's a mechanical server failure you can deploy your server OS again in seconds! Also, you can use version control to do change management. There are many, many benefits; try to think of a few more yourself.

7. Name one advantage of DevOps over Waterfall SDLC.

   Releasing small changes often means you can fix a security bug very quickly. Win!

8. Which of the modern tooling options sounded most interesting to you? Why?

   Only you can answer this.

9. Which of the modern tactics sounded most interesting to you? Why?

   Only you can answer this.

10. After reading this chapter, what do you see missing in your organization? What can you improve, and how can you do it?

    Only you can answer this.

Chapter 9: Good Habits

1. What are some of the risks of technical debt?

   1) Being so far behind in your version of a framework that you need to re-write your entire app in order to upgrade.

   2) Having everything so far behind that it is near-impossible to release bug fixes.

   3) Having 11 different versions of the same framework released in prod for your programming language, a zero day comes out, and you have no idea which one(s) are vulnerable.

2. Should you post private information on social media if you only have friends following you?

   Anything that might embarrass or harm you or your loved ones, get you fired, or can be used against you, should not be put on the internet. Data can be leaked or breached, mistakes can happen, and friends can prove untrustworthy. *Also: the internet never forgets.*

3. Why are multi-factor authentication adoption rates so low? Name three ways we could increase adoption.

   Adoption rates are low because it's extra work and people are lazy and because most people don't understand how much more it protects them and how much risk they are accepting when they put information online.

   We could increase adoption of MFA by

   1) Making it less complex to implement;

   2) Making it mandatory at work;

   3) Providing user training on its value and how to use it.

4. Which password manager do you use? (Note: "I don't use one" is the wrong answer here.)

   I use 1Password, but any password manager is better than none.

5. Which security policy at your office makes it hard to get your job done? Have you spoken to the security team about updating it? Is there a potential compromise that could be made?

   This is something you must answer for yourself. However, an example could be password rotation. It makes it very difficult for the average user to remember their passwords, so they often write them down or use a system of adding a number to the end, which makes the entire situation less-secure.

6. Name an activity you think might make a good "fire drill."

Rolling back a database or application, testing out your Business Continuity (BCP) or Disaster Recovery (DR) plans.

Chapter 10: Continuous Learning

All of the questions in Chapter 10 need to be answered by *you*.
Good luck!

Index